COMMUNICATION

An Introduction to the History of
Writing, Printing, Books and Libraries

Fourth Edition

by
ELMER D. JOHNSON

The Scarecrow Press, Inc.
Metuchen, N. J.   1973

Library of Congress Cataloging in Publication Data

Johnson, Elmer D
    Communication.

    Includes bibliographies.
    1. Libraries--History.   I. Title.
Z721.J6 1973   027'.009   73-83
ISBN 0-8108-0588-X

TABLE OF CONTENTS

*1. what does mean
+ couple of knowledge
peoples university)*

I

COMMUNICATION AND THE LIBRARY

In the history of man's cultural development, the communication of ideas ranks as one of his most significant achievements. Only when man learned to pass on knowledge that he had accumulated did he become distinguished from the lower animals. At first he could communicate through space only so far as sight and sound were perceivable; he could communicate through time only so far as human memory was reliable. Man learned to speak many thousands of years ago; perhaps he developed advanced and complicated languages long before he learned to write. He may even have developed an oral literature that was handed down from generation to generation. He could teach his friends, his sons and his grandsons what he himself had learned, and he could even pass on to them the legends of his ancestors. Man's memory was imperfect, however, and so only the most simple tasks and the most elemental of stories could be passed on before the day of writing. But when man learned to perpetuate his thoughts through some means of writing, he added a new dimension to his means of communication--he could now communicate through both space and time. Assuming durable writing materials and sufficient time, a written message could be transmitted to the end of the earth if necessary; with reasonable care the same message could be preserved to the end of time. The ability to communicate graphically enabled man to transcend his physical limitations and extend the sum total of his accumulated knowledge--or any part of it--both to his contemporaries in space and to his descendants in time. Cultural advances did not need to be relearned by rote in every generation, or forgotten in every catastrophe, but could be preserved and passed on, so that each new generation could begin on the cultural plateau reached by its predecessors. With written records--graphic means of communication--man had reached the point where civilization could begin.

A written record can serve to extend communication in space without being preserved indefinitely in time. A

5

letter, an order, a bill of sale--these often serve their purpose by being written and delivered, received and read.
Once the information is read and acted upon, the message
itself can be destroyed, its mission performed. However,
when information is to be transmitted through time, preserved
for the use of readers yet to be born, then the library, or
its prototype, enters the scene. In its most elementary form,
a library is simply an organized collection of informative
materials. Although non-graphic materials such as museum
objects, botanical specimens, or archeological relics can
also be informative, we usually think of graphic forms of recorded information when we visualize a library.

The earliest "keeper of the written records" merely
stored his materials in a convenient place for future use. As
long as there were only a few manuscripts, organization was
no problem; when the number of items made some arrangement necessary, he experimented with assortment by size or
by shape. Only later did he consider the literary form or
the subject content of his materials and develop an elementary form of classification. When the number of records
stored passed the limit of easy recollection, then he made a
list of them, and the first library catalog or shelf-list was
invented.

The earliest prototypes of libraries probably took
several forms. The temple library developed as a means
of preserving religious scriptures, of standardizing rituals
and ceremonies and of making available enlightening commentaries and explications. The business library began as a
record of partnerships, commercial expeditions, properties
owned, and tributes paid. Palace and governmental collections of records included tax lists, diplomatic correspondence,
royal proclamations, accounts of military adventures, and
international agreements. Even family records might approach library status, with genealogical lists, private business records, deeds, wills and marriage contracts. Whatever the form of these earliest libraries, they contained information that was preserved and used. When succeeding
generations could study the achievements and errors of the
past, then history began and man's prehistoric era was ended.
Henceforth, the library and recorded history were to go
hand-in-hand down through the corridors of time.

The library, however, is only one of many means of
human communication. Man can pass on information to his
fellow man through a variety of methods. Most elementary,
of course, is the simple gesture. It was probably man's

original means of communication. Our earliest ancestors
used the gesture to beckon, to warn, to frighten, to welcome, to approve or to disapprove, and probably for many
other purposes. The Indians of the American plains developed a system of signs and gestures that worked very effectively between tribes who spoke entirely different languages.
Even today the gesture is much more widely used than one
would ordinarily imagine. The policeman on the corner
uses a gesture to direct traffic. Gestures are used as signals in a variety of sports, and in many forms of work,
particularly in the open or where there is much noise, they
take the place of vocal or written commands. Next after the
gesture in the methods of communication used by man comes
the voice, ranging from a simple cry of warning to a complicated speech system, employing thousands of words, and
embellished with supplementary inflections and intonations.
Primitive man used vocal but non-verbal means of communication even before he developed recognizable speech. His
cries of warning, screams of pain, grunts of approval, and
squeals of delight are still used by his civilized descendants
when emotion, or lack of it, precludes more formal expression. Once man had developed a spoken language it served
him for thousands of years as the most effective means of
communication--at least within the range of the human ear.
For amplification of the human voice nothing more complicated than the megaphone, which primitive man approximated
with his cupped hands, was developed until the nineteenth
century. Now the telephone, the radio and the television can
extend the human voice through almost unlimited space in
nearly instantaneous communication, while the various means
of electronic recording, by disc, cylinder, wire or tape,
can preserve the voice through almost unlimited time. Who
would have thought that by 1969 man would walk on the
moon, and would be seen and heard by his fellow men back
on earth while he was doing it!

If man could not extend the range of his voice before
his discovery of electricity, he nevertheless did make excellent use of other auditory means of communication. Various forms of the whistle, the gong, and the drum can be found
in almost all primitive societies, and these means were employed to convey information ranging from the most simple
warning to a rather advanced "drum language" in use among
certain African tribes. A little more advanced form of
communication by sound came with the bell, and this device
has been used for centuries to call worshippers together,
to warn of danger, or to announce victories. Ultimately
from the auditory means of communication came the musical

instruments, wind, string and percussion. From the wooden
whistle have descended the flute and the trumpet, the oboe and
the clarinet and even the saxophone. From the vibrating hunter's bow may have come all the stringed instruments from
the lyre to the violin, and from the banjo to the grand piano.
The hollow log, resounding to the beat of pounding feet or
fingers eventually led to the drum and all of its various percussion descendants. Altogether these musical instruments
added another dimension to man's ability to communicate. If
he could not convey facts or ideas by musical means, he
could at least express his emotions in such a way that his
fellow man could appreciate and enjoy them. Auditory but
non-vocal means of communication have always provided a
considerable portion of man's facilities for reaching his fellow man.

Turning to visual means of communication, man has
used many means of conveying ideas, ranging from the notched
tree designating a trail, or a pile of stones used for a property mark, to the complicated system of ships' flags used to
convey messages at sea. Flags themselves constitute an entire field of symbolic communication, representing such ab-
stract ideas as ownership, nationality, power, prestige, rank
and many more subtle meanings, depending upon their shape,
colors, or position upon a flagstaff. The semaphore and its
related systems of signaling by light constitute a vital means
of communication for both sea and land transportation. Visual symbols and signs are prolific in their relationship to religion, with the cross in its various forms as a prime example. Business men have long used signs, hallmarks,
trademarks and the like, to identify their companies, trade
or products. The barber's pole and the three balls of the
pawnbroker are good examples. With such signs and symbols
reasonably intelligent though illiterate customers would have
little trouble in locating the store, product or service of
their choice. Such non-alphabetic representations can convey information, but they are restricted in their usefulness.
Each one means one thing, or represents one service, but
ordinarily two or more of them cannot be placed together to
convey added or related information. Instead, they would be
confusing if not absolutely meaningless. Unless an elaborate
and prearranged code is known to both sender and receiver,
communicating general information by signs and symbols is
virtually impossible. But when such a code is generally
known, when each symbol or sign represents a specific word
or sound, then we have a basis for a written language.
Primitive man's early pictures became pictographs, his signs

took on specific and widely accepted meanings, and thus a written language was developed. Finally, when these written records were preserved, they formed the bases of archives and libraries.

Approaching the general field of communication from another point of view, all methods of conveying information might be divided into two phases, static and dynamic. Dynamic communication is that which is in continuous process, usually instantaneous, such as human vision, human speech, radio, telephone, television and the like. If you miss a word in a public address, it is gone forever unless a recording has been made. If you miss an action in a circus scene, it is also gone unless it has been photographed by a movie camera or recorded on videotape. Dynamic means of communication are ephemeral without their static counterparts to preserve them. Static tools of communication are those that preserve the message in permanent form: writing, printing, pictures, photographs, sculptures, electronicly recorded impulses and the like. Information communicated by dynamic means lacks durability unless it is captured in some static form. But static means of communication in turn are only as durable as the media in which they are recorded. Furthermore, regardless of the durability of the recording medium, the information itself is useless or difficult to use unless it is arranged into some system for easy location and retrieval of specific items. In other words, we come back to the library--the basic institution for both the preservation of recorded information and its organization into a systematic and usable form. Today's radio news is dynamic communication and today's newspaper is static communication; yesterday's news is available only if it has been preserved. Thus the library, in its function of preserving recorded information in orderly and usable arrangement is a third and vital element of communication. Without it, the other two forms of communication are useful but of minimum value. Dynamic communication is less valuable to man because of its impermanence; static communication is bewildering to him because of its ever increasing bulk and confusion. Only the library, or its counterpart in archive, record file, information retrieval center, or computer memory, can give permanence, order and availability to man's accumulated recordings of knowledge. The library is a means of communication in the sense that it is a storehouse of recorded information, so arranged as to be available for continuous use over an indefinite period of time. It is static communication in its dormant, but potentially vital, form. Just as a motor cannot

run without a source of energy, so the flow of communication
cannot long continue without a constant source of information.
The library is a fundamental source of that information.

Essentially a library is a collection of recorded information. But so is a bookstore, an attic filled with old
letters, or a pile of last week's newspapers on a trash heap.
What distinguishes a library from other collections of recorded knowledge is that it is an organized collection, so arranged that like information is placed together, or at least
so arranged that every item has its definite location and can
be obtained comparatively quickly when needed. To facilitate
this quick retrieval, the information must be indexed or cataloged. The more completely the information is indexed, the
more valuable the collection becomes. The more readily
available the information, the more efficient the retrieval
system, the more valuable the library becomes to its users.
The library catalog with a dozen entries under "horses" may
satisfy the average reader who just wants to read something
about them, but even a hundred entries under the same heading would be confusing, if not hopeless, to the person who
wants information on the diseases of the Percheron draft
horses used in Belgian coal mines during World War I. It
is precisely this feature in the ultimate organization and cataloging of libraries that has led the current generation to a
new point in the history of communication, a point possibly
as significant as that reached with the development of writing or printing. In the midst of the "knowledge explosion"
of the mid-20th century, the librarian and his cohorts are
no longer merely concerned with shelving and relocating
books, but with the storage and retrieval of the information
they contain. The researcher of the mid-1970s does not
want a book that might contain the facts he needs; he wants
the facts themselves, and he is not overly concerned as to
where the facts come from, or how they come to him, so
long as they are reliable. Fortunately, aids to the solution
of the problems of information control are appearing constantly in the form of more and more sophisticated electronic devices. The whole nature of the field of human
communication of factual knowledge is undergoing a revolution, but the vital role of the library in that field, in some
form, is unquestioned.

II

EARLY WRITING

The development of writing, of books and of libraries
has been an evolutionary process. The trail from the earliest cave paintings to the latest electronic devices has been
long but it has been direct and meaningful. Each step has
led logically to the next so that the ladder of man's achievements in communicating with his neighbors has been clear
and substantially continuous. First came speech, then writing, then printing, and now electronic communication. Each,
in its way, has been a miracle.

An early method of communication employed by man
was the gesture, with or without accompanying vocal sounds:
a clenched fist, an upraised arm or a facial grimace conveyed a threat, while an open palm or a smile could be used
to signify peace or friendship. An upraised finger indicated
"one"; all fingers outstretched together could have meant
"many." With dozens of gestures of arms, hands, fingers,
eyes and facial muscles, many different ideas could be conveyed without uttering a sound. With the addition of a few
gutteral grunts, most of the communication necessary for a
primitive society was achieved. Today many primitive or
rural peoples still make good use of the gesture in their
language. Even with a well-developed language, modern
man uses the gesture considerably, all the way from a
simple nod to indicate agreement to the more elaborate
motions of the public speaker or the more subtle move-
ments of the ballet dancer. The gesture, in all its forms,
is fundamental to immediate interpersonal communication.

Along with the gesture, primitive man also developed
a spoken language, at first combining the two, then gradually relying more on the voice alone as he became more
civilized. Just when or how speech originated is lost in
the prehistoric ages. Even the most primitive humans
known to history have had well-developed languages. Some
authorities contend that man's first spoken words were imi-
tative, copying animal or other natural sounds. Others

11

think that interjections, mere cries of alarm or fear, or to
attract attention, were men's first vocal expressions. Undoubtedly nouns and pronouns, the names of people and
things and places, were used very early in the development
of speech, along with simple verbs of action. Adjectives
and adverbs probably came much later, beginning with those
describing size, number and shape. When he could describe
things that were not present, tell of things that had happened
in the past, and give vocal form to his imagination, then
man had developed a true language.

The spoken language, however, was at best only as
durable as sound waves and fickle memories. Stories and
legends could be told and remembered and retold to suc-
cessive generations, but each story teller put his own per-
sonality into his version, so that no listener ever heard ex-
actly what his grandfather had heard before him. A history
and a literature could be preserved without a written language,
but it was a shadowy history and a changeable literature,
subject to the whims and imaginations of the tribal story-
tellers. In order to preserve history as fact instead of
legend, a form of writing was needed, and so the historian
today separates the historic eras from the prehistoric at the
point where written records began to be made and preserved.
Yet it is quite probable that man learned to write in an effort to stabilize his religious practices or to formalize his
business relations rather than to record his history.

Before writing as we know it began, there were
thousands of years during which man used and kept some
kind of account or record. Perhaps his first attempt at
graphic communication was a simple sign, such as an arrow
to point the way that a hunting party had taken, or a clan
symbol, marking the hunting grounds of one tribe to distinguish it from others. Perhaps it was a simple pile of rocks
to serve as a property marker. But very early man began
to draw pictures, and to represent in pictorial form what he
saw around him. The cave man drew the animals that he
saw and hunted. Some of these drawings (the oldest known
dating back only 10,000 to 15,000 years) have been found in
the caves of southern France, Spain and northern Africa.
The earlier drawings are crude and hardly recognizable as
representations, often mere scratchings on rock. But later
examples are often true works of art. The primitive paint-
ers used earth colors and animal-fats in black, white, red
and yellow, to draw very realistic animals and men. Those
in the north African Sahara caves, dated about 4000 B.C.,

often depict social and work scenes involving many people. Were these drawings a means of communication or merely the expression of an artistic impulse? Did they have a religious or ritualistic meaning? Sometimes they seem to be definitely conveying a message, as when the presence of a weapon indicates that an animal has been hunted or killed, or when some indication of numbers seems to indicate a count. Whatever their purpose, these cave paintings definitely provided the artists with a means of expression, factual or imaginative.

Roughly contemporary with these early cave pictures are the marked and colored stones, best known through the "Azilian pebbles" found in the Mas d'Azil area in Southern France. These small stones are marked with curious designs which may represent numbers or other meaningful symbols, or which may have been simply decorative charms. Various suggestions have been made as to their use and meaning. Some scholars believe that they had some magical or religious value, but conveyed no specific meaning; others consider them to be something like property markers, family or clan signs or totems. Still others think they may have been numerical records, indicating the number of animals owned, the number of days passed at some location, or the like. Whatever their purpose, they were an early attempt at graphic expression, and because of the durability of the stone, it is obvious that they were intended to be preserved. Similar primitive paintings or engravings on stone are found in many parts of the world.

Many other articles were used as mnemonic devices by primitive peoples all over the world. These are not means of communication in the fullest sense of the word, but are merely memory aids, serving to remind the initiated of the main facts of a record or story. Among the best known of these mnemonic devices are the quipus or knotted cord pendants of the Peruvian Indians. A quipu, using different colored cords, of different lengths and knotted in different places, was a means of keeping property records and historical chronicles. The reader of the quipu employed it to remind him of numerical information, or even of historical events. The North American Indians had a similar device in their belts of beads or "wampum," in which the color, size and location of the shell beads conveyed meaning. In the Middle Ages, European peasants often used the clog calendar, a notched stick of wood, to serve as a calendar and to remind them of the church festivals and saints' days. In

other parts of the world primitive peoples have made similar
use of carved wood, bamboo or bone, stones or shells,
woven cloth, or inscribed or painted hides and bark. Whatever the form or material used, these mnemonic devices
were means of communication because they did convey meaning to those who were trained to read them.

A step beyond the mnemonic device comes the first
form of what might be called true writing. This is the pictograph. The North American Indian first used the pictograph as little more than a memory aid. For instance, the
"winter count" kept by the Dakota Indians from 1800 to 1870
was simply a series of 71 pictures inscribed on a buffalo
robe. Each picture portrayed the most important event of a
winter and it was enough of a reminder to the tribal chron-
icler to allow him to describe a year's history of the tribe.
An improvement on this was the picture story or message.
By means of simple drawings, easily recognizable as men,
animals, sun, mountains and other common objects, the
Indian could convey a love letter, a report on a hunting trip,
a battle, or even a treaty between tribes. Other primitive
peoples in South America, Africa and Asia have used similar
drawings to record events or convey messages, but pictographs used in this manner still fall short of being an efficient means of communication.

On the other hand, some peoples, such as the Egyptians and the Chinese, began with the same type of pictographs and gradually developed them into true writing, capable of recording history, transacting business and creating a
literature. The Egyptian pictograph at first represented
what it described and no more. Gradually, however, the
pictograph became an ideograph, which conveyed an idea or
meaning other than the object depicted. For example, the
picture of a whip might mean "to dominate" or "to rule,"
while that of the sun could imply "day" or "time," or a
figure of a man with his hand at his mouth could mean "to
eat." We still use ideographs today, although we hardly
ever think of them as such. Many highway signs are ideographs and so are the signs used in mathematics and music.

The Egyptian advanced from ideographs to the next
step in the development of writing: the phonogram, in which
the pictographic symbol took on a particular sound and conveyed that sound-meaning even though the pictorial meaning
might be different. An example in English would be taking
a picture of a bee to represent the verb "be." Next,

pictographs with established phonetic values could be put together to form longer words, as if we were to portray "belief" with pictures of a bee and a leaf.   The Egyptians made good use of this rebus-like written language, but since they had so many words that sounded alike but had different meanings (homophones), they continued to use ideographic signs to distinguish between them.   For example, if the spoken words for "river" and "palace" were the same, they could add an ideograph for water to the phonogram if they wanted it to be read as "river," and a house ideograph if they wished it to be read as "palace."

If the Egyptians had gone one step further the phonograms would have ceased representing syllables and would have retained only their initial sounds, thus becoming a phonetic alphabet.   In this case the pictograph for "bee" would represent only the sound of the consonant "b" and that for the "leaf" might become the "l" sound.   While the Egyptians never quite achieved a true phonetic alphabet, they did develop a set of symbols for some 25 consonants and some 75 other symbols that represented two or three letters each. Both types actually represented syllables rather than letters since vowels were to be understood.   The entire language could have been written with these phonetic symbols, but the Egyptians preferred to continue using a combination of ideographs and phonograms.   The phonetic symbols were employed mainly in transcribing foreign words and for proper names.

The Egyptian pictographic writing is known as hieroglyphic from the Greek words meaning "sacred carvings." There are examples of hieroglyphic writing that date back more than 3000 years before Christ.   The earliest examples found were carved on stone but very early in Egyptian history a writing material made from the papyrus reed was developed.   Many examples of Egyptian papyri have been found, most of them preserved as scraps in the dry desert sands.   A few longer works have been discovered in sealed tombs.   Our word "paper" comes, through the Greek and Latin, from papyrus.   The early hieroglyphic writing, whether on stone or papyrus, was strictly pictorial, but about 3000 B. C. a modified form, less recognizable as pictures, was developed.   This was the hieratic script which was more suitable for rapid writing with brush and ink on papyrus.   Still a third form of Egyptian script was developed about 700 B. C.   This was the demotic writing, a simplified version of the hieratic.   Demotic script was widely used in

personal and business affairs. The hieroglyphic script continued to be used, especially for official and religious writings, until about the fifth century after Christ.

Following the decline of Ancient Egypt the use of
hieroglyphic writing gave way to Greek and Arabic scripts
and for more than a thousand years no one was able to
translate the examples of it that were found. Finally, in
the early 19th century the Rosetta stone, a curiously inscribed plaque which had been uncovered by French soldiers
in Napoleon's attempt to conquer Egypt, was acquired by the
British Museum in London. This stone carried three inscriptions, one in Greek, one in hieroglyphic, and one in
demotic, all apparently giving the same message, a decree
passed in 196 B. C. under the rule of Ptolemy V. The
Greek inscription could be read, but this did not immediately result in deciphering the two inscriptions in Egyptian.
Several scholars studied the stone over a period of years
and finally a young Frenchman, Jean François Champollion,
discovered the key to the hieroglyphics. Champollion guessed
that certain enclosed groups of hieroglyphic characters represented proper nouns and knowing these names from the
accompanying Greek text, he was able to begin assigning
values to the separate Egyptian phonetic characters. His
knowledge of the modern Coptic language, a descendant of
Egyptian, aided him in his work. It was a long task, and
other scholars contributed to it, but Champollion announced
his deciphering of the Rosetta Stone in 1821, and he is
usually given credit for first reading the ancient Egyptian
hieroglyphs. Though our knowledge of the Egyptian scripts
is still not perfect, what we do know has opened up a vast
amount of information concerning the life and history of the
Nile valley peoples. It has also taught us how one people
devised a nonalphabetic system of writing that was so successful that it was used for more than 3000 years.

In the Mesopotamian valley, in what is today Iraq,
another civilization grew up simultaneously with that of
ancient Egypt. This was the Sumerian-Babylonian-Assyrian
civilization which existed from before 3000 B. C. to about
500 B. C. These peoples also developed a system of writing
based on pictographs, but showing little similarity to that of
the Egyptians. The Sumerians and their successors had
little stone and no papyrus, so they turned to clay tablets
for their writing materials. A short pointed stylus of wood
or metal was used to make impressions in soft clay, and
the clay was allowed to harden, or it was baked into bricks

if a permanent record was desired.   The stylus-on-clay method of writing did not lend itself to elaborate pictographs, and
so the Sumerian writing early assumed the form of stylized
diagrams made by short wedge-shaped strokes in the clay.
This writing, known as cuneiform (Latin for wedge-shaped),
was further simplified by the Babylonians and Assyrians until
it showed little or no resemblance to the original picture from
which it developed.   The Babylonians and Assyrians spoke
different languages from the Sumerians but they employed the
Sumerian cuneiform characters for writing, much as the
Japanese use Chinese characters for their quite different
language.   Like the Egyptian, the cuneiform writing developed
through the ideograph to the phonetic syllabary, and never
developed into a true alphabet.   The number of phonetic symbols was, however, reduced to a few hundred by the Assyrians.   After the destruction of Assyria by the Persians in the
seventh century B.C. , the conquerors took over the cuneiform
script and further reduced it to a semi-alphabet of some 43
characters.   Some of these characters represented syllables,
so it was not a true alphabet.   It disappeared in the fourth
century B.C. , and has had no lasting effect in the development of alphabetic writing.

The account of the deciphering and translating of cuneiform is almost as romantic as that of the Rosetta stone.
Examples of the clay tablets had been known for centuries,
and many scholars, including the German, Georg Friedrich
Grotefend, had attempted to decipher them.   Grotefend made
some progress in figuring out the later form of cuneiform,
Old Persian, but it was left to a young Englishman, Sir
Henry Rawlinson, to finally decipher the earlier forms.   Rawlinson, a linguist and army officer, was in Persia in the
early 19th century on an assignment for his government.   Being interested in the extinct languages of the area, he con-
centrated his efforts on a tri-lingual inscription carved on
the Rock of Behistun, a high cliff in the Zagros Mountains
of Northwestern Persia.   The three languages of the inscription turned out to be Old Persian, Mede or Elamite, and
Akkadian or Babylonian.   Working first with the Old Persian
which proved to be an alphabetic language of some 40 characters, Rawlinson and other scholars eventually succeeded in
translating the carvings as a decree of the Persian King,
Darius, of 500 B.C.   Decades later other scientists discovered and translated an even earlier cuneiform language,
Sumerian, and the key to unlock some 3000 years of Mesopotamian history was available.   Eventually thousands of
cuneiform tablets were found in the ruins of ancient

Mesopotamian cities and much that we know about the way of
life of the people who lived then and there is due to the un-
tiring efforts of Rawlinson and his co-workers.

Many other ancient scripts have been discovered, and
where enough examples have been found, or where bilingual
texts are available, most of them have been deciphered. For
example, the Hittites, who lived between the Egyptians and
Babylonians geographically, wrote their language both in a
pictographic script, and in a cuneiform script borrowed from
the Babylonians. The latter has been deciphered, and much
has been done toward reading the pictographs. The latest
success in deciphering an ancient script came in the 1950s
with the reading of the "Linear B" writing of the Mycenaens
who lived on the island of Crete and the adjacent Greek
mainland about 1500 B.C. Michael Ventris, a young English
scholar, deduced that the Linear B language was Greek, or
at least an early form of Greek, and using modern crypt-
analytic methods managed to decipher it in 1952. A similar
script, also found on Crete, is denoted "Linear A" and, being apparently in another language, has not yet been fully
deciphered. Other undeciphered scripts include one found on
the island of Cyprus, and another of the Etruscans who lived
in northern Italy before the Romans. In the Indus valley of
India a pictographic system of writing developed, possibly as
early as 3000 B.C., and this script also advanced to a system of ideographs and phonograms, but there are too few
examples of it available for it to be deciphered. Also at
various other places around the world, including Central
America and Easter Island in the southeast Pacific, examples
of ancient and still unknown forms of writing have been found.
The Mayan writing of Central America was in the form of
elaborate hieroglyphs, and some of the numbers and dates
have been deciphered, although the language itself remains
almost unknown. These and other undeciphered scripts await
another Rawlinson, Champollion or Ventris. In most cases
there are so few examples of a particular type of writing
available that it is doubtful that an accurate reading will ever
be achieved.

Apparently every major civilization, in all parts of
the world, began its writing with pictographs. This was true
in China. Like the Egyptians and Babylonians, the Chinese
never developed an alphabet. However, unlike the Egyptian
and Babylonian, Chinese is a living language and its script
is used today not only by hundreds of millions of Chinese,
but also with minor adaptations by Japanese, Koreans, and

other Asiatic peoples who have used it as the written vehicle
for unrelated languages.   The Chinese script began as pictographs, but by 1000 B. C. it had reached a highly stylized
form in which the original pictures could hardly be recognized.
Actually it developed as a system of phonograms, modified
by ideographs, somewhat as in the Egyptian, but the ensuing
written language was so successful that it has remained virtually unchanged for over 2000 years.   In the past two
decades attempts have been made to substitute a phonetic
alphabet for the more cumbersome ideographic script, but it
remains to be seen if and when this change will be successful.

Most of the world today, however, uses some form of
alphabetic script, and most of these alphabets owe their origin to one developed in the eastern Mediterranean area some-
where between 2000 and 1000 B. C.   The origin of this
Semitic alphabet, as it is usually called, is lost in antiquity,
but there are many theories concerning it.   Many scholars
have held that it was derived from the demotic script of the
Egyptians.   There are similarities between some of the Egyptian phonetic syllables and the early forms of some of the
Semitic alphabetic symbols, but others are quite different.
Other students of the origin of the alphabet point to cuneiform
syllabaries used in the areas where the Semitic peoples lived
as a possible source for the alphabet, while still others point
to early scripts used on the islands of Cyprus and Crete.

A cuneiform alphabet of 30 letters, discovered on clay
tablets found at the site of ancient Ugarit on the Syrian coast,
seems to have been an adaptation of an earlier Semitic alphabet for use on clay, and these tablets have been dated at
about 1500 B. C.   By this date or shortly after, there seems
to have been two varieties of an early alphabet, one known
as the North Semitic and the other as the South Semitic.
From the South Semitic came the later Amharic and Coptic
alphabets used in North Africa, but from the North Semitic
of some 22 symbols came the Phoenician.   The Phoenicians
were a trading people living on the coast of what is now Israel and Syria, and they engaged in a widespread commerce
throughout the Mediterranean world.   Being merchants, they
had contacts with many peoples, including the Egyptians,
Hebrews, Cretans, Cypriots, Hittites, and Babylonians, each
of whom were in some respects more advanced than the
Phoenicians.   Perhaps because they needed a simple script
in their business relationships they were among the first to
make wide use of the alphabet.   At any rate, they spread it
to other peoples, particularly the Greeks.

The Greeks took the phonetic alphabet, adapted it to
their own language, and used it to create a great literature.
The Phoenicians had used an alphabet consisting entirely of
consonants, but the Greeks used some of the Phoenician letters as vowels, added others to represent phonetic values
that were present in the Greek language and not in the Phoenician, and began the custom of writing from left to right.
From Greece, the alphabet passed on to the Italian peninsula,
probably first to the Etruscans and then later to the Romans.
The Etruscans used an alphabet of 26 letters, and wrote from
right to left. The Latins made a few minor changes in the
Greek alphabet, and in doing so produced the Roman alphabet
which by the time of Christ had achieved essentially the form
in which it has passed down to the present. Nearly all
modern West European languages now use the Roman alphabet, some with a few modifications, mostly diacritical.
Some modern East European languages also use the Roman
alphabet, while others, such as Russian, Bulgarian, and
Serbian, have an alphabet developed from the Old Cyrillic,
which grew out of the Greek in a form different from the
Latin. On the other hand, modern Arabic, Hebrew and other
Near Eastern and Southwest Asian alphabets developed from
another descendant of the North Semitic script, or from a
common ancestor.

Writing Materials

In most ancient scripts, the form of the characters or
letters varied with the material on which the writing was
done. Thus the Egyptian hieratic, the Babylonian cuneiform,
and the Greek and Latin capitals were developed to accom-
modate the materials on which they were most effectively
used: papyrus, clay, and stone, respectively. The earliest
writing materials were probably bone or wood surfaces,
marked with charred sticks or sharp stones, but these materials do not lend themselves to preservation, so few examples of such writing are known. Later writing was done
on bark, particularly the inner bark of certain trees, and
on animal hides, sometimes tanned or treated. There was
even writing on early forms of textiles, but none of these
products keep very well, so only scraps of them have been
preserved. But when man began carving on stone, as the
Egyptians sometimes did, a permanent record resulted. Such
carving was difficult and was used only for the most important writings. The clay tablet, used by the Babylonians and
others in their cuneiform writing, was also very durable,

and thousands of them have survived.

For a plentiful and inexpensive writing material, the Egyptians turned to the wild papyrus reeds which grew profusely along the lower Nile. While the papyrus was still young and green it was cut, split, and the pithy inside core was removed and dried. This fibrous core was then pressed flat, laid in strips and covered crosswise by another layer of strips. A light glue or paste was then applied, and the whole was again pressed and dried. The result was a thin sheet of rather porous but durable writing material. The writing surface of the papyrus was then smoothed and polished with a piece of ivory, bone, or shell. The resulting sheets were usually nine to 11 inches long, and five to nine inches wide, although other sizes have been found. When larger sizes were needed, sheets were pasted together and rolled around a central core of wood, metal or ivory. Rolls of more than 100 feet in length have been discovered, although 15 to 20 feet was the length of the average scroll.

The ink used for writing on papyrus was made from lamp-black, or powdered charcoal, mixed with a gum solution, dried into blocks, and then thinned with water for use. Red inks were often used by the Egyptians, and these were made with a gum base, colored by iron oxide or red lead. Other mineral sources were also employed occasionally to provide such colors as yellow (yellow ochre), brown (limonite), or green (malachite). Reed pens, made from dried reeds sharpened to a point, and with the point then chewed or blunted to a soft brush tip, were the writing instruments usually employed with the papyrus.

The papyrus reed was grown mostly in the fertile Nile valley, and hence most of the papyrus was made there. As the demand for it grew it was exported to the other Mediterranean countries. Egypt had something of a monopoly on the production of papyrus and its manufacture became an important industry. Papyrus was made in several grades, and different names were applied to the various types, according to thickness, finish and quality. Trade in papyrus was an important business, and the Phoenicians considered papyrus one of their most important items of commerce. Papyrus was the most widely used writing material in classical Greece and Rome, and although it declined in use after the A.D. 400s, it is known to have been used as late as the 11th century. All in all, it must have served as a major writing material for over 4000 years.

In addition to papyrus, the ancient world also knew
and used another fine writing material. This was parchment,
the specially treated hides of young cattle, sheep and goats.
Dried or tanned animal hides had been used for writing materials for thousands of years, but parchment was a distinct improvement over ordinary hides or leather in that it was thin-
ner, whiter and smoother, and could be used for writing on
both sides. Although tradition has it that parchment was developed in the city of Pergamum, a Greek colony in Asia
Minor, as a competitor for the Egyptian papyrus monopoly,
the true story is more involved. Parchment was probably
developed over a long period of time, and possibly in several
places. However, Pergamum was a center of the parchment
trade by the second century B.C., and the word "parchment"
is derived from the Latin form of "Pergamum." By the second century after Christ parchment was widely used throughout
the Mediterranean world and it remained the major European
writing material throughout the Middle Ages. Like papyrus,
parchment was made in many grades and the term "vellum"
came to be applied to the better grade made from calf-skin.
However, vellum and parchment are often used interchange-
ably for all varieties of the product. Parchment could be
dyed into exotic colors, and also inks of various colors
could be used for writing on it, so many very beautiful manuscripts were produced with it. Parchment also could be
folded more easily than papyrus, and so when the codex or
modern book-form came into use, it tended to replace papyrus
and become the more commonly used manuscript material.
It was widely used in Europe and America as late as the nineteenth century for legal manuscripts and is still occasionally
employed for particularly fine books and documents.

The use of parchment brought a change in the writing
implement. The brush-tipped reed gave way to the sharpened,
split-point reed, and then to the split-feather quill. The
Romans made good use of the quill and our word "pen" comes
from the Latin word for feather. The feather quill was used
as a writing instrument for at least 2000 years, and the
modern metal pen-point is a faithful copy of it.

From Roll to Book

The roll form continued in use long after the development of parchment, but other forms were tried. Smooth
pieces of wood could be written on with charcoal sticks, and
this was an early form of the schoolboy's slate. Later this

wooden slate was covered with a thin layer of wax. Then,
with a wood or ivory stylus, legible impressions could be
made in the wax, which could be smoothed over for re-use.
This "tabula, " from which we get our word "tablet, " had
many uses. It could be used for school practice work, for
figuring accounts in a business house, or for sending letters.
Such waxed tablets were widely used, and examples have been
found on wood, ivory and metal from Egypt, Babylonia, Greece
and Rome. Sometimes the tablet was hinged to another, and
a "diptych" was then formed, looking something like the modern book. A diptych presented two waxed surfaces, face to
face, and thus protected from damage. Sometimes, with
very thin wood, or metal, several waxed "leaves" could be
hinged together and protected by outside covers. This closely
approximated the modern book form.

By about A.D. 100 another book form had become
popular, particularly in Rome. This was the codex, similar
in form to the multi-leaved tabula, and possibly suggested by
it, but made of papyrus or parchment. Several sheets were
folded and then sewn together along the folded edge to form a
quire of eight, 12, 16, or more pages. If necessary, several
quires could be sewn together to form a thicker book. This
form was much easier to read than the roll, especially when
several books were to be compared or consulted together.
Although many papyrus codices have been found, the form was
better suited to parchment and as the codex replaced the roll
as the prevailing book form, parchment rapidly replaced papyrus. When backs and spines of wood or leather were added
to the codex, it reached substantially the form of the modern
book. By A.D. 300s the codex was the most widely used
book form, but the scroll continued to be used for some important documents down through the Middle Ages.

Besides the roll and codex, other book forms have been
used at various times in other parts of the world. For example, an accordian-shaped book has been used in Buddhist
areas of Asia, and can still be found in Tibet. In this book
form long strips of paper or other writing material are folded
like an accordion, so that all of one side must be read before turning to the other. Some early Mayan codices in Central America were also similarly folded. On the other hand,
in other parts of Southeast Asia, the palm-leaf "ola" was a
widely used bookform. This consisted of narrow, oblong
strips of palm leaves, written on both sides, and strung together at both ends. After reading one side of an ola leaf,
the reader turned to the other, and then moved the leaf or

page along the strings so that another page could be exposed.

The origins of some words relating to books and libraries are of interest. The English word "library" comes from the Old French "librairie" which stems from the Latin "librarium," meaning "of books." This in turn comes from the word "liber," Latin for book, but the Latin "liber" originally referred to the inner bark of a tree used as a writing material. The French no longer use "librairie" for library, but instead use it to designate the book-sellers' trade or a book shop. The modern French word for library is "bibliothèque," from the Greek words roughly meaning "book cabinet." Most of the modern European languages employ some form of "bibliothèque" for library, such as the German "Bibliothek" or the Spanish "biblioteca." The English word "book," on the other hand, has an Anglo-Saxon origin, and comes from a word meaning "wooden tablet." This in turn is related to or derived from the Germanic word "boc," meaning "beech tree," also indicating an early use of wood or bark for writing.

Thus, long before the end of the ancient era, man had experimented with various forms of writing and writing materials, and, at least as far as the Mediterranean world was concerned, he had settled down to a system of written communication that was to remain virtually unchanged for a thousand years or more. This system included the phonetic alphabet in its Greek or Latin form, the parchment codex and the ink pen or quill. The physical ingredients were available for the writing of a great literature, and the classics of the Greeks and Romans are eloquent proof that they were well used. That even a fraction of that literature was preserved for future generations is due to our earliest libraries and librarians.

Bibliography
BOOKS

Baikie, James. Egyptian Papyri and Papyrus Hunting. London, 1925. 324 p.
Barber, Charles L. The Story of Speech and Language. New York, 1965. 295 p.
Bodmer, Frederick. The Loom of Language. London, 1944. 692 p.
Budge, Ernest A. W. The Rosetta Stone in the British Museum. London, 1929. 325 p.
Bushnell, G. W. From Bricks to Books. London, 1949. 160 p.

_____. From Papyrus to Print. London, 1947. 218 p.
Cerny, Jareslav. Paper and Books in Ancient Egypt.
    London, 1952. 36 p.
Chadwick, John. The Decipherment of Linear B. London,
    1970.
Chiera, Edward. They Wrote on Clay: the Babylonian
    Tablets Speak Today. Chicago, 1938. 235 p.
Clark, Cumberland. The Art of Early Writing, with Special
    Reference to the Cuneiform System. London, 1938.
    151 p.
Clodd, Edward. The Story of the Alphabet. New York,
    1938. 209 p.
Davies, Nina M. Picture Writing in Ancient Egypt. Oxford,
    1958. 79 p.
Denman, Frank. The Shaping of Our Alphabet. New York,
    1955. 232 p.
Diamond, A. H. History and Origin of Language. London,
    1960. 280 p.
Diringer, David. The Alphabet. 3rd ed. New York, 1968.
    2 v.
_____. The Hand Produced Book. New York, 1953.
    603 p.
_____. Writing. New York, 1962. 201 p.
Doblhofer, Ernst. Voices in Stone: the Decipherment of
    Ancient Scripts and Writings. New York, 1961. 327 p.
Driver, Godfrey R. Semitic Writing, from Pictograph to
    Alphabet. Rev. ed. London, 1954. 238 p.
Etiemble, René. The Orion Book of the Written Word. New
    York, 1961. 114 p.
Frimmer, Steven. The Stone That Spoke and Other Clues
    to the Decipherment of Lost Languages. New York,
    1969. 192 p.
Gelb, I. J. A Study of Writing. Rev. ed. Chicago, 1963.
    319 p.
Goldberg, Isaac. The Wonder of Words. New York, 1938.
    485 p.
Gordon, Cyrus W. Forgotten Scripts: the Story of Their
    Decipherment. London, 1968. 175 p.
Gray, Louis M. Foundations of Language. New York, 1939.
    630 p.
Hogben, Lancelot. From Cave Painting to Comic Strip: a
    Kaleidoscope of Human Communication. New York,
    1949. 286 p.
Hunter, Dard. Papermaking: the History and Technique of
    an Ancient Craft. New York, 1947. 611 p. (See es-
    pecially p. 3-48).
Irwin, Keith G. The Romance of Writing, from Egyptian

Hieroglyphics to Modern Letters, Numbers and Signs.
New York, 1961. 160 p.
Jensen, Hans. Sign, Symbol and Script: an Account of
Man's Effort to Write. 3rd ed. New York, 1969.
613 p.
Jesperson, Otto. Language, its Nature, Development and
Origin. New York, 1964. 448 p.
McMurtrie, Douglas C. The Book, the Story of Printing
and Bookmaking. New York, 1943. 676 p. (See
especially p. 1-39).
Mallery, Gerrick. Picture-Writing of the American Indians.
Washington, 1893. 822 p. (10th Annual Report of the
Bureau of American Ethnology.)
Mason, William. A History of the Art of Writing. New York,
1928. 502 p.
Moorhouse, A. C. The Triumph of the Alphabet. New York,
1953. 223 p.
Ornstein, Jacob. The ABC's of Languages and Linguistics.
Philadelphia, 1964. 205 p.
Pei, Mario. The Story of Language. Rev. ed. Philadel-
phia, 1965. 493 p.
Pumphrey, R. J. The Origin of Language. Liverpool, 1951.
39 p.
Smith, A. M. Printing and Writing Materials, their Evolu-
tion. Philadelphia, 1901. 236 p.
Sprengling, Martin. The Alphabet, its Rise and Development
from the Sinai Inscriptions. Chicago, 1931. 71 p.
Thompson, J. E. S. Maya Hieroglyphic Writing: An Intro-
duction. Norman, Okla., 1960. 347 p.
Tsien, Tsuen-Hsuin. Written on Bamboo and Silk: the Be-
ginnings of Chinese Books and Inscriptions. Chicago,
1962. 233 p.
Ullman, Berthold L. Ancient Writing and its Influence. New
York, 1932. 234 p.
Waddell, Lawrence A. The Aryan Origin of the Alphabet.
London, 1927. 80 p.
Whitney, Elwood. Symbology: the Use of Symbols in Visual
Communications. New York, 1960. 192 p.

PERIODICAL ARTICLES

Carpenter, Rhys. "The Antiquity of the Greek Alphabet,"
American Journal of Archaeology, 37 (1933), 8-29.
Chadwick, John. "Decipherment of Linear B," Natural
History, 70 (1961), 8-19, 58-71.
Diringer, David. "The Origins of the Alphabet," Antiquity,
17 (1943), 77-90.

_____. "Problems of the Present Day on the Origin of the Phoenician Alphabet," Journal of World History, 4 (1957) 40-58.

Edgerton, W. F. "Egyptian Phonetic Writing," Journal of the American Oriental Society, 60 (1940), 473-506.

Hooke, S. M. "The Early History of Writing," Antiquity, 11 (1937), 261-277.

Stieglitz, R. R. "Ugaritic Cuneiform and Canaanite Linear Alphabets," Journal of Near Eastern Studies, 30 (1971), 135-139.

Swanton, John R. "The Quipu and Peruvian Civilization," in: U. S. Bureau of American Ethnology, Anthropological Papers, 26, 587-596.

Ullman, B. L. "The Origin and Development of the Alphabet," American Journal of Archaeology, 31 (1927), 311-328.

III

ANCIENT LIBRARIES

After civilized man began to make and keep written records, the formation of libraries was a logical development. The earliest form of library was what we would today consider an archive, since it was really a collection of government or religious documents. Ancient Egypt, as one of the earliest areas to develop writing, also developed some of the earliest libraries of which we have any record. These libraries were composed of papyrus rolls, and although the earliest ones known were official collections of legal or religious records, some private and business libraries were also known to exist. Ancient Babylonia, in the Mesopotamian valley, also had libraries as early as or earlier than those in Egypt.

The government archives contained mainly official records, correspondence and chronologies, accounting for the events in the reigns of various kings, or the accomplishments of officials in the collection of taxes or the building of monuments. Some records of court cases and chronicles of military expeditions have been preserved, along with some diplomatic correspondence between countries and kings. In the temples, the papyrus "libraries" included church records, religious ceremonies and rituals, and the lives of the various Egyptian gods. Sometimes a school for the training of scribes would be associated with the temple, and thus a collection of texts, or even a separate library, for the use of the student scribes would be maintained.

Some of the wealthier Egyptian nobles and businessmen had private libraries, and since some of these books were buried with their owners in their tombs, we know more about them than we know about the official archives. In tombs that archeologists have opened and examined, "books" of papyrus have been found, tightly rolled and sealed in pottery jars. Some of them contain family records and correspondence, but others include more exciting reading in the form of travel stories, tales of war and adventures, and books of magic. Occasionally there were a few rolls concerned with science,

28

mathematics or medicine, often associated with magic. Probably the best known of all Egyptian books, and the one most
widely found in private tombs was the Book of the Dead. This
was a book of religious ritual designed to guide the souls of
the dead through the underworld to the hall of judgment, where
one's permanent position in the next world was to be decided.
The production of copies of the Book of the Dead was a profitable business, and the length and elaborateness, even the contents, of a copy varied according to the wealth and importance
of the person for whom it was purchased. A copy now preserved in the British Museum is 78 feet long and 15 inches
wide, and contains many colorful illustrations.

Evidences of a few specific Egyptian libraries have
been unearthed by archaeologists. At Tell-el-Amarna, for
example, there was a palace library, dating from about 1350
B.C., that was designated as "The Place of Records of the
Palace of the King." Of its contents, only some clay tablets
containing diplomatic correspondence have survived. In a
temple at Edfu, all traces of books have disappeared except
for a list of them that can still be read on the temple walls.
In the temple of Ptah, at Memphis, remnants of several medical works have been discovered, indicating that this edifice
may have been a temple of physical as well as spiritual
healing.

The "librarian" of the ancient Egyptian library was the
palace or temple scribe, who helped to write and to preserve
the papyrus rolls. In some cases the position of "keeper of
the books" was apparently hereditary, with the task descend-
ing from father to son. Wealthy nobles hired scribes to care
for their books, or had servants trained for the task. In
the library rooms, the papyrus rolls were kept in clay jars,
leather sleeves, or metal cylinders, depending upon the value
of the individual rolls. From one end of the container pro-
truded a title label, with a few key words of the text for
identification. These containers in turn were kept in coffers
or on shelves, but little is known as to how they were arranged or cataloged. In some cases a list of the books in a
library room was inscribed on the wall near the entrance,
as at Edfu.

Since Babylonia and Assyria made their books of baked
clay, literally thousands of them have been preserved. Evidences of many government, religious and private libraries
have been found in the ruins of the Mesopotamian cities. Considering that the major Egyptian collections were largely

archival, the Assyrians may be said to have produced the first
real library. We know that they and their predecessors
achieved very large collections of clay tablets, systematically
gathered and arranged, and including all types of literature.
According to existing records, one scribe in charge of such
a collection was given the title "Man of the Written Tablets, "
nearly 2000 years before Christ. Writing and literature
flourished under the Sumerian kings of around 2100 B.C.,
and it is reasonable to assume that libraries were present
in the schools, palaces and temples of the era. Certainly
the surviving examples of cuneiform "books" from the era
would indicate a systematic means of arranging and preserving them. Apparently the role of the scribe, trained in the
art of writing, also included the librarian's duties in many
cases, but there are indications that some scribes specialized
in keeping the cuneiform tablets in order, and thus might be
considered true librarians.

If we are uncertain of details concerning the earlier
centuries of Sumerian-Babylonian libraries, we reach firmer
ground in the seventh century B.C. During the reign of an
Assyrian king, Assurbanipal (667-628 B.C.), a library was
achieved that would be notable for its size, content and arrangement in any age. Adding to a collection begun by his
grandfather, Assurbanipal gathered in his capital city, Nine-
vah, a library of many thousands of clay tablets. Under the
direction of a royal librarian, a score or more copyists and
clerks were kept busy arranging and caring for the tablets.
Some of the works were historical chronologies and others
were government records and correspondence, but there were
also works on grammar, poetry, history, science, mythology
and religion. Dictionaries of earlier cuneiform languages
were included to aid in the translation and copying of tablets
that had been preserved for hundreds of years by Assurbanipal's time.

The clay tablets of Assurbanipal's library were arranged roughly by subject and lettered on the outside according to their contents. Longer works were written on several
tablets consecutively numbered, and the whole collection of
tablets representing a single work were probably kept together in a separate basket. Apparently works on different
subjects were kept in separate rooms, and a catalog or description of the contents of each room was written on the
door or a nearby wall, giving for each work the title or first
line, the number of lines, and for longer works the number
of tablets upon which it was written. Unfortunately the

Assyrian civilization was virtually destroyed in wars during
the seventh and sixth centuries B.C. and the magnificent library of Assurbanipal was reduced to a pile of rubble. Fortunately for history, the invading Persians simply pushed
down the library walls, so that many of the virtually inde-
structible clay tablets were preserved for some 25 centuries
until they were unearthed by archeologists in the 19th century
and later. Many thousands of these cuneiform finds are preserved in the British museum in London.

     Other outstanding collections of clay tablets have been
found in the ruins of various Mesopotamian cities, including
Ashur, Ur, Nippur and Kish, indicating that there were
probably other public or private libraries dating back to 2000
B.C. In recent years discoveries of Hittite ruins to the west
of Mesopotamia have brought to light another ancient civilization that made use of clay tablets and cuneiform writing. A
library of Hittite tablets, including a few "catalog" tablets,
or lists of writings, has been found in what was apparently
their capital or major city. Still another library has been
found near the Mediterranean coast in the ruins of the ancient
city of Ugarit (modern Ras-Shamrah), and this too consisted
of cuneiform tablets. In fact there were apparently two
major libraries in Ugarit; one was a government archive while
the other was apparently a temple library. Cuneiform tablets
have also been found on the islands of the eastern Mediterranean, such as Crete and Cyprus, indicating that this medium
of written communication found acceptance far from the Mesopotamian area of its origin.

     Although Greece had a written language by the seventh
century B.C. or earlier, and a relatively prolific literature
by the fifth century B.C., we have little real evidence of libraries in that era. The ruler Pisistratus, tyrant of Athens
from 560 to 527 B.C. is reported to have collected books for
a private or perhaps even a public library, but this is considered unsubstantiated by most historians. The works of
the philosophers and dramatists, such as Plato and Euripides,
indicate a wide acquaintance with earlier works, but the
existence and size of their libraries is largely conjecture.
For Aristotle's library we are on somewhat firmer ground,
but even here we know little of its actual contents or final
disposition. We do know that Aristotle collected books on
many subjects, used them widely in his lectures and writings,
and even loaned them to his students and friends. His own
numerous writings would have made a quite sizable collection. At his death he left his library to his follower,

Theophrastus of Lesbos, who in turn willed it to Neleus of Scepsis. After that its fate is uncertain. Part of it may have eventually reached Rome or the Alexandrian Library, but if so the individual manuscripts lost their identity in larger collections. The fact that it was kept together as long as it was indicates its value and its importance as a collection. Other Greek scholars who are credited with owning fairly notable private libraries include Euthydemus, poet and collector of Homer, Larensis of Athens, Demosthenes the orator, and Euclid the philosopher.

In addition to private libraries there were also public collections in Greece by the fourth century B.C. There was a public library in Athens that contained copies of the current Greek dramas of Aeschylus, Sophocles and Euripides, and made them available to readers who could not afford to own copies. The texts of the dramas so preserved were also "official" ones, thus making the public collection serve as something of a registry office as well as a library. By the next century, public, private and school libraries were available in Athens and the other larger Greek cities, so that scholars from all over the Mediterranean world converged upon that area for study and research.

Libraries were also established in the Greek colonies in Asia Minor, Egypt and Sicily, and it is an odd fact that more is known about some of these colonial libraries than about those in Greece proper. Antiochus the Great (223-187 B.C.) established a library at Antioch in Syria, and Euphorion of Chalcis was appointed librarian there. Archaeologists have uncovered the ruins of this library building and have found there mosaic representations of scenes from Homer and Euripides. Eumenes II, who lived from 197 to 149 B.C., and who reigned as king of Pergamum in Asia Minor, established a library in his capital city. Book scouts were sent to all parts of the Greek world to purchase or copy literary works, and the library at Pergamum grew rapidly. According to Plutarch, it contained over 200,000 rolls at its height, all housed in a beautiful temple dedicated to the goddess Athena. Crates of Malos was associated with this library and may have compiled an extensive catalog of it. The Roman ruler Antony is supposed to have taken the Pergamum Library, or a large portion of it, as spoils of war in 41 B.C. and presented it to Cleopatra of Egypt.

The greatest library of the ancient world also stemmed from the Greek cultural domination of the eastern Mediterrane-

an, and grew up at Alexandria in Egypt in the third century
B.C., under the rulers Ptolemy I and II. Actually the Alexandrian Library consisted of two, and possibly more, collections.
The larger and more famous was in the Museum, a school
or assembly of scholars patterned after Aristotle's school in
Athens, while a smaller one was in the temple dedicated to
the Egyptian god Serapis. The former is sometimes called
the Brucheium, while the latter is termed the Serapeum. At
their height around 200 B.C., the collections together are
supposed to have contained several hundred thousand rolls.
To enlarge the libraries, the Ptolemaic emperors acquired
books from all the known world, in Egyptian, Greek, Latin,
Hebrew and other languages. In most cases translations
were made into Greek, and different copies of individual
works were compared and edited in order to achieve the most
authentic texts. In addition to obtaining copies of works for
research and preservation, scribes on the staff of the Alexandrian libraries also made copies for sale, thus making the
institution a publisher as well as a library. One of the most
important works attributed to the Alexandrian scholars is the
translation from the Hebrew of the first Greek version of the
Old Testament, the Septuagint, so-called from the 70 scholars
who are supposed to have worked on it.

    Several outstanding names in Greek literature have
been connected with the Alexandrian library. Demetrius of
Phalerum, a statesman and orator, was one of the early fig-
ures connected with the library; he is in fact credited by some
writers with having planned and organized it. Zenodotus of
Ephesus, a noted grammarian, was an early librarian and so
were Aristophanes of Byzantium, a lexicographer, and Appol-
lonius of Rhodes, a poet. One of the most important names
connected with the Alexandrian library is that of Callimachus
of Cyrene. It is not certain just what his connection was, but
it is known that he compiled a catalog or bibliography, probably of the holdings of the library, that was widely known and
used in his era. The "Pinakes," as Callimachus' catalog was
called, was an author list, arranged into major subject or
form groups, such as epic poetry, dramatic poetry, laws,
philosophy, history and oratory. In addition to the bibliographical details concerning each work, Callimachus added bits
of information concerning the author, and short excerpts or
summaries of the works themselves. One author gives the
sub-title of the Pinakes as "Tables of all those who were
eminent in any kind of literature, and of their writings."
Though the work, which was reported to have been contained

in 120 rolls of papyrus, has been lost, excerpts from it appear
in the books of later authors.

The ultimate fate of the Alexandrian Library is almost
as uncertain as the names of its librarians. At its height it
attracted scholars from all over the Mediterranean world,
and there are many references to it in the works of classical
authors. Apparently at least part of the Brucheium was
burned in the fighting between the Egyptians and Romans in
47 B.C. Whether or not its losses were replaced by Antony's
gift of the Pergamum Library, it or a replacement was still
flourishing in Alexandria as late as A.D. 200s. Its significance gradually declined, however, and a fire in A.D. 273
may well have ended the library in the Brucheium. The library in the Serapeum was probably destroyed in A.D. 391
under the orders of the Christian Emperor Theodosius, who
considered it a pagan influence. Tradition also tells of an
Alexandrian Library destroyed by the Moslem conqueror Omar
in A.D. 642, but this was probably a Christian library that
had been established later on the site of the Serapeum.

In the two centuries immediately before the Christian
era, libraries were present in most if not all of the major
cities of the Greco-Roman world. Athens had a flourishing
book trade, and copies of almost any known literary work
could be purchased there. A school founded there by the
Ptolemies contained a large library and on the Island of
Rhodes a similar institution of learning was built around a
noted library. Fragments of a catalog of this library have
been found, indicating that the books were arranged by subject.
An inscription found on the Island of Cos shows that a library
there was built around donations of books and money from the
citizens of the island. Other Greek libraries of note were
located at Corinth and Delphi in Greece, and at Ephesus and
Smyrna in Asia Minor. In the later Roman conquests, many
of these libraries were destroyed or carried off as spoils of
war to Rome.

The Romans took from the countries they conquered many
cultural developments. Not only did they acquire the idea of
libraries, but the books themselves were taken from Greece,
Asia Minor and Egypt to fill the shelves of Roman libraries.
In many cases educated citizens were carried along as slaves
to become the scribes, teachers and librarians of Rome.
Roman culture was thus heavily indebted to Greece and Egypt,
but in libraries as in law the Romans improved on their
predecessors.

In the second century B.C., the Roman general Paulus, who had defeated the Macedonians, brought home a Greek library as his personal spoils of war, and in the next century, Sulla and Lucullus did the same. Sulla set up his collection of manuscripts in a special room in his palace, and employed Tyrannion, a former Greek slave, as his librarian. Lucullus went on from his conquests to become an ardent collector of books, and threw open his library to all scholars who came to use it. A few years later Julius Caesar drew up plans for a public library in Rome, patterned after the great Alexandrian Library, and commissioned Terentius Varro, an ardent book collector, to assemble it. Caesar's library never materialized, but it may have provided the plan for the library founded by Caius Asinius Pollio about 39 B.C. on the Aventine Hill, and including many works from the collections of Sulla and Varro. Each of these, like most later Roman libraries, was divided into two sections, one each for Greek and Latin books. Following Augustus, many of the later emperors founded libraries, either in Rome or in other cities, so that by A.D. 350 or so, there were reported to be no less than 28 public libraries in Rome alone. Possibly the most famous of the classical Roman libraries was the Bibliotheca Ulpiana, founded by the Emperor Trajan around A.D. 114. Housed in the Forum of Trajan, this library consisted of two rooms, each 60 by 45 feet, on opposite sides of a colonnaded court. Busts of important Greek and Latin authors stood guard over their respective works. In the center of the court was a huge stone replica of a papyrus scroll, symbolic perhaps of Trajan's own history of his wars. The Ulpian Library had the odd fate of being housed, at least temporarily in the fourth century, in the Baths of Diocletian. Since there were reading rooms and lecture halls along with the Baths, this was really more of a gentleman's club than a public bath, so the Library was not too much out of place.

The public libraries in Rome approached the modern conception of public libraries in that they were not only publicly owned, but they were freely used by anyone who could read, and it was not uncommon to see both noblemen and slaves using them at the same time. In organization, the Roman libraries were apparently patterned after those of Greece and Egypt, with the rolls arranged according to subject or title on shelves or in bins. The average book was rolled on a wooden core and preserved in a leather wrapper, or perhaps in an earthen jar, but the more valuable and more elaborate works were sometimes wrapped around an

ivory center and preserved in bronze cylinders. By the third
century after Christ, Roman libraries began to contain folded
or bookform codices. Ordinarily books had to be used in the
library or in adjacent reading areas, but there are a few
references in classical literature to books being taken out by
important scholars or noblemen.

There were several types of library workers in the
Roman libraries and under some emperors there was even an
imperial library administrator who supervised all the public
libraries in Rome. Each library in turn had its own administrator or procurator who apparently concerned himself with
acquisition and administrative duties. The more direct work
with the books was done by workers of various grades, including many slaves. Some of them worked only with Greek
books, while others worked with Latin. Some were copyists
and transcribed additional works, while still others were
translators. It is interesting to note that some of these
classical library workers were women.

Many Roman private libraries were almost as large
and elaborate as the public libraries. Cicero had a large
book collection of his own, and Serenius Sammonicus, of the
third century was reported to have built up a library of over
60,000 volumes. Epaphroditus, who lived during the reign of
Nero, left a collection of 30,000 rolls. In the ruins of Herculaneum, a city destroyed in the eruption of Mount Vesuvius in
A.D. 79, there has been found the remains of a large private
library. This collection of some 1700 volumes was found in
a room about 12 feet square with the walls lined with book
cases all the way to the ceiling. The rolls were charred and
in very bad condition, but careful treatment has made many of
them readable. Apparently this collector specialized in the
works of the Epicurean philosophers, and there is some evidence that the owner was the philosopher Philodemus. The
collecting of books and the building of private libraries became such a fad among the wealthy noblemen and merchants
of Rome that Seneca is supposed to have said, "Nowadays a
library is considered a necessary ornament with which to
adorn a house, along with hot and cold baths." The libraries
of the wealthier nobles had librarians of their own, usually
educated slaves, trained to keep them in order and to copy
works from other sources.

Closely connected with libraries, then as always, was
the book manufacturer and the book seller. In prosperous
times, the demand for copies of books was so great that the

wholesale publishing of certain works became profitable.   An
enterprising bookseller would hire a number of scribes, or
perhaps purchase slaves who could write a good hand, and
set them to copying the book in demand.   One would read
from the text, while ten or 12 writers would copy, and a
proofreader stood by to assure the accuracy of their work.
There were a number of such book manufacturers in Rome,
some of whom were renowned for the quality of their publishing.   There was no copyright to prevent anyone from copying
any work, but in many cases prominent authors allowed their
works to be copied and sold by only one dealer, thus making
him in effect their sole publisher.   Adjoining the booksellers'
shops were posts on which lists of books for sale were placed.
On market days public criers were sometimes employed to
stand before the shops and proclaim the volumes for sale.
Some of the larger bookshops had recital rooms where would-
be authors could read or recite their works to anyone who
cared to listen.   If a listener was captivated enough by the
recital to purchase a copy, a scribe was set to work to produce it.

        The great age of Roman libraries lasted some 500 years,
but like so many other ancient book collections, those of
Rome were all destroyed sooner or later.   Even while Rome
was still strong and powerful, accidental fires consumed
several famous libraries.   In A.D. 80, a catastrophic fire
destroyed the Octavian Library along with several temples
and theatres.   In 192, the great Palatine Library was burned,
and also the library of the Temple of Peace.   But the great
loss of Roman libraries came in the fifth century with the
fall of Rome itself.   Waves of barbarians swept over the
Italian peninsula, and virtually all vestiges of the once great
civilization were destroyed.   Most of the libraries disappeared
more from neglect than from fires or vandalism, but the effect was the same.   What we know of Roman libraries comes
from the archaeological remains, particularly those of the
buried cities of Pompeii and Herculaneum, or from the brief
statements about them in the surviving works of the great
Roman writers that were preserved elsewhere.   Fortunately,
the writings of the Latin historians, poets and philosophers
were well known in Greece and Asia Minor, and it was largely in those places that they survived when Rome itself was
ransacked.

        One interesting library of the early Roman era was
that of a religious group in what is now Israel.   This group,
thought to have been the Essenes, led a monastic-like existence

from about 125 B.C. to about A.D. 70, and the remains of a
library of their writings have been discovered.   These "Dead
Sea Scrolls" found at Qumran were largely parchment rolls
stored in clay jars, although some were papyrus and at least
one was on thin copper.   This "library" was largely theological in nature, containing most of the books of the Old
Testament along with scriptural commentaries.   Now housed
in an Israeli museum in Jerusalem, these ancient manuscripts are considered one of the greatest archeological discoveries of the 20th century.

     The early Christians also began to collect their scrip-
tures into religious libraries; several of these are known to
have existed by about A.D. 200.   Probably the earliest one
was formed by a colony of Christians in the Egyptian city,
Alexandria, but Bishop Alexander of Jerusalem formed one
there in the late third century.   Clement of Alexandria, a
contemporary, quoted from over 300 authors in his writings,
indicating that he had a rather large library at his disposal.
Eusebius, writing his history of the Christian Church about
330 used a library at Caesarea, and St. Jerome used the same
collection later.   After 325, when the Roman Emperor Constantine recognized the Christian church and founded the city
of Constantinople, the collecting and preserving of Christian
literature proceeded in the churches and monasteries of the
eastern Mediterranean world.   Some of them were destroyed
by the Moslems in the seventh century, but Constantinople
itself survived until 1453.

     After the Emperor Constantine transferred his capital
to Constantinople, many libraries of notable size were developed there.   A royal library was begun soon after 325 and
within a decade contained over 4000 volumes.   By the middle of
the next century it contained over 100,000 volumes, and was
at that time probably the greatest library in the world, but
like its Roman counterparts, it too suffered from a disastrous
fire in A.D. 477.   By this time, however, there was a large
university in Constantinople with a sizable library of its own.
It flourished for several centuries, with special collections
in law and medicine.   Still a third major library was that of
the Patriarch of the Eastern Church at Constantinople, while
other temple, monastery and school libraries were to be
found throughout the Eastern Roman or Byzantine Empire.
Altogether, these libraries made Constantinople a great cultural center for more than a thousand years.   Though more
Greek than Latin, the Byzantine culture preserved much of
the Roman heritage, sometimes in complete works, but more
often in excerpts or epitomes.   In the field of law, Con-

stantinople actually contributed to the Roman heritage, since it was here that the great Code of Justinian was compiled rather than in Rome itself, although it was of course based on the earlier Roman law.

The libraries of Constantinople were rivaled in the seventh and later centuries by the new ones springing up in the Moslem world that developed to the east and south. The followers of Mohammed esteemed the book second only to the sword, and although for the majority of the people there was only one book, the Koran, there were many scholars who translated, studied and preserved the classical literature of the Greeks and Romans. As early as 689 there was a library and archival collection at Damascus, then the center of the Moslem empire, and in the next century there were libraries in most of the Moslem cities from central Asia to Egypt. Baghdad, for example, had both public and university libraries, with the public one open to all who could read, and with the university library providing copying and translating services for scholars. Mathematics, medicine and most of the sciences were particularly well represented in the Moslem libraries, but there were also poetry, geography and history, and the pseudosciences of alchemy and astrology.

By the tenth century the Moslem culture had spread throughout North Africa and into Sicily and Spain, and for several centuries there were magnificent libraries and universities in Moslem cities from Bokhara, east of the Caspian Sea, to Cordova in Spain. The Moslem libraries contained books in scores of languages and by hundreds of authors from England to India. Many of their books, particularly copies of the Koran, were works of art, beautifully written, decorated and bound. Unfortunately, these libraries too were destined to be destroyed by the 14th century. Civil wars, Christian crusaders, and the Asiatic hordes of Genghiz Khan and Tamerlane all combined to destroy Moslem libraries, and scarcely one in a hundred of their books have survived in even a single copy.

The Far East, too, had its cultural centers. There were schools and libraries in China long before the Christian era. The Chinese had a written literature as early as 1500 B.C., and their "classical" era of philosophy and history, beginning by 1000 B.C., reached its height in the fifth century B.C. with Confucius. Official libraries and archives for the use of scholars were widespread, but in 213 B.C., the "Burning of the Books" by a zealous emperor almost wiped out the collective literary heritage of the earlier centuries.

Under the Han dynasty, from about 200 B.C. to A.D. 280,
state archives and libraries again flourished, and an attempt
was made to obtain copies of all written works in the empire
to be organized, cataloged, and made available to government
officials and scholars. In A.D. 79, a great convocation of
scholars was called together to edit and confirm the texts of
all surviving historical literature. It was said that when the
national capital was moved in A.D. 50, from one city to
another, it took 2000 carts to move the books and manuscripts.
Early Chinese writings were on bamboo and silk, but paper was
invented about A.D. 105 and cultural contacts were established
with India, and at least temporarily with Rome. The introduction of Buddhism into China from India resulted in an increased
interest in scholarship and learning, and consequently in the
collection of books into religious and scholarly libraries.
Wars, revolutions and accidental fires took their toll over the
centuries on Chinese libraries, but a strong cultural continu-
ity was maintained to give China what is probably the oldest
continuous civilization in the world.

Generally speaking, the ancient library was a product
of its civilization. It appeared whenever a people had reached
the point where they had writing materials, a written
language, and records to preserve. It progressed in size,
complexity and elaborateness as civilization itself advanced. It
suffered from natural disasters and from man-made wars.
Centers of learning shifted as the tides of war built new
capitals on ancient ruins--and made ruins out of old capitals.
Whenever a civilization was overthrown by a more primitive
people, books and libraries disappeared and ignorance returned. If our study of ancient libraries teaches us nothing
else, it shows us that the library in some form is a necessary part of any advanced human society. The preservation
of recorded knowledge is vital to cultural growth and progress.

Bibliography
                         BOOKS

Boyd, Clarence B.   Public libraries and Literary Culture in
        Ancient Rome. Chicago, 1915.   69 p.
Brassington, William S.   A History of the Art of Bookbinding,
        with Some Account of the Books of the Ancients.   Lon-
        don, 1894.   270 p.
Budge, E. A. W.   The Literature of the Ancient Egyptians.
        London, 1914.   272 p.

Bushnell, G. H.   The World's Earliest Libraries.   London,
    1931. 58 p.
Clark, J. W.   The Care of Books: an Essay on the Develop-
    ment of Libraries and their Fittings. Cambridge,
    England, 1902. 352 p.
Clift, Evelyn H.   Latin Pseudepigraphia: a Study in Literary
    Attributions. Baltimore, 1945, 158 p.
Cress, F. M.   The Ancient Library of Qumran and Modern
    Biblical Studies. New York, 1958. 196 p.
Dahl, Svend.   History of the Book. New York, 1958. 279 p.
Dunlap, Leslie W.   Alexandria: the Capital of Memory.
    Emporia, Kansas, 1963. 25 p.
Edwards, Edward.   Memoirs of Libraries. London, 1858.
    (Reprinted New York, 1968. See particularly v. 1.,
    p. 1-82.) 2 v.
Fiore, Sylvestro.   Voices from the Clay: a Study of Assyro-
    Babylonian Literary Culture. Norman, Okla., 1965.
    254 p.
Hessel, Alfred.   A History of Libraries. New Brunswick,
    N. J., 1955. 198 p.
Holliday, Carl.   The Dawn of Literature. New York, 1931.
    367 p.
Johnson, E. D.   A History of Libraries in the Western World.
    Metuchen, N. J., 1970. 521 p. (See p. 1-109.) 2nd ed.
Kenyon, Frederick G.   Ancient Books and Modern Discover-
    ies. Chicago, 1927. 83 p.
Kenyon, Frederic G.   Books and Readers in Ancient Greece
    and Rome. Oxford, 1932. 136 p.
Kramer, Samuel N.   From the Tablets of Sumer. Indian
    Mills, Colorado, 1956. 293 p.
Laessoe, Jorgen.   People of Ancient Assyria, their Inscrip-
    tions and Correspondence. New York, 1963. 169 p.
Lanciani, Rodolfo.   Ancient Rome in the Light of Recent
    Discoveries. Boston, 1900. 329 p. (See p. 178-205.)
Maspero, Gaston.   Life in Ancient Egypt and Assyria. New
    York, 1912. 376 p. (See p. 287-302 on "Assurbanipal's
    Library.")
Myer, Isaac.   The Oldest Books in the World. New York,
    1900. 502 p.
Nichols, C. L.   The Library of Rameses the Great. Boston,
    1909. 43 p. (Reprinted Berkeley, Calif., 1964.)
Parsons, Edward A.   The Alexandrian Library. New York,
    1952. 468 p.
Pedley, Katharine G.   The Library at Qumran. Berkeley,
    Calif., 1964. 23 p.
Platthy, Jeno.   Sources on the Earliest Greek Libraries.
    Amsterdam, 1968. 203 p.
Pinner, H. L.   The World of Books in Classical Antiquity.

Leiden, 1958. 64 p. 2nd ed.
Putnam, George H. Authors and Their Public in Ancient
    Times. New York, 1894. 326 p.
Reynolds, L. D., and Wilson, N. G. Scribes and Scholars.
    Oxford, 1968. 192 p.
Richardson, Ernest C. Beginnings of Libraries. Princeton,
    1914. 176 p. (Reprinted Hamden, Conn., 1963).
Richardson, Ernest C. Biblical Libraries. Princeton,
    1914. 252 p. (Reprinted Hamden, Conn., 1963.)
Richardson, Ernest C. Some old Egyptian Libraries. New
    York, 1911. 93 p. (Reprinted Berkeley, Calif., 1964.)
Thompson, James W. Ancient Libraries. Chicago, 1939.
    120 p. (Reprinted Hamden, Conn., 1962.)
Van Hook, LeRue. Greek Life and Thought. New York,
    1923. 329 p. (See p. 114-121 on "Greek Libraries.")

PERIODICAL ARTICLES

Buksh, S. K. "The Islamic Libraries," Nineteenth Century,
    52 (1902), 125-139.
Davis, D. G., Jr. "Christianity and Pagan Libraries in the
    Later Roman Empire," Library History, 2 (1970),
    1-10.
Dunlap, Leslie W. "The library at Nineveh," Stechert-Hafner
    Book News, 15 (1961), 81-83.
Guppy, Henry. "Human records, a survey of their history
    from the beginnings," John Rylands Library Bulletin, 27
    (1942), 182-222.
Highet, Gilbert. "The Wondrous Survival of Records," Horizon,
    5 (November 1962), 75-94.
Irwin, Raymond. "Callimachus," Library Association Records,
    58 (May 1956), 168-173.
Johnson, E. D. "Ancient Libraries as Seen in the Greek and
    Roman Classics," Radford Review, 23 (1969), 73-92.
Kleberg, Tonnes. "Bibliophiles in Ancient Rome," Libri,
    1 (1950), 2-12.
Mackensen, Ruth S. "Background of the History of Moslem
    Libraries," American Journal of Semitic Languages and
    Literature, 51 (1934-35), 114-125; 52 (1935-36), 22-33,
    104-110.
Miller, Walter. "Hadrian's Library and Gymnasium,"
    Art and Archaeology, 33 (1932), 89-91.
Rau, R. V. "Did Omar Destroy the Alexandrian Library?"
    Nineteenth Century, 36 (1894), 555-571.
Reichman, Felix. "The Book Trade at the Time of the
    Roman Empire," Library Quarterly, 7 (1938), 40-76.
Root, Robert K. "Publication before Printing," Publications

of the Modern Language Association, 28 (1913), 417-431.

Sperry, John A. "Egyptian Libraries: a Survey of the Evidence," Libri, 7 (1957), 45-55.

Weitemeyer, Mogens. "Archive and Library Technique in Ancient Mesopotamia," Libri, 6 (1956), 217-238.

Wilson, N. G. "The Libraries of the Byzantine World," Greek, Roman and Byzantine Studies, 8 (1967), 53-80.

Witty, Francis J. "The Pinakes of Callimachus," Library Quarterly, 28 (1958), 132-136.

Wyss, Wilhelm V. "The Libraries of Antiquity," Living Age, 306 (1923), 217-249.

IV

BOOKS AND LIBRARIES IN THE MIDDLE AGES

After the fall of Rome in the fifth century, Europe entered 900 years or more of the Dark Ages and the cultural progress that Rome had made largely disappeared. True, in parts of the former Western Empire, particularly in southern France and eastern Spain remnants of Roman civilization survived into the seventh century. Also in Greece, southern Italy, Sicily and southern Spain, the nearness of, or actual control by, Byzantine and Moslem cultures provided a stimulus that kept libraries and learning alive, but for the great majority of Europe, the denomination of the era as "dark ages" is essentially correct. The classical libraries created by the Romans were destroyed, scattered, or allowed to decay, so that only a few copies remained of the thousands of manuscripts that had made Rome a center of learning. Not until the modern era would there again be libraries in most of Europe to compare with those of imperial Rome, and not until the Renaissance would there be very much added to the secular literature that Greece and Rome had left to posterity. Even before A. D. 500, papyrus had largely given way to vellum and parchment as writing materials, and the roll had been replaced by the codex, which remained the major book form of the Middle Ages. But making books was still a laborious process of writing and binding books by hand, and there was no major change in these processes until the inventions of printing in the 15th century. This hand-making of books became an art, however, and in illustrating, illuminating and binding, the best medieval manuscript books equal or surpass anything produced today.

In the midst of the Dark Ages, there were several forces at work, though not always together, to preserve something of the culture of Rome and Greece, and to keep alive the learning of that advanced age. The institution usually credited with preserving books and learning during the Middle Ages, and in western Europe, is the monastery, and undoubtedly it did play a major role. But the monastic libraries were primarily concerned with the Bible and religious literature. Aside from texts employed in teaching

the Latin language, and a few classical authors read for
moral lessons, the preservation of secular literature in the
monasteries was usually incidental. Private book collectors,
present to some degree throughout the Dark Ages, also took
part in preserving the classics, especially the secular ones.
These private book collectors were wealthy merchants or
noblemen, occasionally an abbot or bishop of the church, and
particularly in the cities around the Mediterranean. Some of
them collected manuscripts for show and prestige, but, whatever their motives, they did acquire, preserve and have
copied many notable works. After the 11th century, the
medieval university took its place as an active participant in
collecting, editing and copying the earlier authors. As already mentioned, the Moslem world from Asia to Spain did
its share in preserving works of the classical authors, as did
also the Byzantine civilization around Constantinople. Occasional enlightened monarchs, the Charlemagnes and Alfreds,
whose reigns stand out like beacons in an otherwise gloomy
era, also aided in the collecting of books and the preservation of knowledge.

The monastery had its beginnings in the eastern Mediterranean area and in North Africa long before the fall of
Rome. In addition to the Essenes other Jewish and early
Christian groups found that religious worship could best be
carried on in a relatively isolated community. During the
second century, monks of the Coptic Christian sects were
forming monasteries in Egypt and manuscripts of the early
Christian writings stocked their libraries. Several other
Christian monasteries were formed in the area from Egypt
to Greece before the fourth century, and there was a monastery at Marseilles on the Mediterranean coast of France
around A.D. 410, but the most significant movement in European monastic history began in Italy in the sixth century.
One of the most important of these early Italian monasteries
was that at Monte Cassino, found about 530 by St. Benedict.
Just when a library was founded at Monte Cassino is uncertain, but St. Benedict's rules of monastic life included regular reading, especially at meals and during the evenings, so
books must have been available. Cassiodorus, a noble who
had served with the ruler, Theodoric the Goth, retired from
his office in 554 to live as a monk on his estate in Calabria
in southern Italy. Here at Vivarium, as he called his combination of monastery, scriptorium and theological school,
he began a library with his own collection of manuscripts
and spent the remainder of his long life in promoting learning. He continued to collect manuscripts, both religious and

secular, and trained monks in the art of copying them, until he had a library of at least 300 titles. Cassiodorus wrote several works himself, including a lengthy History of the Goths, and a handbook of monastery rules and regulations known as the Institutiones. This work included a section on the proper use of the monastery library, and a bibliography of religious and secular literature that may have been a checklist of the library then at Vivarium. Unfortunately, Cassiodorus' library did not long survive him, but his Institutiones did survive, and this work remained a popular volume in monasteries throughout the Middle Ages.

Oddly enough, the spread of monasteries into the remainder of Europe came not so much from southern Italy as from Ireland. That island had been converted to Christianity in the fifth century, and by the end of the sixth it was the cultural center of northern Europe, with flourishing monasteries and schools attended by students from all over Europe. Missionaries from Ireland, including Saints Columba and Columban, established monasteries in Scotland, England, France, and other parts of Western Europe. Among these monasteries were Iona in Scotland, Lindisfarne in England, Luxeuil and Corbie in France, Gall in Switzerland, Würzburg in Germany, and Bobbio in northern Italy. Libraries were founded in each of these institutions very early in its history, and soon they were cultural centers in their respective areas. Books for these early monastic libraries were obtained from Ireland or from the older religious libraries in southern Italy. The monks who obtained or copied them often made long and dangerous trips just to secure a needed text or even to compare one copy with another. A story is told of one bishop in southern France detaining a traveler by force until his scribes could complete the copying of a book that he was carrying.

The spread of the monasteries, and hence of monastic libraries, was greatly encouraged by the establishment of the various orders on monks. The Benedectine order, one of the earliest, was particularly interested in books and learning and each of their monasteries was required to have a library. Some of the more important Benedictine monastic libraries were those at Monte Cassino in Italy, Fleury and Cluny in France, and Peterborough in England. The Augustinians and the Dominicans were also great lovers of books, and their libraries ranked second only to those of the Benedictines. The libraries of the Cistercians were designed wholly to assist in their religious studies, and

contained almost no secular literature, but those of the Car-
thusians were more worldly and as much as a third of their
works might treat of nonreligious subjects. Even the Franciscans, who disavowed most worldly goods, made an exception of books, and their monasteries developed libraries
nearly equal to those of other orders.

Whatever its order, the monastery usually included
special locations or quarters for its library and scriptorium.
The latter was a work-place where books were copied, illuminated and bound. In some cases a group of writers or
"scriptores" sat or stood at sloping desks and copied, hour
after hour, as another monk read to them. More often, the
copyist was his own reader, and only one copy could be
made at a time. A copyist could spend months, or even a
year, in the careful copying of one volume. After the text
was copied, the pages might go to an artist-monk who would
illuminate them with ornamental drawings for the capital letters and along the borders. If these illuminations were in
red, as they often were, they were termed rubrications, and
the artist was a rubricator. Other colors, including gold
and silver, were used in more ornate works and sometimes
the parchment or vellum itself was tinted. The art of book
illumination reached a high level during the later Middle Ages
but many of the earlier works were also noted for their
beauty. The Lindisfarne Gospels, produced at the monastery
of Lindisfarne in north England before A. D. 700, survives
in the British Museum as an example of this era. Even
more beautiful is the Book of Kells, a copy of the four gospels made in an Irish monastery about A. D. 800. This has
been called one of the most beautiful books ever produced,
and is now preserved in the library of Trinity College,
Dublin.

The bindings of books produced in the monasteries
also reached near perfection. They were made of fine
leathers and textiles, sometimes even of gold or silver.
Precious stones were sometimes set in bindings or into the
metal clasps that held the heavier books together. For
larger books, the covers were sometimes made of wood,
covered with leather or cloth. The leather bindings were
ornamented with fancy toolings, either "blind" as the plain
toolings were called, or with colors or gold foil pressed
into the embossings. More valuable books, and sometimes
the more frequently consulted books, were often chained to
the tables or lecterns upon which they lay, or fastened to
shelves with chains long enough to reach a nearby desk or
table.

In the early Middle Ages, the books in the monastery libraries were still kept in chests rather than upon shelves or lecterns. The book chest was known as an armarium, and thus the early monastic librarian was designated an "armarius. " Other medieval terms for the librarian were "bibliothecarius, " and "custos librorum" or keeper of the books. In later periods, and in some monasteries, the position of librarian might be combined with that of the director of singing or "precentor. " Whatever his title, he usually had other duties besides "keeping the books" and might supervise the scriptorium and book bindery as well.

Catalogs of the monastic book collections were usually little more than accession lists. Some of them have survived, and from them we can tell a little about the contents of the average medieval library. The books of the Bible, usually in St. Jerome's translation into Latin, were always present, often in multiple copies. Next in importance came the commentaries on the Bible and the lives of the saints. The early Christian writings were usually present, with St. Augustine being a favorite. His City of God was probably the most popular single work other than the Bible. Secular works were usually kept separate from the works on theology, but there were generally few of them. Among these there would usually be works on philosophy, science and medicine, with even a few books on magic. Only a few of the classic authors were ordinarily present and these often varied widely from monastery to monastery. Cicero and Seneca were popular, along with Vergil and Horace and the historians Sallust and Suetonius. In the later medieval period, the works of Ovid and Juvenal became more popular and Greek writers, particularly Aristotle, became better known, at least in Latin translation. The Latin secular writers were studied by the monks in order to gain greater facility in reading Latin and thus to be able to read the religious works in that language more readily. Each monastery usually contained some works on local history and the writings of local authors, but for the most part the monastic library in England was apt to be very similar in contents to that in France or Italy. Sometimes secular works were preserved unintentionally when the parchment on which they were written was washed or erased, and a religious work written over it. The original writing would not be completely obliterated and could later be read after special treatment. Such accidentally preserved manuscripts are called "palimpsests. "

The usual method of acquisition for monastery libraries was by copying.   A manuscript could sometimes be borrowed for copying, and on other occasions a monk would be
sent from one monastery to another to copy literary treasures.
Sometimes such trips would take a monk from Ireland to
Spain, or from Poland to Italy, just to obtain a copy of a
needed work.   If funds were available, copies of some works
could be bought, and generous friends sometimes donated
books from their own libraries.   Bequests of books on the
death of noblemen, merchants and church officials often increased the size of monastic libraries.   Sometimes these
gifts were substantial and consisted of whole private libraries, but often they consisted of only one or two books.   On
the other hand, books were sometimes removed from monastic libraries by force, either by raiding armies or avaricious
rulers, and it was not unknown for books to be given by a
monastery to a prince or bishop, just to obtain his favor.

As monastery collections grew larger, methods had to
be devised for arranging and separating the books.   Separa-
tion by language, or into religious and secular divisions, or
by size of volume were methods employed at various times
and places, and later there were attempts to arrange books
by major subjects.   Occasionally books were arranged solely
by donor, thus keeping gift collections together, regardless
of subject.   Whatever the arrangement, the only catalog was
a list of books, sometimes by author, sometimes by title or
first line, and usually not even alphabetical.   Usually these
lists were used more for inventories than for finding purposes.   Ordinarily the books in the library were available only
to the monks or their students, but there are accounts of
"inter-library loans" between monasteries, and of borrowings
of books by important personages.   In the latter case, a sum
of money or a book of like value might be left as deposit for
the volume borrowed.   In the early Middle Ages, when books
were few, works were assigned to individual monks for reading by the season, or even by the year.   At appointed times,
all books would be returned and new ones issued.   Virtually
the entire collection might thus be in use at any given time.
As collections grew each reader might have a greater choice.
As the custom of chaining the more valuable books arose,
the collection would be divided into those chained and those
available for use elsewhere.   These "circulating" books
would probably be duplicates or less valuable works.   It
should be pointed out that in almost every monastery there
were periods in which the monks would be uninterested in
their library, and its condition and size would deteriorate,

only to be rebuilt when more interested leaders took over.
There are several accounts of medievial travelers finding a
noted library, such as even that at Monte Cassino, in a
deplorable condition.

In the midst of the Dark Ages, the reign of the Frank-
ish emperor, Charlemagne (742-814), stands out as far as
books and learning are concerned. Charlemagne himself was
something of a scholar, and he felt a need to improve and
spread learning in order to hold his large and sprawling empire together. He gathered a personal library of note but he
is mainly remembered for the palace library which he directed to be collected, not only from his realm but from other
lands. Important works in Italy and Spain were copied for
Charlemagne's library, and at least one volume came from
the imperial library at Constantinople. Once the books were
gathered, scholars were put to work collating and comparing
texts to test their authenticity and to remove interpolations
added by over-enthusiastic copyists. The style of writing was
improved during this period and a new script, usually termed
the Carolingian minuscule, was developed for use by the court
scribes. This script proved so popular that it remained in
use for several hundred years. The word "Carolingian"
came from the Latin form of the Emperor's name, while
"minuscule" identified the script as being in small letters
rather than the "majuscule" or capital letters in general use
since the days of the Romans. Libraries and learning went
through a premature renaissance in the days of Charlemagne,
and scholars from Greece to Britain visited his capital at
Aachen to use the palace library there.

Among the scholars attracted to Charlemagne's court
was the distinguished English Monk, Alcuin (735-804). Alcuin had helped to build the monastery library at York,
England, into one of the best libraries in Europe, and had
become renowned as a religious leader and teacher. Charlemagne first called on Alcuin to direct a school which had
grown up around his court. This school seems to have been
something of an informal college for the training of officials
and nobles, but it also attracted lay scholars and religious
leaders. Upon the success of this educational venture,
Charlemagne encouraged the establishment of similar schools
throughout his realm, which then included most of western
Europe. Alcuin advised that if a library and scriptorium
were established at any given place a school would naturally
grow up around it.

Later Alcuin became the abbot of St. Martin of Tours in southern France, and there he established a model library for a religious institution. He made his church library something of a source collection, where authorized texts of the Bible and other religious works were kept for copying by anyone who could visit or pay for a copyist. But Alcuin never forgot the book treasures of the library at York, and he asked Charlemagne to send scribes to copy those "flowers of Britain" so that he could be surrounded with them in his abbey at Tours. Charlemagne and Alcuin stand out in the field of library history, but like others before them, their efforts did not long survive. Charlemagne's grandson, Charles the Bald, preserved the palace library, but after his death the feudal wars and Viking invasions that swept much of western Europe destroyed most of the schools and libraries that Charlemagne had begun.

In the 11th and 12th centuries the monasteries of Germany and central Europe, especially those at Fulda, Corvey, St. Gall and Regensburg, were active in building and preserving libraries. In these institutions, which were generally schools as well as monasteries, the position of "librarius" became established as the custodian of the books. It was his duty to arrange the books, to see that sufficient copies of the more important texts were available, to keep records of use, and in general to carry out the usual functions of a librarian. The library cooperated closely with the scriptorium, and books borrowed from other monasteries could be copied for the collection. One of these 11th-century monastery librarians has left us a list of his 64 readers and their reading for one Lenten season. Needless to say, most of the works read were religious. Twenty-two monks chose works of the early Christian writers, such as St. Jerome and St. Augustine. Twelve chose commentaries on the Bible written by medieval scholars, while 11 others took works on monastic life and discipline. Nineteen were reading works of church history such as those of Bede, Orosius and Eusebius, or minor theological works. Only one individual was reading a secular writer, and he was perusing the works of the Roman historian, Livy.

Closely akin to the monastery library was the cathedral library, which developed largely after the eleventh century. Since the cathedral was the seat of a bishop and a religious center, it was often connected with a theological school and its library was for the use of students as well as for the church officials. The cathedral libraries were often

larger and broader in content than those of the monasteries.
In some cases there might be three collections of books associated with a cathedral--a main theological library; a
group of service books, often chained, for public use; and
a library for the use of the student priests. Some of the
better known cathedral libraries were those at Durham,
York and Canterbury in England; at Notre Dame, Orleans and
Rouen in France; at Bamberg and Hildesheim in Germany;
and at Barcelona and Toledo in Spain. The cathedral libraries were usually larger than those in the monasteries, but
they were fewer, and their general effect on the cultural
history of western Europe is less noticeable. However they
do serve in a sense to bridge the gap, both chronologically
and culturally, between the monastic library and the medieval
university.

Although in the later Middle Ages a cathedral library
might have over a thousand volumes, most medieval libraries
numbered their books in the hundreds. The monastery library at St. Gall in Switzerland had only 300 volumes in the
ninth century, while that at Reichenau in Germany had only
413. The famous Benedictine monastery at Bobbio in northern
Italy possessed 650 books three centuries after its founding,
and in the 12th century, that at Cluny in France had 570.
The cathedral library at Durham had only about 600 volumes
in 1200, while that at Rouen in France was even smaller.
It should be pointed out that the medieval volume was often
quite large, containing many times as much material as the
classic papyrus roll. Also, it was common to have several
separate works bound together into a single volume, so that
the number of titles in a library would often exceed the number of volumes. A 15th-century catalog of the library at
Peterborough in England seems to indicate that there were
1695 separate works bound into only 344 volumes.

In the sixth and seventh centuries, Spain had a flourishing Latin culture similar to that of southern France. In
Seville, for example, Bishop Isidore (ca. 600-635) collected
a large library and wrote numerous books, while in other
Spanish cities there were notable church and private libraries. The Iberian peninsula was conquered by the Moslems in
the eighth century, but this soon resulted in another highly
developed civilization with such cities as Toledo, Seville and
Córdoba becoming centers of culture and learning. The University of Córdoba in the tenth century was one of the three
greatest Moslem universities, and there were lesser colleges
at Salamanca and other Spanish cities. No less than 70

important libraries were reported in Spain during the tenth to 12th centuries, many of them filled with rare and beautiful books. Book collectors, both official and private, obtained their literary treasures from as far away as India and England. The technique of paper-making entered western Europe through Spain, brought by Arabs who learned of it from the Chinese in the eighth century. The ornate Morocco leather book bindings were also introduced to Europe in the 11th century or so. The Spanish Moslems were not only collectors of books, they were writers as well, and they produced many of the important medieval works in science and philosophy. By the late 12th century, however, Moslem civilization in Spain was on the decline, and there were political and religious leaders who ordered books destroyed and who banned writing contrary to the prevailing religious beliefs. Later on, wars among the Moslems, and between the Moslems and Christians, destroyed still more books and libraries. By the 16th century, when King Philip II was gathering materials for a royal library, he found that the only source for books on the Moslem history of Spain was North Africa, because all Arabic books in Spain had been destroyed.

From the fall of Rome to the 1100s, education in western Europe was largely in the hands of monasteries. Cathedral schools developed after the tenth century, but their emphasis was largely on religious education. Even in the monasteries most of the instruction beyond the elementary years was theological, but it was usual for the monks to give the rudiments of schooling to the sons of neighboring noblemen, and sometimes to promising sons of poorer parents. Some of the monastic orders encouraged education, and during the reigns of some enlightened monarchs there were brief periods of educational progress. In the later middle ages, schools for the training of clerks for the growing business firms were begun in some of the cities; but reading, writing and arithmetic were about the extent of their studies. Whatever the type of school, lessons were memorized and recited by rote; independent thought or reading outside the prescribed texts was not encouraged. The quality of teaching was usually poor, and the few great teacher-scholars, such as Peter Abelard (1079-1142) in Paris, and John of Salisbury (d. 1180) at Canterbury, stand out far beyond their fellows. By the late 11th century, however, a few of the schools were reaching into higher education, and in Paris degrees of bachelor of arts were being given at the completion of a prescribed series of studies.

The development of the medieval universities, in the
12th century and later, changed this pattern and raised the
level of learning in western Europe to a point where the
Renaissance could begin. The earliest universities of note
were those in northern Italy at Bologna and Padua, and
these grew largely out of informal groups of students who
hired learned men to teach them. Law, both civil and religious, and medicine were subjects that were much in demand and competent teachers were scarce. When a group of
teachers, each teaching a different subject, met with their
students with some regularity in one location a "university"
was born. Later on, the power to grant degrees was obtained from civil or religious authorities or both, and a
more formal course of studies was required. Generally
speaking, however, the medieval university student usually
studied under one teacher until he felt that he had learned
all he could from that source, and then went on to another.
Before a degree could be received, an examination before a
group of the masters or teachers had to be taken and passed.
The university idea spread throughout all of Europe, and by
1500 there were some 50 or 60 of them, scattered from
Spain to Scandinavia and from England to Poland.

In these early universities there were no libraries as
such, in fact there were no campuses or stately buildings as
are usually associated with universities. Each master had
a collection of books which he might lend or rent to his students. Each student, in turn, had to buy not only his textbooks, but also any other book he might wish to read, unless
he could borrow or rent it from a master or bookseller.
Only the most wealthy of students could afford to own all the
texts he might wish to study, so the book rental trade was
brisk. Usually the university authorities controlled the book
trade in order to guarantee the authenticity of the texts and
the booksellers, or "stationarii," were licensed by them as
were the dealers in parchment and other writing materials.

As the universities grew in size, they usually came
to be divided into colleges, and it was in these colleges that
the earliest academic libraries were begun. It became the
custom for each college to provide books for its students,
and wealthy friends and alumni often donated books to the
collections. At the group of colleges that came to be known
as the University of Paris, the library of the Sorbonne College was an early outstanding one. By 1322 the Sorbonne
Library had over a thousand volumes, and by 1400 it had
established a circulating collection which could be taken from

the library by the students after the payment of a deposit.
By 1480, this library was housed in a separate building,
with a main reading room 12 by 40 feet. A set of rules for
the use of the Sorbonne Library has been preserved, and although some of them sound odd, many are still familiar to
library users today. A few of these rules (adapted from
Nathan Schachner: The Medieval Universities, p. 329) were:

> Each student had a key to the library, and no
> one else could enter the library except with a
> student or faculty member.
> No student could enter the library unless wear-
> ing cap and gown.
> It was forbidden to write on the books, or tear
> out leaves.
> As far as possible, silence was to reign in the
> library.
> Books containing condemned doctrines could be
> read only by professors of theology and then only
> when necessary.

In organization, the university library was similar to
that of the monastery, except that its books were kept in
divisions according to the subjects taught in the colleges or
faculties. At first there were no sub-classes to these
groups, and books were arranged only according to size and
accession. For storing the books, the change from chests
to lecterns and bookshelves was a gradual one, but by the
end of the Middle Ages, as books became more common,
shelves were in general use. Subject catalogs were, of
course, unknown, but book lists, similar to those in the
monastery libraries, were maintained and a number of these
have survived down to the present. In the Sorbonne Library,
and probably in others, the different faculties were distinguished by colors, and each book was marked with the color
of its appropriate faculty. Sometimes additional letters or
numbers were employed to indicate the shelf or section
where a book was shelved. Interestingly enough, there was
an attempt at a "union catalog" in 14th-century England.
Some unknown scholar, possibly a Franciscan monk in
London, compiled a Registrum Librorum Angliae, which was
an attempt to list all of the known copies of the works of
some 90 authors and libraries in which they could be located.
Some years later the list was extended by John Boston of
Bury (ca. 1410) to include the works of about 600 writers
located in 180 different libraries. This work contained not
only authors, titles and locations, but a short biographical

account of the author as well.   This is a treasure of English
bibliography prior to 1400.

     In addition to the early universities at Paris and in
Italy, other notable ones with important libraries were those
at Cracow (1364), Prague (1366), Heidelberg (1386), Oxford
(1412), and Cambridge (1425).   The dates given are those in
which general libraries are known to have been functioning,
although separate college libraries often preceded those of
the universities.   University College at Oxford had a library
as early as 1280, and possibly as early as 1249.   Richard
de Bury, Bishop of Durham, planned to leave his library to
Durham College, Oxford, but unfortunately his death resulted
in the scattering of most of his books.   De Bury was a
leading religious figure of his day, a government official at
one time and an ardent book collector.   He collected books
through dealers in London and in Europe, through his trips
to the continent, and through gifts of his many friends and
co-workers.   His account of why and how he collected books
is told in his work entitled Philobiblion; or, The Love of
Books, written about 1345.   In the will of Thomas Cobham,
Bishop of Worcester, books and money were left to start a
general library for Cambridge University, but it was nearly
a century later before one was effectively functioning there.
An interesting "special library" of the late Middle Ages was
the Guildhall Library of London.   This collection, largely a
legal library, was supported by the lawyers and merchants
of London and was the recipient of many gifts and bequests
after its founding about 1420.

     A few significant private libraries are known to have
existed throughout the Middle Ages, but toward the end of
this era the number of such collections increased noticeably.
Notable among them were those of the Italian authors
Petrarch and Boccaccio and of several members of the
Medici family.   Petrarch (1304-1374) began collecting books
as a boy, and covered much of Europe in his search for
manuscripts in his later life.   He is particularly noted for
his part in rescuing and preserving some of the works of
Cicero and Vergil, and for donating much of his library to
the city of Venice.   Poggio Bracciolini (1380-1459) was
another noted Italian book collector who learned Greek and
visited Constantinople in order to enrich his library.   It
was Poggio who found priceless Latin manuscripts, some of
them unique copies of classic writers, decaying in an attic
at St. Gall in Switzerland.   Cosimo de' Medici (1389-1464)
began several libraries during his lifetime, including the

noted one in the Convent of San Marco in Florence, to which
he gave 400 books. Many of his books came from the library
of Niccolò de' Niccoli (1363-1437), who had spent a lifetime
collecting rare books, and whose treasures included many
unique volumes. Federigo, Duke of Urbino, founded the
famous Urbino Library of Greek and Latin classics in the 15th
century, largely with gifts from his own private collection.
For both the Medicis and Duke Federigo, Vespasiano da
Bisticci (1421-1498) served as book agent and collector.
Vespasiano was something of a scholar and editor as well as
an international book dealer, and he kept a staff of writers
busy making copies of important works which he found in his
travels throughout Europe.

Some of the most noteworthy of medieval private libraries were those of the royalty and nobility. King Matthias
Corvinus of Hungary, who ruled from 1458 to 1490, collected
a remarkable library for his time and area. It was reported
to contain 50,000 separate items. Although this is probably
an exaggeration, there is no doubt that he did amass a sizable library. He maintained groups of copyists, illuminators
and binders in both Buda, his capital, and in Florence, in
order to provide for his collection the finest copies of the
most authentic works available. Although most of his books
were destroyed by the Turks when they invaded Hungary in
1526, some 125 volumes have survived. Charles V of France
(1337-1380) collected a library which was housed in the
Chateau du Louvre in Paris, and which was administered by
a full-time librarian. Another French ruler, Philip the
Good, Duke of Burgundy, (1396-1467), was also a noted collector. He had libraries at Dijon, Paris, Bruges and
Antwerp. His stated goal was to acquire the largest and
finest library in the world and to that end he employed a
regular staff of copyists, illuminators and translators.

Many private collectors donated their libraries to
university or public libraries. Robert de Sorbonne, in 1250,
gave his library to the college that took his name in Paris,
and Humphrey, Duke of Gloucester, gave his library to Oxford University early in the 15th century. His contemporary,
William Gray, Bishop of Ely, made a collection of Greek
and Latin classics and later donated them to Balliol College,
also at Oxford. In Central Europe, the German collector,
Johannes Sindel, gave some 200 volumes in the fields of
medicine and mathematics to Charles University in Prague.
Unfortunately, many of these medieval libraries, whether
private, university or church, were later destroyed or

scattered in political and religious wars. Neglect and abuse
added to the toll, so that today in most cases only a few volumes survive from what were once large and magnificent
libraries.

One library of the Middle Ages that deserves special
notice was that of the Popes in the Vatican at Rome. Tradition has it that the early Popes had begun a Vatican library
even before the end of the Roman Empire, but the history of
these early papal collections is obscure. We know that there
was a papal library from the sixth century on, and that particularly under Pope Zacharias (741-752) it received important
accessions from the earlier monastic collections. Because of
the struggles within the Church in the 13th and 14th centuries,
few if any of the original volumes were preserved. A new
Vatican Library was begun in the early 15th century, and this
library grew into importance under the direction of Pope
Nicholas V (1447-1455) who had been a book collector of note
before becoming Pope, and his librarian, Giovanni Tortelli
of Arezzo. Nicholas donated to the library his own volumes,
particularly of Greek classics which he had had translated
into Latin. At his death the collection contained some 1200
volumes and it was further increased by Pope Sixtus IV
(1471-1484) to about 3500 volumes. About this time the collection was divided into a main library for the use of monks
and scholars and a smaller private library for the pope.
The papal library served as the central library of the Roman
Catholic Church and as such it preserved the most authoritative texts of all the major Christian writings. Copies of religious works were produced continuously for distribution to
churches and monasteries throughout the Catholic world, and
duplicates were kept for loan or deposit in other church libraries. Though the Vatican library never reached great size
before the modern era, the high quality and value of its
holdings made it one of the most important libraries in the
world.

While Europe was in its Dark Ages, other parts of the
world were experiencing high levels of civilization and producing great libraries. The Byzantine world, centered around
Constantinople, continued to have universities, monasteries,
and churches with notable libraries until its fall to the Turks
in 1453. For several centuries the Moslem civilization,
stretching from India to Spain, was far superior to western
Europe in learning, particularly in medicine and science, and
its libraries contained books in the tens of thousands. Baghdad was a center of learning in the ninth century, with one

traveler reporting that it had 30 libraries open to the public.
Egypt had strong universities and libraries in the tenth to 12th
centuries. There were many prominent private libraries belonging to Moslem noblemen, and Arabic traders carried
camel loads of books with them, to read and to sell, in their
commercial ventures from the central Asian deserts to the
north African. India, too, had libraries, particularly during
the reign of the Mogul emperors who built a large imperial
library and archive at Delhi during the 15th and 16th centuries.
Japan had a "House of Papyri" as early as the eighth century.

It was, along with Arabia, in China that learning
flourished while Europe lay in ignorance. It was in China
where the book reached its height in cultural significance.
There were government libraries, libraries associated with
centers of learning, and hundreds of private libraries, both
large and small. Yang Ti, emperor in the early seventh
century, hit upon an excellent way to augment the size of the
imperial library. He rounded up scholars in all fields, and
ordered them to write books in their specialties. The major
Chinese libraries were staffed not only with workers who cataloged, arranged and circulated books, but with editors, proof-
readers, and collators who guaranteed the authenticity of the
texts. Calligraphers, artists in the writing of books, added
to the beauty of the Chinese texts. As in the West, there
were periods when learning was not encouraged in China, but
generally speaking the era from 500 to 1500 was considerably
more progressive there than in Europe.

Wherever the medieval library, in Islam, Asia or
Europe, it was closely paralleled by the commercial book
maker and bookseller. Although the majority of books were
in the hands of religious or official libraries, there were
private book collectors, and there was profit to be made in
providing books for libraries, schools and scholars, particularly after the tenth century. The professional copyists,
the book publishers of their day, might not rival the monks
in the accuracy or artistic perfection of their works, but they
could compete in school texts. As a matter of fact, the
monasteries themselves sometimes turned to the professional
copyist for the books for their shelves. The private book
makers produced most of the secular literature of the day,
even though there was not very much of it. The copyist
usually flourished in the towns, and by the later Middle Ages
he could be found, accompanied by parchment makers, book
binders and illuminators, in organized guilds or companies.
In London, for instance, there were about 1400 separate and

powerful guilds for the text-writers or copyists, for the lim-
ners or illuminators, and for the binders. The bookseller,
on the other hand, was often a lone hand, although he might
have agents in other towns. Usually he could be found in the
larger cities, or around universities and monasteries, and he
often added to his income by renting books to students who
could not afford to buy their own texts. In 1323, there were
no less than 28 booksellers in the vicinity of the University
of Paris, some of them offering as many as 125 texts for
rent. On a higher level, commercially speaking, were the
international book dealers, sometimes really smugglers, who
could obtain for a Paris or London customer a rare text from
Constantinople or Córdoba and who handled books and manuscripts in the same manner that they would costly fabrics or
works of art. Some of these book men, for example, Vespasiano, were scholars and by securing the texts of the classics
from the East and making them available in Western Europe
they contributed substantially to the beginning of the Renaissance.

Even ordinary books were luxuries in the Middle Ages.
It has been estimated that in current values, an average volume in the 12th century would have sold for about $200. A
tenth-century sale of a single book of sermons brought a
price of 200 sheep and three barrels of grain, while a complete Bible was traded for a house and lot. In the 14th century, a two-volume missal was sold for 200 gold francs and
a century earlier another was traded for an extensive vine-
yard. It should be pointed out that these were probably highly-
illuminated and ornately bound works, but the fact remains
that almost any book was expensive. Also, one element in
the value of medieval manuscript works was the degree of
accuracy of its contents. A book that had been carefully col-
lated with more than one other copy, or one whose authenticity had been certified by a reputable scholar, was obviously
of greater value since it could be used as a master work
from which other copies could be made.

Despite the scarcity of books and the smallness of
libraries in western Europe, the cultural centers of the
Middle Ages did bridge the gap between the ancient and the
modern worlds. Whether in monastery or cathedral, university or bookshop, a representative proportion of the classics
was preserved despite the ravages of wars and time. It
has been estimated that not more than 10 per cent, and
probably much less than that, of the major works of Greece
and Rome have been preserved, but if it were not for those

works we would know virtually nothing of their history and
culture. The art of communication through the written word
declined considerably after the fall of Rome, but it was never
completely lost. The western world owes an eternal debt of
gratitude to the scholarly monks, the princely book collectors,
and the industrious copyists who preserved those priceless
records of the past.

Bibliography
                          BOOKS

Addison, Julia D. Arts and Crafts in the Middle Ages.
    Philadelphia, 1908. 298 p. (See p. 326-364 on books
    and manuscripts.)
Beddie, J. S. Libraries in the Twelfth Century: their Cata-
    logs and Contents. Boston, 1929. 23 p.
Cassiodorus, Senator. An Introduction to Divine and Human
    Reading. New York, 1946. 283 p.
Clark, J. W. The Care of Books. Cambridge, England,
    1902. 352 p.
_____. Libraries in the Medieval and Renaissance Peri-
    ods. Cambridge, England, 1894. 61 p.
DeBury, Richard, Philobiblion; or, The Love of Books.
    London, 1925. 148 p. (Originally published 1473; many
    other editions.)
Diringer, David. The Hand Produced Book. New York,
    1953. 603 p.
Duckett, Eleanor S. Alcuin, Friend of Charlemagne. New
    York, 1951. 337 p.
Dunleavy, Gareth W. Colum's Other Island: The Irish at
    Lindisfarne. Madison, Wisc., 1960. 149 p.
Edwards, Edward. Memoirs of Libraries. New York, 1969.
    2 v. (Originally published 1859).
Guppy, Henry. Stepping Stones to the Art of Typography.
    London, 1928. 45 p.
Herbert, John A. Illuminated Manuscripts. London, 1912.
    135 p.
Hessel, Alfred. A History of Libraries. New Brunswick,
    N. J., 1955. 198 p.
Holzknecht, Karl J. Literary Patronage in the Middle Ages.
    Philadelphia, 1923. 258 p.
Humphreys, K. W. Book Provisions of the Medieval Friars.
    Amsterdam, 1964. 150 p.
_____. The Library of the Franciscans of the Convent
    of St. Anthony, Padua, at the Beginning of the Fifteenth
    Century. Amsterdam, 1966. 206 p.

Johnson, Elmer D. History of Libraries in the Western
    World. Metuchen, N. J., 1970. 521 p. (See p. 87-
    162.
Johnston, Edward. Writing and Illuminating and Lettering.
    New York, 1939. 500 p.
Ker, Neil R., ed. Medieval Libraries of Great Britain:
    a List of Surviving Books. 2nd ed. London, 1964.
    424 p.
Kibre, Pearl. The Intellectual Interests Reflected in Librar-
    ies of the 14th and 15th Centuries. New York, 1946.
    40 p.
_____. The Library of Pico Della Mirandola. New York,
    1936. 330 p.
Laurie, S. S. The Rise and Early Constitution of the Uni-
    versities. New York, 1891. 293 p.
Madan, Falconer. Books in Manuscript. London, 1920.
    208 p.
Merryweather, Frederick. Bibliomania in the Middle Ages.
    New York, 1900. 322 p.
Middleton, J. M. Illuminated Manuscripts in Classical and
    Medieval Times. Cambridge, England, 1892. 270 p.
Mitchell, Sabrina. Medieval Manuscript Painting. New York,
    1965. 212 p.
Norris, D. M. A History of Cataloging and Cataloging
    Methods, 1100-1850. London, 1939. 256 p.
Ogilvy, J. D. A. Books Known to the English, 597-1066.
    Cambridge, Mass., 1967. 320 p.
Orcutt, W. D. In Quest of the Perfect Book. Boston, 1926.
    (See especially p. 109-150.)
Putnam, G. H. Books and Their Makers During the Middle
    Ages. London, 1896. 2 v. (Reprinted New York, 1964.)
Savage, Ernest A. Old English Libraries: the Making, Col-
    lecting and Use of Books During the Middle Ages.
    London, 1911. 298 p. (Reprinted New York, 1970.)
_____. The Story of Libraries and Book-Collecting. New
    York, n. d. 230 p.
Schachner, Nathan. The Medieval University. New York,
    1938. 388 p.
Taylor, Archer. Renaissance Guides to Books. Berkeley,
    Calif., 1925. 130 p.
Thompson, J. W. The Medieval Library. Chicago, 1939.
    694 p. (Reprinted New York, 1957. 702 p.)
Thornton, J. L. Chronology of Librarianship. London,
    1941. 266 p.

PERIODICAL ARTICLES

Beddie, J. S. "Ancient Classics in the Medieval Libraries,"
    Speculum, 5 (1930), 3-20.
Buksh, S. K. "The Islamic Libraries," Nineteenth Century,
    52 (1902), 125-139.
Connolly, Brendan. "Jesuit Library Beginnings," Library
    Quarterly, 30 (1960), 243-262.
Garrod, H. W. "The Library Regulations of a Medieval
    College," The Library, 7 (1927), 312-335.
Jackson, Sidney L. "Cassiodorus' Institutes and Christian
    Book Selection," Journal of Library History, 1 (1966),
    89-100.
Ker, N. R. "Cathedral Libraries," Library History,
    1 (1967), 38-45.
Koch, Theodore W. "New Light on Old Libraries,"
    Library Quarterly, 4 (1934), 244-252.
Mackensen, Ruth S. "Four Great Libraries of Medieval
    Baghdad," Library Quarterly, 2 (1932), 279-299.
Schutz, Geza. "Bibliotheca Corvina," Library Quarterly, 4
    (1934), 552-563.
Winger, Howard W. "Regulations Relating to the Book Trade
    in London from 1357 to 1586," Library Quarterly, 26
    (1956), 157-195.
Winkelmann, John II. "The Imperial Library in Southern
    Sung China," Library Quarterly, 39 (1969), 299-317.

V

EARLY PRINTING

The 15th century saw the coming of the second most important event in the development of graphic communication, and thus in the history of books and libraries. The first, of course, was the development of writing; the second, the development of printing in western Europe. Ordinarily we say that Johann Gutenberg invented printing around 1450 in Mainz, Germany. However, there is much more to the story than that; there were others involved besides Gutenberg, and we should say "printing from movable type" in order to be reasonably accurate about the date. Actually, if we define printing in its simplest form as making an impression of intelligible characters by one object upon another, then printing began long before the Christian era. The Babylonians and Egyptians used metal or wooden seals for impressing pictures and pictographs upon clay or wax. The Babylonians even used a seal-cylinder, by means of which an entire paragraph could be rolled out on a clay tablet with one turn of the embossed cylinder. The Chinese used similar seals for centuries, and by the fifth century after Christ they were using inked seals for printing on paper, rather than the plain seals for making impressions on clay or wax. These inked seals were made of wood and hence produced a primitive form of wood-cut. A variation of this came from stone inscriptions, from which paper copies could be made by rubbings. The Japanese adapted the use of seals and wood-cuts from the Chinese, and by 770 the Empress Shotoku had ordered the distribution of a million Buddhist charms that had been "printed" by impressions from a wood-cut. These charms were on paper 18 inches long by two inches wide, containing about 150 separate characters, and they were designed to be distributed from shrines throughout the country. Since the date of this Japanese charm is fairly well authenticated, it is certainly one of our earliest known examples of printing.

Wood-cut printing continued to develop in China in the eighth and ninth centuries until it reached a rather high de-

gree of perfection. Carefully carved wooden blocks could
contain an illustration and a half page or more of Chinese
characters, so that the appearance of a modern page could be
achieved. Several pages, side by side on a long sheet of
paper could produce a printed "book" or scroll. The earliest
known example of this form of printing is the Diamond Sutra,
printed in 868 and discovered in a cave in northwestern China
in 1907. A sutra was a Buddhist holy book, and this particular one was printed on a roll 16 feet long and one foot wide.
It was carefully and neatly done, indicating that such printing
was an accomplished art by that time.

The Chinese not only originated block printing, but
also an early form of printing from movable type. Since the
Chinese writing was based on a phonetic syllabary rather
than on an alphabet, one piece of type could be used to print
a whole word. Experiments with individual pieces of type for
each character, with the type made of baked clay, and held
in place by wax or tar, were made as early as the 11th century. Later these types were locked together in a metal
form, inked and pressed upon the paper much in the manner
of modern print-making. Fonts of the clay type were kept on
hand, but unusual or little-used characters could be formed and
baked relatively quickly as needed. Some two centuries later
the Chinese printers were trying movable types made of tin
or wood, but printing from wood blocks remained the usual
form of duplicating written materials in China and movable
type did not gain wide acceptance until centuries later. It
should also be noted that the Chinese did not develop a printing press such as Gutenberg was to pioneer in Europe. The
Chinese were able to do a remarkable amount of printing by
means of their wooden blocks, including many-volumed encyclopedias and sets of reference works. They also printed
paper money in millions of copies, especially from the ninth
to the 13th centuries.

Other neighboring nations besides Japan also borrowed
printing from the Chinese. Koreans by the 15th century, but
still before Gutenberg, were printing hundreds of copies of
books from movable metal type. But the Koreans also used
type slugs containing whole word characters, so they fell
short of the workable system later developed in Europe, and
their system of printing fell into disuse in the same century
that saw it rise. The Uigurs, a people of central Asia, also
adopted printing from the Chinese, and used it for their written language which was alphabetical. But, so carefully did
they follow the Chinese system that they made individual type

slugs for entire words, rather than for the individual letters
of their alphabet.   Despite these attempts at printing from
movable type, and they were continued sporadically over several centuries, most printing in East Asia continued to be done
by wood-blocks until European machinery and methods were
introduced in the 1800s.

Inevitably the channels of trade carried Chinese inventions westward, and printing was no exception.   From central
Asia it spread to Persia, thence to Asia Minor and finally to
Egypt.   Paper money was printed in Persia in 1294, and
scraps of printed materials found in Egypt may date from an
even earlier period.   But the Moslem religious leaders frowned
upon printing and even block printing seems never to have
been popular in the Arabic world.   Thus one possible link
between Chinese and European printing is difficult to prove,
but it is known that block printing was being practiced in
western Europe by the late 14th century.   One interesting
product for which block printing was readily adaptable was
playing cards.   The origin of card games is definitely Chinese, where they were first called "sheet dice."   They were
in use there by the tenth century or earlier.   Playing cards
may have reached Europe through the returning Crusaders,
who had first seen them in Asia Minor, or they may have
come through the Russians who were under the influence of
the Mongols in the late 13th and early 14th centuries.   At any
rate, block printed playing cards were in use in Western
Europe by the 1300s and along with them came block printed
religious items, such as pictures of the saints.   Whether
cards or pictures, these were made from rather crudely
carved blocks, but they did provide multiple copies of a
graphic work, and as such they were the immediate forerun-
ners of printing.

Whether or not there is a direct connection between
early printing in China and that later developed in Europe,
there is no doubt about the spread of another phase of book-
making from East to West.   This was the manufacture of
paper.   Papyrus, parchment and vellum were all comparatively expensive, and for a process that made hundreds of
copies of a work in a short time, a cheaper writing material
was necessary.   It has been estimated, for example, that it
would have taken the hides of 5000 calves to provide the vellum necessary for printing just 35 copies of the Gutenberg
Bible.   Many surfaces have been tried in various countries
for writing, including wood, clay, stone, metal, hides, silk,
bamboo, papyrus and bark, but all were either too scarce or

too bulky for use in mechanical printing. Several primitive
peoples, including the natives of Mexico and the Southwest
Pacific, developed sheets of matted vegetable fibers that were
elementary forms of paper, but the Chinese were the first
to make a really workable product. As early as A.D. 100s
they had experimented with paper made from silk, tree bark,
and hemp. Later cotton and linen rags were used, and by
the fifth century paper of good quality was commonplace in
China. This paper was made by soaking and pounding the
raw materials until the individual fibers were separated. A
thick mixture of these fibers with water was made and then
a fine meshed screen was dipped into the mixture. As the
screen was lifted a thin layer of the fibers adhered to the
screen, and when this layer was dried and peeled off it made
a single sheet of paper. Later the paper was pressed and
sometimes rubbed with stone to give it a smooth, hard finish.

Traveling westward along the routes of trade and war,
the art of manufacturing paper was introduced to the Arabs in
Samarkand in 750 by Chinese prisoners of war. A paper mill
had begun operation in Baghdad in 793. In the ninth century
paper was being made in Egypt, and by the 11th century in
Morocco. The first paper manufactured in Europe was in the
province of Valencia, in Moslem Spain before 1150; in 1276
a paper mill began operation near Ancona, Italy. Paper was
first manufactured in France in Troyes, in 1348, and in
Nürnberg, Germany, in 1390. None was made in England
until 1494, when John Tate established a mill in Hertfordshire,
nor in Russia until 1576, but of course paper was being used
in all of these northern European countries for many years
before it was actually manufactured there. The oldest extant
European paper document comes from Sicily and is dated
1209. The first paper to be used in Europe came from the
Moslem cities, particularly Damascus, and an early name
for paper in Latin-speaking countries was "charta damascena."
In the 14th and 15th centuries, France became the most
important paper-maker in Europe. The source materials
used were rags, sometimes of cotton or silk, but more often
of linen or hemp, and the process was much the same as
that employed for centuries in China. Oddly enough paper
did not receive a warm welcome in Europe despite its comparative cheapness as a writing material. Religious and
governmental leaders opposed its use, particularly for important documents, and for many years it was illegal to use
paper for official manuscripts.

From the playing card and religious print, it was only

a short step to the block printing of small books, with each
page being made as a single print. As in the early block
printed books in the Far East, these pages usually consisted
of a large picture and a few words. The earliest known block
books date from the mid-15th century, although it is quite
probable that others were produced earlier. The process of
making the block book began with the wood-cut of picture or
text or both. The block was inked and the paper was placed
upon it and rubbed lightly to insure a clear impression. This
block-printing process was used for small books that could be
produced relatively cheaply and distributed widely. Many of
them were on religious themes, such as the Pauper's Bible,
a collection of Bible verses with pictures, designed for
children or near-illiterates. Other block books were elementary school texts, particularly Latin grammars. Such
works continued to be printed for some time after the development of printing from movable type, and apparently they
were well used since only a few of them have survived.
Though it was only a poor beginning, block book-making undoubtedly pointed the way for the printed book, or to be more
exact, for the book printed from movable type.

One other predecessor of printing that should be mentioned is textile printing. It seems that wherever textile
fabrics have been developed, methods of impressing designs
on them have soon been achieved. Primitive textile printing
was practiced in Egypt early in the Christian era, and examples dating from the sixth to the eighth century have been
found in Egypt, India, China, and Germany. However, the
art of textile printing was apparently lost in Europe for centuries, and re-discovered around 1300. This process of
printing upon cloth was very similar to that of printing upon
paper, that is it was done by pressing a carved, inked block
upon cloth supported by another wooden block. It appeared
in Europe along with the early wood-block prints, or possibly
earlier, and although it was a matter of printing patterns
and designs rather than words and pictures, it was still a form
of transferring an impression and it was for many years more
widely used than printing on paper.

The development of printing from movable type centers around the activities of Johann Gensfleisch zum Gutenberg and in order to understand his role in this historic oc-
casion it is necessary to know a little about the man himself.
He was born about 1400 (some sources say 1397) in Mainz,
Germany, and seems to have come from a well-to-do family.
About 1434 he left Mainz and took up his residence in Stras-

bourg, where he entered into a partnership with several
craftsmen, workers in gold and other metals.   During his
years in Strasbourg, Gutenberg became involved in several
lawsuits, both in business and domestic matters (he was sued
for breach of promise by one Strasbourg lady), and thus his
presence there is a matter of record.   At some time while
in Strasbourg, Gutenberg began experimenting with printing
from movable type, but just when is a matter of question.
About 1440, he was sued by two of his ex-partners for failing
to teach them a secret process, unnamed but usually thought
to have been printing.   One source says that he had a press
constructed in 1438, and was then purchasing lead, which
would seem to indicate that he was already casting type.
There are also a few fragments of printing which some authorities believe were printed by Gutenberg in Strasbourg,
but there is no general agreement on this.   By 1448, however,
Gutenberg was back in Mainz, and by 1450, he was definitely
in the printing business as several of his contemporaries
later recorded.   In 1452, already indebted to Johann Fust, a
wealthy merchant, Gutenberg took that gentleman into partnership with him.   By this time the press was in operation,
but apparently it brought little remuneration to Gutenberg,
for by 1455 he was so indebted to Fust that he made over his
share of the business to Fust and his son-in-law, Peter
Schöffer.

Schöffer was an experienced calligrapher, and would
become one of the first designers and casters of printing type.
From the Gutenberg press, now the property of Fust and
Schöffer, there came in or about 1456 the famous Gutenberg
Bible, sometimes called the "42-line Bible" from the number
of lines of type per page.   This edition of the Bible was no
experimental affair; it is undoubtedly one of the finest pieces
of printing ever done.   It does not seem reasonable that a f
first printed book could be such an example of perfection, so
it must be assumed that many years of experimentation and
trial and error were necessary before a printing press could
be developed to do such fine work.   Apparently these years
of experiment without income impoverished Gutenberg, and
his creditors and business successors reaped the benefits of
his work.

No single piece of printing actually bears the imprint
of Gutenberg, but from careful study of the available records
most authorities agree in crediting him with several items,
and of course it is quite possible that dozens of minor books,
pamphlets, and broadsides printed by Gutenberg may have

been lost or worn out in later years. The first dated piece of
printing was an indulgence, a broadside church form, printed
in 1454, apparently by a Gutenberg press operated by Peter
Schöffer. It is thought that the 42-line Bible was completed
by 1456 since, although it bears no date itself, a copy was
illuminated and bound by Heinrich Cremer in the summer of
that year according to a note in the copy still preserved in
the Bibliothèque Nationale in Paris. This Gutenberg Bible
was most probably completed and sold by Fust and Schoeffer,
but the press, the type, and possibly even the composition
were the work of Johann Gutenberg. A Psalter, published in
Mainz in 1457, is the first work to bear the imprint of Fust
and Schöffer.

Did Gutenberg really invent the printing press? The
best evidence is that he did--or at least he first put together
the combination of type-casting, movable type, screw-press
and quick-drying ink necessary for a workable printing press.
A skilled metal worker, he developed methods of typecasting
that made it possible to cast large numbers of precisely-made,
uniform type. Since the water soluble ink used in wood-block
printing was not satisfactory for press-work, Gutenberg also
encouraged the development of an ink that was thick and yet
quick-drying for use on the presses. Finally, he developed
the press itself, no doubt using for a prototype the screw-
press that had long been used in leather-curing and wine-
making. The finished product made it possible to lock the
type into forms so that sheets of paper could be rapidly inserted and removed, producing many copies of the same impression in a very short time. This press also made it possible, with good paper and ink, to print on both sides of the
paper--quite a change from the old block-printing methods.
Putting all these things together, and making them work,
constituted Gutenberg's invention, and its perfection was
definitely a notable achievement in man's history. Gutenberg
may have been the printer of the Catholicon, a work published
in Mainz in 1460, but his later life is very obscure. It is
generally believed that in 1465 he became a pensioner at the
court of Count Adolph of Nassau and that he died in Mainz in
1468.

Other European countries also claim the invention of
printing. The Netherlands in particular has a case for one
Laurens Koster (or Coster), who is alleged to have used a
printing press with movable type as early as the 1430s. There
is little proof to support this claim, although there is evidence, somewhat crude, that someone was experimenting

with printing in the Netherlands about the same time that
Gutenberg was developing his press.   One other interesting
claimant to Gutenberg's fame has come from France, where
in 1444-46 at Avignon, one Procopius Waldfoghel, a silver-
smith, was experimenting with "alphabets of steel," with
which he claimed to be able to "write artificially." There is
no evidence to show that Waldfoghel ever did any printing.
Other even more vague and unsubstantiated claims to the invention of printing come from other cities in France, Germany, Italy and Czechoslovakia.   Until and unless some more
substantial discovery is made in the history of early printing,
Gutenberg's position seems secure.

Whatever doubts there may be about Gutenberg's printed works, there is no doubt that successful printing was in
operation in Mainz either before or shortly after 1450, and
that from this city it spread fairly rapidly to the rest of
Europe.   In 1462 a feudal war between two competing claim-
ants for the archbishopric of Mainz resulted in the capture of
the city by one force and the disruption of the printing industry there, at least temporarily.   Some of the printers,
trained in the shops of Fust and Schöffer, were unemployed
and had to look elsewhere for jobs.   Others may have been
forced to leave because they had opposed the victorious bishop.
At any rate, they left Mainz and carried their knowledge of
the art of printing to other parts of Europe.   A French
writer described this exodus in 1470:

> There has been discovered in Germany a wonderful
> new method for the production of books, and those
> who have mastered this method are taking their
> invention from Mainz out into the world somewhat as
> the old Grecian warriors took their weapons from
> the belly of the Trojan horse.   The light of this
> wonderful discovery will spread from Germany to
> all parts of the earth [Putnam, Books and Their
> Makers. . . , vol. 1, p. 359, reproducing a letter
> from Wilhelm Fichet to Robert Gaguin].

It was natural that the nearby German towns should
receive printing shortly after it had been perfected in Mainz,
and this seems to have been the case.   There were printers
in Strasbourg by 1460, in Bamberg by 1461, and in Cologne
by 1466 or earlier.   Some of the German printers crossed
the Alps and set up the first printing presses in Italy.   Conrad
Sweynheym and Arnold Pannartz left Mainz and started a
printing establishment at Subiaco, near Rome, either late in

Table 1

THE SPREAD OF PRINTING IN EUROPE

Date	Country (modern name)	City	Printer
1445-53?	Germany	Mainz	Johann Gutenberg
1454?	Germany	Mainz	Fust & Schöffer
1458?	Germany	Strasbourg	Johann Mentelin
1461	Germany	Bamberg	Albrecht Pfister
1464?	Italy	Subiaco	Swenyheym & Pannartz
1465	Germany	Cologne	Ulrich Zell
1466?	Switzerland	Basel	Berthold Ruppel
1467	Italy	Rome	Sweynheym & Pannartz
1468	Germany	Augsburg	Gunther Zainer
1468	Czech.	Pilsen	(unknown)
1469	Italy	Venice	John of Spires
1470	Germany	Nürnberg	Johann Sensenschmid
1470	Italy	Venice	Nicolas Jensen
1470	France	Paris	Martin Crantz, Ulrich Gering, Michael Friburger
1470	Netherlands	Utrecht	Gerardus Leempt & Nicholas Ketalaer
1471	Italy	Milan	Antonio Zarotti
1471	Italy	Naples	Sixtus Riessinger
1471	Italy	Florence	Bernardo di Cennini
1473	France	Lyon	Wilhelm König
1473?	Hungary	Budapest	Andreas Hesse
1473?	Belgium	Louvain	John of Westphalia
1474	Spain	Valencia	Lambert Palmart
1474	Poland	Cracow	Casper Hochfelder
1476	England	Westminster	William Caxton
1478	England	Oxford	Theodoric Rood
1480	England	London	John Lettou
1482	Austria	Vienna	Stephen Koblinger
1482	Denmark	Odense	Johann Snell
1483	Sweden	Stockholm	Johann Snell
1489	Portugal	Lisbon	Rabbi Elieser
1491	England	London	Richard Pynson
1491	England	Westminster	Wynkyn de Worde
1491	Switzerland	Basel	Johann Froben
1494	Turkey	Constantin.	David ibn Nachmias
1563	Russia	Moscow	Ivan Federov

1464 or early in 1465. Later they moved on to Rome and
printed in that city for several years. Other Italian cities
had printing presses by the 1470s, including Venice, where
the industry flourished--Naples, Florence, and Genoa. Basel
in Switzerland had printing by 1465, Paris in 1470, Utrecht
in 1473, and Cracow by 1475. The art was slower in reaching
the Baltic countries and the Balkans. It was the 1480s before
there were presses in Denmark (where paper was not manufactured until 1635), Norway and Sweden, and not until 1494 did
printing reach Constantinople. The first printing in England
was done in 1476 or early in 1477 and in Spain by 1474. There
were reports of three printers going to Moscow in 1490 but
the first known printing in the Russian capital was not until
1563. By 1500 there had been more than 1700 presses in
operation in over 300 cities in western Europe and they had
turned out over 40,000 separate works or editions in more
than 15,000,000 copies. These works printed before 1500 are
known as incunabula, from the Latin word for "cradle," refer-
ring to the books produced in the infancy of the art of printing.

Outside of Europe, the printing press reached Turkey
in 1503, Palestine in 1563, India in 1556, and Japan in 1590.
Printing in the New World reached Latin America almost a
century before it began in English America. Mexico had a
printer in the 1530s, and Peru in the 1580s. In the English
colonies the first printing press reached Massachusetts in
1639. Elsewhere, printing began in the Philippines in 1602,
and in Iran in 1640. The western printing press finally
reached China in 1644.

Even before 1500, many printers had become outstanding artists in their profession and some of the most beautiful
works of typography ever produced had appeared. Printers in
Italy early assumed a lead in the new industry, and among
them Aldus Manutius and the Frenchman Nicolas Jenson stand
out. Jenson's press was in Venice. He produced more than
150 different books, all printed in a clear, very legible type
which he designed himself. Just as Gutenberg's type was
based on the gothic handwriting then prevalent in Germany, so
Jenson based his "Roman" type on the script used by the
humanist scholars of northern Italy. Aldus Manutius, also of
Venice, was known for his development of italic type from the
slanted script used in Italy for informal writing, and for the
printing of small, well-made but relatively cheap, editions of
Greek and Latin classics. Most early printers preferred the
large, folio format for their books, or at least the quarto,

but Aldus turned to the octavo, a small, hand-sized volume
that was easy to hold and to read. Most modern books are
in the octavo size. More than any other of the early printers,
Jenson and Aldus were responsible for popularizing the
printed book and thus helping to spread learning. Both men
were scholars as well as printers and they edited the books
that they published. One of the greatest achievements of Aldus
Manutius was the collection of the many fragments of Aristotle's works into as nearly complete an edition of his works
as was then possible. He is also remembered for the founding of the Aldine Academy for the study of Greek and Latin
classics, but this did not survive long after his death in 1515.

Among the early German printers, the Koberger family
of Nürnberg stand out for the quantity if not for the quality of
their work. They printed on a large scale, running several
presses, with a large number of workmen each trained in a
special task. They tended to specialize in religious works
and textbooks, and by 1500 had 24 presses in operation in
Nürnberg and nearby towns. Many of their books were profusely illustrated with woodcuts. One of the Kobergers' most
famous works was the Nürnberg Chronicle, which was an illustrated history of the world. It was very elaborate, with
almost 2000 illustrations, but it is interesting that the same
woodcut was often used several times to depict different people or different scenes. The Kobergers promoted their business effectively with published catalogs, and used salesmen
to peddle their books throughout Europe. Johann Snell, of
Lübeck, Germany, had a similar but smaller establishment
with branches in Denmark and Sweden.

Among other early European printers of importance
were several generations of the Estienne family of France,
Beginning with Henri Estienne in 1502, and for nearly 150
years, this family produced, in Paris and Geneva, some of
the finest books ever published. Another famous printing
concern, lasting for 300 years or more, was the House of
Plantin in Antwerp, begun by a Frenchman, Christophe Plantin, in 1555. It was noted for excellent printing into the 19th
century. The Elzevir press in Leiden produced over 1600
books in five different languages in a little over a century of
operation. Switzerland considers Johann Froben, who printed
in Basel from 1491 to 1527, one of its greatest printers.
Froben surrounded himself with scholars, including Erasmus,
and undertook to produce only the best of printing and the
most authentic of texts. Among his most notable publications
was a Greek New Testament in nine huge folio volumes. Froben

also published some of the earliest works on medicine and
science, part of which were illustrated with woodcuts by
Hans Holbein.

Closely associated with printing throughout its history
has been the art of type-founding. Early printers like Gutenberg and Jenson were also type-founders, but by the 16th
century, type designing and casting was becoming a separate
trade and types were being created specifically for printing.
Much of the type used by Aldus Manutius, particularly the
italic, was the work of Francesco Griffo of Bologna. Two
Frenchmen stand out for their contribution to early type designs. One of these was Robert Granjon, who specialized
in italic type faces, and the other was Claude Garamond, who
developed a clear, open roman character, based somewhat on
the Jenson type. Both styles of type were widely used by
contemporary printers, and after a revival of interest in the
19th century, adaptations of these types are still popular.

Printing was relatively late in reaching England, the
first printing being done there only by 1477. The first
English printer was William Caxton, a well-to-do merchant
who had been conducting a business in Bruges, Belgium. He
apparently learned the art of printing during a visit to medieval Germany's largest city, Cologne, probably at the press
of Ulrich Zell, established in 1464. At the request of Margaret, Duchess of Burgundy, who was English born, Caxton
had translated from the French a popular book on the Trojan
wars, entitled Recuyell of the Historyes of Troye, and he
printed some copies of this in Brugge (Bruges) in or before
1475. Caxton then decided that printing could be a profitable
trade, and so in 1476 he returned to England and set up his
printing business at Westminster, near the abbey. There his
first dated printing was another translation, The Dictes or
Sayinges of the Philosophers, 1477. There were probably
earlier publications in pamphlet or broadside form from the
Caxton press, but none of them has survived. Before his
death in 1491, Caxton printed more than 100 different works,
including the poems of Geoffrey Chaucer, and other works of
English literature. As a printer, Caxton was not an artist
and his works fell short of perfection, but as an editor and
publisher he did much to standardize the English language and
preserve its literature. Caxton used several typefaces at different times, but the one for which he is best known is the old
English black-letter, a heavy almost gothic type that was
copied by other early English printers and is still sometimes
used.

Caxton's successor was Wynkyn de Worde, who had
been his assistant almost from the first.   Wynkyn de Worde,
a native of Worth, in Alsace, was in many ways a better
printer than Caxton and his output in numbers was large, but
in the early history of English printing he is overshadowed
by Caxton.   The first printer in London proper was John Lettou, in 1480.   William de Machlinia, Richard Pynson, and
Julian Notary also printed in London before 1500, and other
presses were established in Oxford in 1478 and in St. Albans.
All were foreigners except Caxton and possibly the printer of
St. Albans, whose identity is unknown.   On the whole, early
English printing is typographically undistinguished when compared to that produced on the continent during the same period.
With the possible exception of Wynkyn and Pynson (who between
them published about two-thirds of the English output between
1500 and 1530), the early English printers seem to have been
journeymen rather than masters and never to have brought
their trade to perfection.

The total product of the 15th-century presses is
astounding numerically, and equally amazing is the quality
and variety of the matter printed.   Although many works have
undoubtedly been lost, it is apparent that practically every
piece of literature then known in the western European languages, or in Latin or Greek, plus many in Hebrew, must
have been printed in that prolific half-century.   There were
nearly 500 editions of the Bible, or its parts, with several
hundred more religious works such as breviaries, hymnals
and prayer-books.   With the various editions of the works of
the saints and those of the early Christian philosophers, the
grand total of religious works formed about half of the output
of the 15th-century presses.   About 10 per cent of the incunabula were books of church or civil law, including commentaries and textbooks.   Another 20 per cent or so were
works of literature, both classic and medieval, while all the
sciences together made up not quite another 10 per cent.   The
remainder were divided among elementary textbooks (mostly
Latin grammars), history, travel, and miscellaneous.

Some of the authors and titles that enjoyed popularity
before 1500 included, among the Latin classics, the works of
Cicero, Vergil, Ovid, Seneca, Horace, Juvenal, Persius and
Terence, in roughly that order.   From the Greek, there were
the works of Aristotle, Aristophanes, Aesop, Homer, Galen,
Theophrastus, Theocritus, and Euripides.   Among the medieval writers there were Petrarch, Boccaccio, and Dante,
with the works of the first named going through some 40

editions prior to 1500. In history, the Nürnberg Chronicle
was one of the most important books produced but there were
similar contemporary works. In the sciences there were volumes on agriculture, astronomy, mathematics, medicine and
alchemy. Several contemporary romances were published,
including an early best-seller by Aneas Sylvius, entitled Concerning Two Lovers. Christopher Columbus' Letter Concerning the Newly Discovered Islands was a popular item in the
1490s, and went through 12 editions, despite the fact that it
was only a four-page leaflet. Of English authors published before 1500, perhaps the most significant was Geoffrey Chaucer,
whose Canterbury Tales were printed by Caxton.

All things considered, the art of printing made great
progress in its first half century. The first colophon, giving
publisher and date of publication, appeared in 1457 in a psalter
printed by Fust and Schoeffer in Mainz. Wood-cut illustrations were added to books printed from movable type in 1461,
and copper engravings were used as early as 1476. The
first elementary form of a title page appeared in 1463, the
first table of contents in 1470, and even attempts at indexes
were made by 1480. The printing press itself had reached
a form by 1500 that was to change very little in the next
300 years, and typography in general had reached a state of
near perfection that has been improved upon only in the last
century. Though the making of books was still a laborious
job, involving much hand work, it was far superior to handwriting, and the literate world would no longer be handicapped
through lack of reading material. The invention of the printing press brought about a cultural revolution hardly surpassed by any other single development since the beginning of
writing. Henceforth communication of men's ideas through
either space or time would have a rapid and relatively inexpensive vehicle. The Reformation begun by Martin Luther in
the 16th century proceeded and expanded with the full support
of the printing press. Even in the 18th century it is difficult
to understand the winning of American Independence without
the widespread support engendered through the thousands of
printed copies of Thomas Paine's Common Sense, and Thomas
Jefferson's Declaration of Independence. Books, pamphlets
and broadsides, journals, magazines and newspapers, all
products of the printing press, played a major role in changing political, cultural and social history. And the accumulation, preservation and distribution of this mass of printed
material was to radically change the character of the library
and the librarian.

Bibliography
                          BOOKS

Aldis, Harry G. The Printed Book. Cambridge, England,
    1951. 142 p.
Blake, N. F. Caxton and His World. London, 1969. 256 p.
Bland, David. The Illustration of Books. New York, 1954.
    160 p.
Blum, Andre. On the Origin of Paper. New York, 1934.
    79 p.
_____. The Origins of Printing and Engraving. New York,
    1940. 226 p.
Buehler, Curt F. The Fifteenth-Century Book: the Scribes,
    the Printers, the Decorators. Philadelphia, 1960.
    195 p.
_____. The University and the Press in Fifteenth-
    Century Bologna. South Bend, Ind., 1958. 195 p.
Bullock, Warren B. The Romance of Paper. Chicago, 1940.
    154 p.
Butler, Pierce. The Origin of Printing in Europe. Chicago,
    1966. 155 p. (Original ed., 1940.)
Carter, Thomas F. The Invention of Printing in China and its
    Spread Westward. Rev. ed. New York, 1955. 293 p.
Chappell, Warren. A Short History of the Printed Word. New
    York, 1970. 259 p.
Clair, Colin. A Chronology of Printing. New York, 1969.
    228 p.
_____. History of Printing in Britain. Oxford, 1965.
    314 p.
Dahl, Svend. History of the Book. 2nd English ed.
    Metuchen, N. J., 1968. 299 p.
DeVinne, Theodore L. The Invention of Printing. New York,
    1969. 556 p. (Original ed., 1876).
Diringer, David. The Illuminated Book: its History and Pro-
    duction. New York, 1958. 524 p.
Dowding, Geoffrey. Introduction to the History of Printing
    Types. London, 1961. 278 p.
Duff, E. Gordon. Early Printed Books. New York, 1968.
    219 p. (Original ed., 1893).
Goldschmidt, E. P. The Printed Book of the Renaissance.
    Cambridge, England, 1950. 92 p.
Greenwood, David. Chronology of Books and Printing. New
    York, 1936. 186 p.
Handover, P. M. Printing in London from 1476 to Modern
    Times. Cambridge, Mass., 1960. 224 p.
Hind, Arthur M. An Introduction to a History of Woodcut.
    New York, 1935. 2 v.

Hirsch, Rudolf. Printing, Selling and Reading. Wiesbaden,
    1967. 165 p.
Hunter, Dard. Paper Making; the History and Technique of
    an Ancient Craft. New York, 1947. 611 p.
Jennett, Sean. Pioneers in Printing. London, 1958. 196 p.
Laufer, Berthold. Paper and Printing in Ancient China.
    Chicago, 1931. 33 p.
Lehmann-Haupt, Helmut. Gutenberg and the Master of the
    Playing Cards. New Haven, 1966. 83 p.
Levarie, Norma. The Art and History of Books. New York,
    1968. 315 p.
McKerrow, Ronald B. An Introduction to Bibliography for
    Literary Students. Oxford, 1927. 359 p. (See p. 38-
    144.)
McMurtrie, Douglas C. The Book: the Story of Printing and
    Bookmaking. New York, 1943. 676 p.
Orcutt, William D. The Book in Italy During the Fifteenth
    and Sixteenth Centuries. London, 1928. 220 p.
_____. Master Makers of the Book. New York, 1928.
    271 p.
Oswald, J. C. A History of Printing. New York, 1928.
    403 p.
Putnam, G. H. Books and Their Makers During the Middle
    Ages. London, 1896. 2 v. (Reprinted, New York, 1964).
Scholderer, Victor. Printers and Readers in Italy in the
    Fifteenth Century. Oxford, 1949. 23 p.
_____. Johann Gutenberg, the Inventor of Printing.
    London, 1963. 32 p.
Simon, Irving B. The Story of Printing, from Woodblocks
    to Electronics. New York, 1965. 128 p.
Steinberg, S. H. Five Hundred Years of Printing. New
    York, 1959. 286 p.
Stillwell, Margaret B. Incunabula and Americana. New York,
    1931. 483 p.
Updike, Daniel B. Printing Types, their History, Forms
    and Use. Cambridge, Mass., 1946. 2 v.
Williamson, Derek. Historical Bibliography. London, 1967.
    129 p.
Winship, George P. Johann Gutenberg. Chicago, 1940.
    38 p.
_____. Printing in the Fifteenth Century. Philadelphia,
    1940. 158 p.
Wroth, L. C., ed. A History of the Printed Book. New
    York, 1938.

PERIODICAL ARTICLES

Buehler, Curt F.   "Aldus Manutius: the First 500 Years,"
    Papers of the Bibliographical Society of America, 44
    (1950), 205-215.
Daniel, Henry.   "The Koreans Were Ahead of Gutenberg,"
    Natural History, 60 (1951), 376-378.
Deland, Judson.   "The Evolution of Modern Printing,"
    Journal of the Franklin Institute," 207 (1931), 209-34.
Guppy, Henry.   "Stepping Stones to the Art of Typography,"
    Bulletin of the John Rylands Library, 12 (1928), 83-121.
Hirsch, Rudolf.   "Printing in France and Humanism, 1470-
    1480," Library Quarterly, 30 (1960), 111-123.
Prostov, Eugene V.   "Origins of Russian Printing," Library
    Quarterly, 1 (1931), 255-277.
Stuart, D. M.   "William Caxton, Mercer, Translator, and
    Master Printer," History Today, 10 (1960), 256-265.
Uhlendorff, G. A.   "The Invention of Printing and its Spread
    till 1470," Library Quarterly, 2 (1932), 179-231.

VI

EUROPEAN BOOKS AND LIBRARIES, 1500-1900

The total cultural effect of the invention of printing can hardly be overestimated. The coming of printing revolutionized communication and made it possible for the dissemination of new ideas to thousands of people instead of a few score. Information on new discoveries could be made quickly available, but also the age-old truths of the classics and the scriptures could reach more people. Learning, long shut up in monasteries and in a few schools, emerged to become something that anyone with interest and initiative could pursue. Printing furthered the Renaissance that had already begun and facilitated the Reformation that soon followed. With more books being printed and read and more people becoming educated, the Dark Ages rapidly came to an end. The printing press, probably more than any other factor, was responsible for the beginning of the modern era.

In particular, the printing press changed the world of books. This change was achieved gradually over a period of a half century or more as the products of the presses were increasing and filling the book-shelves of Europe. The bookseller ceased being a dealer in manuscripts, scarce and costly, and instead could stock and sell the newly printed books in large numbers. Journeymen booksellers peddled their wares from town to town and from village to village. Later on, with the publication of cheaper works, the chapman followed with his penny chap-books to sell to the poorest reader. The new trades of printer, bookbinder, paper-maker, woodcut artist, type-maker, copper-plate engraver and bookseller added numbers to the rapidly growing middle class. Though few publishers became really wealthy, the book business was economically as well as culturally a successful innovation.

In the library itself, the coming of the printed book brought many changes, but not at first. In fact, many 15th-century librarians and book collectors refused to have the printed books in their libraries. In their eyes, the printed page was merely a poor imitation of the real thing.

Gradually, however, the book replaced the manuscript and in
time the latter became a valuable rarity rather than an object
of ordinary use. When they did come into the libraries, books
were kept on open shelves rather than in chests or on lecterns.
The library was separated from the scriptorium and, indeed,
the latter disappeared, with some monasteries acquiring printing presses instead. Printed books were plentiful enough to
be loaned for use outside the library walls, and hence the
public circulating library became a possibility. The typical
16th-century library became the oblong room with books
around the wall, and with tables for readers in the center, or
perhaps cases for displaying historical objects. The library
room came to have stipulated times for opening, with a librarian or keeper on duty. With books in larger numbers,
new methods of classification and arrangement had to be devised and various experiments were made in this direction.
Whatever the system used, whether by subject, size or
source, something in the way of a catalog or finding list was
usually available. Many libraries now numbered their holdings in thousands rather than hundreds and by 1600 at least
a beginning had been made toward the modern library.

The books themselves varied widely in content and
size in the early centuries after the beginning of printing.
Many of them were still huge folios, resembling the bound
volumes of manuscripts, but there were also the small
popular books printed by Aldus Manutius in Italy, by the
Elzevir Press in Holland, and by others. Religious works
still outnumbered all others, and the classics were still
popular, but contemporary works ranging from science to
superstition to travel to romance were also widely published.
The medieval wood-cut gradually gave way to the copperplate
engraving, but not until the former had reached a high stage
of perfection under such artists as Hans Holbein and Albrecht
Dürer. Bookbindings ranged from the paper back through
the simple unlettered vellum to the highly ornate gold-em-
bossed leathers. Printing types were changed, except in
Germany and to some extent in England, from the black-
letter or gothic types to lighter, more legible ones. Printing
as an art tended to decline in Italy, Germany and England,
but it flourished in France and the Low Countries, reaching
a high point in those areas in the 17th century. In the
printing of the Plantin and Elzevir families the copperplate
engraving came into its own.

Since the Renaissance had begun in the Italian peninsula, and since the printing industry had achieved an early

popularity there, it was only natural that Italian libraries
prospered in the 15th and 16th centuries. Several outstanding libraries were established long before the printing press,
and one, the Biblioteca Capitolare of Verona, claims to be
the oldest library in the world in continuous operation, dating
from the fifth century. But as books became more plentiful,
and as profitable trading centers developed at Venice, Genoa,
Florence and Naples, merchant princes were produced with
sufficient interest and funds to collect books and endow libraries. A few wealthy nobles, who had searched monastery
libraries from Greece to England to purchase, purloin or
copy manuscripts for their collections now added printed
books to their libraries and opened them to the public or
gave them to public institutions. The Medici family of the
15th and 16th centuries contained several book collectors,
and their books, after many vicissitudes, found their way to
the Laurentian Library in Florence which was opened to the
public in 1571 in a building designed by Michelangelo.
Another great Italian library was that of St. Mark (Biblioteca Marciana) in Venice. It was based on the 15th-century
collection of Cardinal Bessarion and was housed in its own
building about 1550. In 1609, the Ambrosian Library (Biblioteca Ambrosiana) was opened to the public in Milan,
largely through the efforts of the scholarly Archbishop of
Milan, Federigo Borromeo. This library, which contained
some 15,000 manuscripts and 30,000 printed volumes, was
almost unique in that it was open to the public a few hours
a day, although its treasures were protected behind brass
grills. Connected with the Ambrosian Library was a college of
doctors which was really a group of scholars engaged in, or
directing, research. For a time a printing press was provided to make available the results of their studies. The
National Library of Florence had its beginnings in 1714 with
a gift of books from the library of Antonio Magliabecchi,
while that in Turin was founded in the 1720s by Vittorio
Amadeo II. Girolamo Casanato opened his library (the Biblioteca Casanatense) in Rome in 1701, and Bologna's central
university library was founded in 1721 by Count Marsigli. At
Cosena, in northern Italy, the Biblioteca Malatestiana was
completed in 1452 by the local duke, Malatesta Novelle, and
this library, including building, furniture and books has been
preserved to the present day. These and a few other endowed and university libraries in Italy grew slowly during
the 18th and 19th centuries, often losing books by theft, war
or carelessness, but just as often being renewed by valuable
gifts. By 1900 they constituted some of the most valuable
libraries in the world, but public and school libraries were

virtually non-existent in most of Italy.

    Among theological libraries, the most important by
far was that of the Vatican in Rome. After many reverses
in the Middle Ages, the Vatican library began to grow rapidly in the 16th and 17th centuries. In 1527, much of the library brought together under Pope Sixtus IV was destroyed
when Rome was sacked by the armies of the Holy Roman
empire, but it began to grow again, particularly under Pope
Sixtus V (1585-90). Many treasures from monastery libraries found their way to the Vatican in this era as gifts to the
various popes. Occasionally whole libraries were added at
once, as when Fulvio Orsini bequeathed his library of some
500 manuscripts and 200 printed books in 1600. In 1623,
Maximilian, Duke of Bavaria, took the Palatine Library of
Heidelberg as spoils of war and gave it to Pope Gregory XV.
In 1658, the Library of Urbino, founded by Duke Federigo,
added some 1900 manuscripts to the Vatican collection. Still
another great library, that of Queen Christina of Sweden
containing over 2,000 manuscripts, was added in 1690.

    From this period onward, the course of the papal li-
brary has generally been one of continued improvement in
size and value, except for a brief set-back in the early 19th
century. During the latter days of the French Revolution the
invading French armies took over 500 choice volumes from
the Vatican Library and carried them to Paris. Fortunately
most of them were returned after the Bourbon kings returned
to power in France in 1815. Many of the Vatican librarians
have been of high quality, including several outstanding
writers and scholars such as the 16th-century church historian, Baronius. In the 18th and 19th centuries, steps were
taken to arrange the growing collection into useful order.
Printed books were separated from the manuscripts, and
among the latter the codices were separated from the rolls.
Further division was made by languages, and the more valuable tomes were enshrined in separate cases. Unfortunately,
the Vatican library's treasurers were not readily available,
and under some popes it was virtually unused. Still, in
contents and potential it was by 1900 one of the most important libraries in the world. It contained then over 400,000
printed books including 4000 incunabula; and more than 30,000
Latin, 4000 Greek, and 3000 Oriental manuscripts, with the
latter division including Hebrew and Coptic. Under Pope Leo
XIII (1878-1903), both printed books and manuscripts were
made available to scholars, and a large reading room was
provided. Its modern history dates from this era. So

important has the Vatican Library been considered in the development of the Catholic Church that many of its most important leaders have been honored with the post of chief librarian, and several of these have been promoted, in time,
to the position of pope.

The libraries in France after 1500 owed much to
Italian precedents, just as did its medieval libraries. The
French tended to improve or broaden the Italian beginnings,
and to promote a profession of librarianship that was hardly
achieved in Italy. France had the advantage over Italy of
being a unified nation, at least after the 16th century and
this gave rise to a French national library. Since the days
of Charlemagne at least, the French rulers had owned
royal private libraries and under several of them, particularly Charles V (1337-1380) and Louis XI (1423-1483), important collections were made. The library of Charles V,
housed in one of the towers of the Louvre, numbered nearly
1000 volumes. Francis I (1494-1547) strengthened the
Bibliothèque du Roi (as the Bibliothèque Nationale was then
called) by ordering that one copy of each book printed in
France be deposited there, and by establishing the position
of royal librarian. One of the first to hold this position was
Guillaume Budé, a noted scholar, and under his direction
the library was enlarged and arranged into something resembling a true library.

Although the Bibliothèque du Roi grew slowly, it suffered from several moves both in and outside of Paris, and
not until 1731 did it find a more permanent home on the rue
Richelieu. In 1692 it had been opened to the public twice
weekly, but this was rarely used and it was not until 1735
that it was permanently opened to readers. The first printed
catalog in 1622 listed some 6000 volumes, over half of
which were manuscripts, but after that most of the growth
was in printed works, and by 1700 there were over 70,000
volumes, occupying 22 rooms on two floors. During the
French revolution, its name was changed to the Bibliothèque
Nationale, and its size was increased considerably by books
seized from the nobility, the suppressed monasteries, and
from churches. It is estimated that over 100,000 printed
volumes and 70,000 manuscripts came into the French national
library during the Revolution and Napoleonic eras; by 1815 it
contained over half a million volumes. A few of these were
later returned to their original owners, but the 19th century
saw continued growth so that by 1900 the Bibliothèque Nationale was probably the most important library in the world.

Under the administration of the great librarian, Léopold
Delisle (1874-1905) the library's arrangement and usefulness
came to equal its size, and it served, directly and indirectly,
as a model for research libraries all over the world.

An early rival of the French national library was the
Bibliothèque Mazarine, formed by the scholar-librarian
Gabriel Naudé for Cardinal Mazarin in the early 17th century.
Naudé and his agents searched all over Europe for books and
manuscripts to add to the cardinal's library, and by 1650 it
contained some 40,000 volumes, most of them richly bound in
leather and stamped with the Cardinal's seal. Naudé, in addition to compiling and arranging the Mazarin library, also
wrote one of the earliest books on library science. This
was his Avis pour Dresser une Bibliothèque ("advice on
establishing a library"), published in 1627. In this work,
Naudé proclaimed the necessity for having all types of books
in a library, new and old, rare and common, sacred and
profane. He recommended a system of classification based
on the faculties or branches of knowledge commonly taught
in the universities, but he subdivided these into smaller classes for convenience. He hoped the Bibliothèque Mazarine
would become a universal library, preserving the literary
heritage of all peoples, and open to all users, and he set out
to make it so. Unfortunately, the library was virtually
destroyed in the 1650s by Mazarin's political enemies, only
to be partially reconstituted a decade later. After the cardinal's death, his library was bequeathed to the Collège de
Mazarin and still later it became the property of the French
government. It became one of the major libraries of Paris
and by the end of the 19th century contained over 250,000
volumes.

Another outstanding library in Paris was the Bibliothèque de l'Arsenal, formed in the 18th century by the Marquis
de Paulmy (1722-1787). Being a man of wealth, Paulmy was
able to acquire whole libraries at a time, and before his
death had built up a library of over 150,000 volumes, one of
the largest private libraries of all times. Before his death
the library was sold to the Count d'Artois, and during the
French Revolution it was taken over and opened to the public
as a national library. Growing rapidly through gifts and
purchases in the 19th century, the Bibliothèque de l'Arsenal
has developed largely as a humanities collection, and under a
series of scholarly librarians such as Charles Nodier (1822-
1844), it was by 1900 one of the major libraries in the world
in the fields of literature and drama.

One of Paris' great libraries that began as a monastic collection was the Bibliothèque St. -Geneviève. This began in 1624 as the library of the abbey of the same name, but by 1710 it was a semi-public library of some 40,000 volumes. It lost some volumes during the French Revolution, but continued to grow in the 19th century and by 1900 was a famous reference collection of 300,000 volumes.

Elsewhere in France, most of the notable libraries of the 16th to 19th centuries were either those of the universities or of the nobles. Some of the towns developed publicly owned collections at an early date, such as the Bibliothèque Municipale, founded in Troyes in 1651, but these were more in the nature of museums than libraries. Rouen claims the oldest municipal library in France, dating from 1634, but formed from an earlier cathedral collection dating back to the 12th century. During the French Revolution, many religious libraries, both monastic and cathedral, were confiscated by the state and turned into public libraries. Since that time most library development in France has been on a national basis, except for private universities and endowed institutional collections. Such "public" libraries as developed in France, either before or after the Revolution, tended to be the reference, non-circulating type, and although often containing valuable volumes, they were poorly cataloged, non-circulating, and of little use to the general public. School and public library service as it is known in America today was virtually non-existent in France before the 20th century.

In Germany there was no national unity until the 1870s and so each German state developed its own library, with many of them deservedly famous. Early Prussian princes had built up in their capital at Königsberg the "Silver Library" noted for its ornate bindings in silver, but it was under the rule of Frederick William of Brandenburg, the Great Elector, that the State Library of Brandenburg was opened in Berlin in 1661. Before his death, the Great Elector had built this collection to more than 20,000 volumes and 1500 manuscripts, all cataloged neatly by the librarian, Christoph Hendreich. This library had its ups and downs, but it was strengthened under later Prussian rulers until by 1790, under Frederick the Great, it contained some 100,000 volumes. After 1870 it became the Imperial Library of Germany, housed in what once had been the royal stables, and containing over 1,000,000 volumes and more than 30,000 valuable manuscripts. Duke Albrecht V (1550-1579) founded the State Library of Bavaria at Munich with his own private library as a nucleus. It was

housed in a separate building in 1575, and contained over
20, 000 volumes by 1600. During the Napoleonic wars many
thousands of volumes from closed monasteries found their
way to the Munich library, and it grew tremendously. During the 19th century its famous librarian was Johann Andreas
Schmeller who arranged and cataloged much of the collection.
By 1900, it contained over a million volumes.

     Julius, Duke of Brunswick, founded the Duke's Library
at Wolfenbüttel in 1558, and in the next century Duke August
himself compiled a catalog of this library that contained
nearly 4000 pages. In the next century, the philosopher Leibniz was librarian from 1690 to 1716 and he recataloged the
collection and classified it in a system of 20 main divisions
of knowledge. In the later 18th century the dramatist Gotthold Lessing was also librarian for a few years, and succes-
sive dukes added to the collection by purchase and seizure.
Housed in its own building from Leibniz' day onward, the
Wolfenbüttel Library was one of the greatest of the German
princely libraries, finally becoming the property of the state
in 1954. In Bamberg the State Library dates back to a collection formed by the Emperor Henry II in the 11th century.
Although never large in size, it contained priceless manuscripts, and, surviving wars and famines, it remains one of
the oldest libraries in continuous existence in Central
Europe.

     By the 18th century the other German states and prin-
cipalities also had libraries, usually founded by the nobility,
and many of them grew into considerable size by the 1800s.
Their holdings included many valuable manuscripts and early
printed works, but they were not usually available except to
favored friends of the rulers. The German merchant princes
early joined the political and religious leaders in the creation
of scholarly libraries, and many of these reached considerable size. For example, Ulrich Fugger (1526-1584), merchant
of Augsburg, added to a collection begun by his father and
grandfather. His descendants continued to enlarge this
family library, and it came to include thousands of volumes.
When it was finally broken up, parts of it went to three
major libraries: the Austrian National Library, the Bavarian
National Library, and the Palatine Library at Heidelberg.
The Schedel family library at Nürnberg, begun by Herman
Schedel in the 15th century, also grew into thousands of vol-
umes in several generations, and eventually ended up in the
Bavarian National Library at Munich. In the 18th century,
Johann Frederich von Uffenbach collected books systematically,

buying them on tours all over Europe, until he owned over
20,000 volumes, many of them extremely rare. On his death
his library went to the University of Göttingen. Collecting
books became the vogue for wealthy men, and even for some of
those not so wealthy, if current accounts can be believed.
The printing presses were turning out books in volume; booksellers and the annual book fairs at Leipzig and Frankfurt
made them readily available, and for those with means it
was not difficult to accumulate sizable libraries. Many
modern European, and some American, libraries owe their
treasures to the collecting activities of these German noblemen and merchants.

     One phase of library history that was common down to
the 19th century was the confiscation of books as spoils of
war by conquering armies. Sometimes, of course, books
were destroyed by pillaging soldiers who did not appreciate
their value, but often they were carefully gathered by agents
of the victorious king or prince and carried off with full
honors to become parts of the captor's library, or of some
institutional collection where he chose to place them. The
fate of the Palatine library of Heidelberg has already been
mentioned, and other examples are not rare. The armies
of King Gustavus Adolphus of Sweden in the 17th century
collected books from libraries all the way from Finland to
Czechoslovakia and presented them to Swedish libraries,
especially to the University of Uppsala. The French Revolution resulted in the greatest redistribution of books in history,
as valuable works were taken from individuals and libraries
all over France and placed in public collections. Napoleon's
armies extended the seizure of books to all of western Europe
as his empire grew, but some of these were later returned.
In other wars and revolutions literally thousands of books
changed hands and thousands more were destroyed, with
monastery and church libraries suffering particularly in the
religious wars that followed the Reformation. Some of the
important library moves were made voluntarily, as when
Queen Christina of Sweden took with her into exile a large
part of the Swedish royal library and eventually gave it to
the Vatican.

     Besides the state libraries and private collections al-
ready mentioned, there were other types of libraries developing in Germany in the 16th and 17th centuries. The Protestant church libraries replaced the monastery libraries to
some extent. Martin Luther taught that everyone should
read the Bible and he translated it into German so that it

90 Communication

could be read by the common people who could not read Latin. He encouraged the Lutheran churches to provide books for the people to read, and popular libraries, small but useful, grew up in the local parishes. They were quite different from the old monastery collections in that they consisted of printed books, and they were apparently well used by the parishioners. Another type of popular library was the municipal or "alderman's library." One of these was founded at Nürnberg in 1445, but most of them date from later centuries. They were usually housed in the city hall, and many of them soon deteriorated due to lack of care and use, but particularly in the larger towns they grew into the significant municipal reference libraries of the 19th century. At Jena, Heidelberg, Göttingen and Konigsberg, to mention only a few of the more prominent universities, there developed scholarly libraries far superior to those in most other European countries. At Göttingen, for example, the university library was founded about 1737, reached 60,000 volumes before 1800, and over half a million by 1900. The university library at Leipzig was founded in 1543, and with the addition of many valuable private collections over the centuries it too had reached a half million printed volumes by 1900, with thousands of valuable manuscripts in addition. Not only were the university libraries valuable in terms of holdings, but they were well organized and directed by scholar-librarians who operated them according to definite library procedures, and kept their treasures available for use. Usually, however, they were operated as reference libraries rather than as circulating collections, and were often of little use to the average student.

Among the German scholars who gave at least a portion of their lives to librarianship was Gottfried Wilhelm von Leibniz (1646-1716), also noted as a philosopher, mathematician, theologian and diplomat. Leibniz became acquainted with libraries during a stay in Paris and he may have worked for some time in the royal library there. At any rate he later went to Hanover as librarian and privy counsellor to the Duke of Brunswick. Still later he was librarian at Wolfenbüttel, and at that library he created an alphabetical catalog and directed the construction of one of the earliest buildings ever designed strictly for library use. Leibniz was a theoretical as well as a practical librarian, and he is remembered for his general philosophy of librarianship. In his writings he advocated a public library that would be both a research center and a popular reading collection. He also called for strong public support of libraries. He deplored those who judged a library by its number of books only, or by the fineness of its bindings, and said that the only true evaluation of a library was by the quality of the books in it and by the extent to which they were used. In addition to his alphabetical catalog of authors, he recommended a subject catalog or index, and also a chronological list of the books by date of publication. Many of Leibniz' ideas about library service were more fully realized by German librarians of the 18th and 19th centuries.

An outstanding German scholar-librarian of a later date was Fritz Ebert, who headed the Wolfenbüttel Library in the early 19th century. In his book, The Training of the Librarian, Ebert was rather critical of the average library of his day. In particular, he found the usual university library to be poorly organized, in charge of inexpert personnel, and filled with treasures that were all but lost for the average reader who used the library. He was a little more charitable to the municipal libraries, but these too he felt had suffered from maladministration and untrained workers. He urged that librarianship be raised to the status of a full-time, trained profession, but unfortunately few people agreed with him at that time. Ebert was something of a perfectionist and a bit over-critical perhaps, but his points were well taken. Like Leibniz, he was ahead of his time. The German dramatist, Johann Wolfgang von Goethe (1749-1822), was for a time in charge of the libraries at Weimar and the University of Jena, and took an active interest in their growth and organization.

Despite Ebert's criticism, the German libraries of the 1800s were probably the best in the world. The variety in kinds of libraries, the number of all types, the size of the major collections, the professional interest and ability of the librarians, and the financial backing afforded by church, state and wealthy patrons, all combined to make this possible. By the early part of the 19th century, German librarians were already familiar with such library developments as circulating libraries, popular reading rooms, published bibliographies and catalogs, inter-library loans, and even union catalogs. It must be admitted, however, that libraries for popular use lagged considerably behind those designed for scholarly and reference service. By 1900, all types of libraries, even special libraries and children's collections, were present in Germany, and most of them were well used. As an example, in that year some 268 libraries containing together more than 5,000,000 volumes in Berlin alone. In Munich, a much smaller city, there were 46 libraries, with all told more than 2,000,000 volumes and over 60,000 manuscripts.

In other parts of Europe libraries progressed in varying
degrees after the coming of printing, with the west and north
in general being far ahead of the east and south. In Austria,
the Royal Library was founded by the Emperor Maximilian I in
1493, although not much of it was surviving when Hugo Blotius
became the royal librarian in 1575. Under Blotius, the library
was cataloged and gradually enlarged until by 1600 it contained some 10,000 books and 1500 manuscripts. One of its
early librarians was Enea Silvio Piccolomini, who later became Pope Pius II. In 1727, with some 90,000 volumes, the
Austrian Royal Library moved into a new building especially
designed for it, and under the Emperor Joseph II, its size
was doubled with books taken from closed monasteries. The
legal deposit law, requiring one copy of each printed book in
the Empire to be placed in the Royal Library, had been passed
in the late 16th century, but the results of this law, in terms
of books received, were most noticeable in the 19th century.
By 1900, the Austrian "Hofbibliothek" as it was then called,
contained over 1,000,000 volumes, along with thousands of
valuable manuscripts, including one of the largest collections
of Egyptian papyri in existence. Other important libraries in
Austria developed at the Universities of Vienna, Graz, and
Innsbruck. Empress Maria Theresa opened the library in
Innsbruck in 1746, while that at Vienna dates back to a joining
of faculty libraries in the university in 1545, and that at Graz
was founded in 1585.

In Belgium, the Royal Library at Brussels began in
1837, but it was based on the library of the Dukes of Burgundy,
which was formed in the 15th century. It progressed rapidly
and by 1900 it contained over 500,000 printed books and
28,000 manuscripts. The municipal library at Antwerp was
opened in 1609, and is one of the oldest continuously operating municipal libraries in Europe. There were important
university libraries at Ghent and Louvain, and large municipal libraries at Brussels and Liège. Most of the other Belgian towns had small municipal collections, but like those in
comparable German towns they were largely for reference
use and enjoyed little patronage.

In the Netherlands, the Royal Library was founded in
1798 on the basis of the library of the Princes of Orange and
several smaller collections. Its holdings in incunabula were
especially valuable, and it too reached the half million mark
by 1900. The University of Utrecht Library was begun in
1636, but many of its books came from an earlier collection

gathered by the town fathers. The University of Leiden was virtually built around a library donated by the First William of Orange in 1575, while the University of Amsterdam Library grew out of a theological collection originating in the 15th century.

Some of the older and more important libraries in the Scandinavian countries are: the University of Copenhagen Library, founded in 1482; the Royal Library of Denmark, 1539; the Free Public Library of Oslo, 1780; the University of Oslo Library, 1811; and, in Stockholm, the Royal Library of Sweden, 1585. The University of Uppsala, containing probably the oldest library in Sweden, was founded in 1477 and greatly enlarged by Gustavus Adolphus in 1620. It had over 30,000 volumes by 1700, most of them in Latin. Legal deposit privileges on all books printed in Sweden brought more rapid growth in the 18th and 19th centuries, so that by 1900, with student and faculty libraries included, Uppsala had over 500,000 books at its disposal. In Finland, the University of Helsinki Library, which also serves as the national library, was founded in 1828. In all the Scandinavian countries, the movement toward popular libraries and reading rooms in towns and provinces became particularly strong after 1850.

In Spain and Portugal, the private libraries of the medieval scholars declined as the Moslems were driven out between the 12th and 15th centuries, and although Christian monastic and church libraries developed in the same period, they did not compare with those of France or Germany. In Spain the National Library dates from a palace collection formed by Philip V in 1711, but it grew so slowly that a catalog formed in 1760 lists only about 2000 volumes. In the 1800s it fared better, particularly under the librarianship of the bibliographer Manuel del Valle, and by 1900 it contained some 500,000 volumes and thousands of manuscripts. Also in Madrid, the Central University Library, founded in 1508, was noted for its collections on Spanish history and literature. One of the most notable libraries in Spain is that of the monastery at San Lorenzo del Escorial, near Madrid. This institution was founded by Philip II in 1565, and its library received his personal attention. Many medieval manuscripts from the library of the Spanish kings of Naples were added to it, along with other whole collections that came by purchase or gift. Considered a royal library until 1885, when it came under the control of Augustinian monks, the Escorial library grew only slowly in the 18th and 19th centuries, but its modern history has been one of cataloging, restoring and preserving its thousands of treasures. Today it is one of the most beautiful libraries in Europe in regard to both books and furnishings.   An outstanding Spanish library that began as a private collection is the Biblioteca Colombina in Seville, founded by Columbus' son, Ferdinand, in the early 1500s. Ferdinand Columbus willed his library to the Chapter of Seville Cathedral, whose history for some 400 years was one of ups and downs.   Only some 5000 volumes remain from the original collection, but this still makes it a valuable library.

In Portugal, the National Library, founded in Lisbon in 1786, is the most valuable single collection, although the municipal library at Oporto almost equalled it in size in the 19th century.   The university at Coimbra dates from the 1200s, but its various book collections were first brought together in a separate library building in 1717.   In the 19th century the university library received many valuable works from closed monasteries, and the legal deposit law kept it up-to-date so far as Portuguese publications were concerned.   Several other universities in Spain and Portugal had notable collections of books and manuscripts by the 1800s, including those at Seville, Barcelona and Salamanca, although lack of staff and organization often left their services inadequate.   Public library service was also virtually unknown until the 20th century.   On the other hand the nobility, and an occasional merchant prince, compiled a number of outstanding private collections, many of which eventually entered public ones.

In Russia, the greater libraries date for the most part from the 1700s, growing out of private collections or from libraries taken as spoils of war.   The Imperial Library in St. Petersburg (now Leningrad) began with the seizure of several libraries in Latvia in 1714 by Peter the Great.   It was little more than a royal private library, however, until 1794, when Catherine the Great added to it a library of nearly 300,000 volumes seized in Warsaw at the time of the dismemberment of Poland.   In the 19th century the Russian Imperial Library was enlarged by the legal deposit of two copies of each book printed in Russia, and through the acquisition of other large collections donated by merchants or nobles.   By 1900 it was one of the largest libraries in the world, with nearly 2,000,000 volumes and over 30,000 manuscripts.   Count M. A. Korf, librarian from 1849 to 1861, was responsible for modernizing the collection, and organizing it along the lines of the British Museum.   One of the great acquisitions of the Imperial Library was the Tischendorff collection of Near Eastern manuscripts, including the Codex

Sinaiticus, one of the earliest known versions of the Bible.
Other important libraries in Russia before 1900 included the
Academy Library in St. Petersburg founded in 1725; the University of Moscow Library (1755); and the Public Library of
Moscow, which evolved from a library founded in 1689.
Other large Russian cities, such as Odessa and Kharkov, also
began municipal libraries in the 19th century, the former in
1830 and the latter in 1886. Russian churches and monasteries often had sizable religious book collections, and the
nobility occasionally amassed large private libraries, but
public and school libraries in the modern sense lagged behind
western Europe in the 1800s.

The same was true in the remainder of Eastern Europe, and also in the Balkans, where the Turkish domination or
influence lasted well into the 1800s. Bulgaria, for example,
had many private and monastic libraries before the 15th century, when the area fell under the rule of the Ottoman Turks.
Libraries and learning then declined until the late 19th century when independence was achieved. The public library
in Sofia became the Bulgarian national library in 1879, and
reading clubs became quite popular throughout the country
before 1900. In Rumania modern library history began in
1831 with the establishment of a public library in Bucharest.
Poland's University of Cracow began in the 1300s, but with
the exception of a few other academic, monastic and private
collections, there was little significant library development
until the 20th century.

In other parts of the world, the library scene between
1500 and 1900 was varied, but generally far behind that of
western Europe or the United States. In Asia, the Buddhist
world, stretching from India to Japan, encouraged learning
and usually provided small religious collections in its numerous monasteries. Burma, for example, had many religiously
oriented village schools, each with a few books, as early as
the 17th century, with larger libraries in the older monasteries, and a royal library in the nation's capital. As of the
late 1700s, it was noted by a European traveller that Burma
probably had a higher rate of literacy than most European
countries. As European influence spread into south and east
Asia in the 18th and 19th centuries, western-type libraries
were begun in some of the coastal cities, as in the case of
the famous Raffles Library of Singapore. Both in China and
Japan, there were government libraries, and some large private collections, but until the introduction of western-style
printing in the 1800s, books were usually few and not widely
available.

In Africa, modern library service also generally came with European intervention. The wonderful libraries of the Moslem era in North Africa generally declined or disappeared before 1500, and there is a gap in library history until the 19th century. The National Library of Algeria was founded in 1835, but was small in size during the remainder of the century. The National Library in Cairo was established in 1870, and the Municipal Library of Alexandria in 1892. Ethiopia has several ancient book collections, particularly in the Coptic Christian monasteries. On the west African coast, some libraries were established in the European colonies, such as that at the Fourah Bay College in Sierra Leone in 1837, or at the American-oriented University of Liberia in 1862. Even in the Republic of South Africa, library history begins largely with the 19th century, especially with the South African Public Library begun in Capetown in 1818. South Africa also made good use of subscription libraries in the late 1800s and these provided most of the popular reading. Australia had little in the way of public library service until after 1850, when state or "public" libraries were established in each of the six major political divisions. There were more of the official or reference type, however, and most popular reading for the Australians came from social or "mechanic's" libraries in the towns and villages.

Returning to the European scene, the invention of printing spurred other developments in the world of books besides the growth of libraries. In particular, there were new forms of reading matter such as periodicals, newspapers and encyclopedias. The periodical began with the pamphlet of the 16th century, developed into a sporadic series of related pamphlets, then into annual or biennial "registers" of the news, and finally, by the late 1600s, into the regular periodical. Three of the earliest periodicals were the Journal des Scavans, which began publication in France in 1665; the Transactions of the Royal Philosophical Society in England in the same year, and a journal in Latin, the Acta Eruditorium, which began in Germany in 1682. The newspaper developed from the newssheet or broadside of the 16th century and had become fairly common by the late 17th. As early as 1548, a newsletter was issued by a Frankfurt printer for a short time, and several similar publications appeared briefly before 1600, but the first regularly published newspaper is usually considered to be the Avisa Relation oder Zeitung, published in Strasbourg in 1609. The Netherlands soon became an early center for newspapers, with its lack of censorship, and both French and English newspapers were published there for distribution in those countries. "Corantos" or newspapers added a new

element to public communication, that of "news" or the latest
information quickly disseminated. The impact of the printed
word was enlarged more than ever, and, on the practical
side, the ambitious printer had a new source of income.

The encyclopedias, created by almost a school of
writers in the 17th and 18th centuries, were an outgrowth of
ancient and medieval attempts at collecting all available
knowledge into one book or set of books. In 1630, Johann
Heinrich Alsted published in Switzerland what was probably
the first modern encyclopedia. He arranged his reference
work topically, under seven major heads with some 35 sub-
divisions. Later in that century, two Frenchmen, Pierre
Sayle and Louis Moreri, both produced encyclopedias, with
that of Bayle being usually considered the most authoritative.
In 1704, John Harris published his Lexicon Technicum; or,
An Universal English Dictionary of Arts and sciences, arranged alphabetically. In 1728, Ephraim Chambers, with
the aid of many other English scholars, produced his two-
volume Cyclopedia, which was more complete and scholarly
than that of Harris. Using a French translation of Chambers as a base, Denis Diderot and other continental scholars
produced the famous Encyclopédie which appeared in 30 volumes in Paris between 1750 and 1780. By the end of the
18th century, the new encyclopedia had reached virtually its
modern form, complete with illustrations, long articles by
authorities, alphabetic arrangement and cross references.

Generally speaking, the 16th and 17th centuries brought
the art of printing to a stage of perfection that was not surpassed in the 18th or 19th. The copper-plate engraving
largely replaced the wood-cut in the 1500s, it was not until
the 1800s that other methods of reproducing pictures were
developed. Printing in more than one color was tried even
before 1500, but perfection in this type of work was not
achieved until some 300 years later. The center of printing
in Europe moved from Germany to Italy, and then in the
1600s to France and the Low Countries. The whole era
from 1500 to 1800 saw only slow progress in the book world,
including libraries. Once the library had adapted itself to
the changes brought on by printing, there was relatively little
improvement in functions or services and not much in the numbers or size of libraries. The major European libraries
grew gradually but in a haphazard manner. In the 19th century, however, the industrial revolution brought tremendous
changes to the printing industry, while the growth of democra-
cy and education brought improvements just as important to

the world of libraries. Books were being printed by the millions, and libraries were preserving them by the hundreds of thousands. More important, though, the library was coming to be used more than ever, and was becoming recognized as a popular educational institution rather than a store-room for rare books.

Bibliography
                    BOOKS

Burton, Margaret. Famous Libraries of the World: Their History, Collections and Administration. London, 1937. 458 p.
Dahl, Svend. History of the Book. 2nd English ed. Metuchen, N. J., 1968. 299 p.
Dana, John C., and Kent, Henry. Literature of Libraries in the 17th and 18th Centuries. New York, 1907. 536 p. (Reprint, 1967.)
Edwards, Edward. Libraries and Founders of Libraries. London, 1864. 503 p. (Reprinted Amsterdam, 1968.)
_____. Memoirs of Libraries. London, 1859. 2 v. (Reprinted New York, 1964.)
_____. A Statistical View of the Principal Libraries of Europe and America. London, 1849. 48 p.
Elton, C. E. The Great Book Collectors. London, 1893. 228 p.
Esdaile, A. J. K. National Libraries of the World: Their History, Administration, and Public Service. London, 1957. 413 p.
Hessel, Alfred. A History of Libraries. New Brunswick, N. J., 1955. 198 p.
Hobson, Anthony. Great Libraries. New York, 1970. 320 p.
Johnson, Elmer D. A History of Libraries in the Western World. Metuchen, N. J., 1970. 521 p.
Koch, Theodore W. The Imperial Public Library at St. Petersburg. New York, 1915. 35 p.
Krieger, Bogdan. Frederick the Great and His Books. New York, 1913. 24 p.
Lomeier, Johannes. De Bibliothecis. . . (Chapter 10 translated by John W. Montgomery as: A Seventeenth Century View of European Libraries. Berkeley, Calif., 1962. 181 p.).
Naudé, Gabriel. Advice on Establishing a Library. Berkeley, Calif., 1950. 110 p. (Original ed., 1650.)
Newman, L. M. Leibniz (1646-1716) and the German Library Scene. London, 1966. 53 p.

Norris, Dorothy M. A History of Cataloging and Cataloging
    Methods, 1100-1850. London, 1939. 246 p.
Ogle, J. J. The Free Library, its History and Present Con-
    dition. London, 1897. 344 p.
Orcutt, W. D. The Magic of the Book. Boston, 1930.
    315 p. (See particularly p. 63-104.)
_____. Master Makers of the Book. New York, 1928.
    271 p.
Pottinger, David. The French Book Trade in the Ancient
    Regime, 1500, 1791. Cambridge, Mass., 1957. 363 p.
Rice, James. Gabriel Naudé. Baltimore, 1939. 134 p.
Savage, Ernest A. The Story of Libraries and Book Collect-
    ing. New York, 1909. 230 p.
Thornton, J. L. Chronology of Librarianship: An Introduc-
    tion to the History of Libraries and Book-Collecting.
    London, 1941. 266 p.
_____. Selected Readings in the History of Librarianship.
    London, 1967. 2nd ed. 408 p.
Tisserant, Eugene. The Vatican Library. Jersey City,
    N. J., 1929. 31 p.

PERIODICAL ARTICLES

Christiansen, Claude H. "Classification and Cataloging in
    the Scandinavian Countries," Library Quarterly, 1
    (1931), 436-454.
Clarke, Jack A. "Gabriel Naudé and the Foundations of the
    Scholarly Library," Library Quarterly, 39 (1969), 331-
    343.
Garnett, Richard. "Librarianship in the 17th Century," in his
    Essays in Librarianship and Bibliography, London,
    1899, 174-190.
Jackson, S. L. "Highlights of Continental Librarianship,
    1680-1789," Journal of Education for Librarianship, 11
    (1971), 344-350.
Gosnell, Charles F. "Goethe the Librarian," Library Quar-
    terly, 2 (1932), 367-374.
Hoffman, Herbert H. "Co-operative Acquisition in German
    Research Libraries, 1800-1930," Library Quarterly,
    34 (1964), 249-257.
Montgomery, John W. "Luther and Libraries," Library
    Quarterly, 32 (1962), 144-147.
Munthe, Wilhelm. "The Library History of Norway,"
    Library Journal, 45 (1921), 19-24, 57-62.
Reichman, Felix. "Three Hundred Years of the Prussian
    State Library," Library Quarterly, 32 (1962), 225-230.
Rostenberg, Leona. "The Libraries of Three Nuremberg

patricians, 1491-1568," Library Quarterly, 15 (1945), 131-138.

Schwiebert, Ernest G. "Remnants of a Reformation Library," Library Quarterly, 10 (1940), 494-531.

Spratt, H. P. "Some Libraries of Northern Europe," Library Quarterly, 4 (1934), 467-486.

Stummvoll, Josef. "Austrian Libraries, Past and Present," Library Quarterly, 20 (1950), 33-38.

Trenkler, Ernest. "History of the Austrian Nationalbibliotek," Library Quarterly, 17 (1947), 224-231.

Wehmer, C. "History of German University Libraries," Library Trends, 12 (1964), 496-506.

Wood, Raymond F. "Berbrugger, Forgotten Founder of Algerian Librarianship," Journal of Library History, 5 (1970), 237-256.

VII

ENGLISH BOOKS AND LIBRARIES, 1500-1900

Until the 16th century, libraries in England developed much the same as those on the continent. There were the early monastery and cathedral libraries, the beginnings of the university libraries, and a few private collections worthy of note. After about 1500, however, English libraries began to develop in a manner of their own.

Both the book arts and libraries in England were severely retarded in the 1530s and 40s by the Act of Dissolution, which under Henry VIII separated the Church of England from the Roman Catholic Church. Much of the property of the Church was transferred to the King, and in the process, many monastery libraries were broken up and their contents sold or destroyed. At first the university libraries and Oxford and Cambridge seemed to benefit from this destruction of monastic collections, and the cathedral libraries also managed to escape at first. But under Edward VI there was a purge of all theologically undesirable works from the universities and cathedrals and their turn came to suffer. When this literary purge was over, the Cambridge University Library contained only 19 of the 330 manuscripts previously held, while Oxford lost almost all of its library. All over England it was estimated that at least a quarter of a million books were lost or destroyed. In the printing world things were almost as bad, since nothing could be printed without the consent of the government. The accession of Elizabeth I in 1558 brought an end to this tragedy, but not until many literary treasures had been lost and library development had received a costly set-back.

The Elizabethan period saw a considerable revival in the English literary world and a period of relative progress for libraries. Collectors began to regather the scattered volumes, to obtain copies of others from Europe, and to reprint many of the scarce printed works. Writers and publishers found more freedom in their activities, so that the

"age of Shakespeare" was an outstanding one in English literature.   Among the libraries, that of Oxford University was slow
to recover after the purges of Henry and Edward, and it was
not until the turn of the century that it was greatly enlarged
and strengthened by Sir Thomas Bodley (1548-1613). Bodley,
having achieved success in business and diplomacy, retired in
the 1590's and devoted himself to building up the book collection at Oxford.   In a few years, the library contained over
2000 volumes, and a regular librarian was employed.   In
1613 an annex was added, and by 1620, the librarian, Thomas
James, could report that his library contained 18,000 volumes.   So important were the efforts of Bodley that the university's central library took his name, and to this day it is
known as the Bodleian Library.   Many other accessions came
in the 17th century, including 1300 manuscript volumes from
the collection of Archbishop Laud, and 8000 volumes donated
by a lawyer, John Selden.   The addition of all current books
printed in England by the legal deposit act of 1610 also added
to the growth of the collection.   By 1700, the Oxford University Library was by far the largest and most important in
England.

The Cambridge University Library did not fare as well
in the 17th century as did the Bodleian, but it did grow.   In
the late 1500s, it had been revived with a valuable gift of
books and manuscripts from the library of Matthew Parker,
Archbishop of Canterbury, and in 1632, a large group of
Arabic manuscripts from the collection of Thomas Erpenius
of Leiden was added.   During the Civil War and Commonwealth period, 1641-1660, the fortunes of the Cambridge Library varied, sometimes losing, sometimes gaining a few
volumes.   After the Restoration of Charles II, it received
some royal attention, and in 1666, Bishop Tobias Rustat
presented an endowment of £1000, the proceeds from which
were to be used for the purchase of books.   Several other
important gifts and bequests of books were received before
1700, including a collection of 4000 volumes given by Henry
Lucas.   In addition to their university libraries, Cambridge
and Oxford also had significant libraries in many of their
constituent colleges.   In many cases, these college libraries
had endowments of their own, and were better off financially
than the central collections.   The college library contents
were usually more restricted in subject than that of the university library, and their use was generally limited to the
students and faculty of the particular college.

In Scotland, the University of Glasgow Library,

founded in 1453, was an important educational asset in the
16th and 17th centuries.   It received important gifts from
Bishop James Boyd in 1627 and from Zachary Boyd in 1651.
The University of St. Andrews is known to have had a library
as early as 1478, but its organization as a university collection dates from 1611.   Edinburgh University Library was
founded in 1583, largely from a gift of funds and books from
Clement Little, a wealthy merchant and lawyer.   In 1637 it
had 2410 volumes, according to a catalog completed that
year, and by 1700 there were over 11,000 volumes.   A fourth
Scottish university, at Aberdeen, had a college library in
operation in 1495, and a university library by 1634, but it
never equalled the others in size or importance.   In 1710,
after the union of Scotland and England to form Great Britain,
the Scottish universities were permitted by the Copyright Act
to receive one copy of every work printed in the nation.

    In Ireland, the library of Trinity College at Dublin be-
gan with a gift of books by the English army after a victory
over the Irish at the battle of Kinsale in 1601.   By 1604 this
collection had 4000 volumes, and it gradually became the most
important library in Ireland.   James Ussher, later Primate
of Ireland, directed the early growth of this library, and on
his death in 1655, willed his own library of some 7000 volumes
and 600 manusoripts to it.   In 1732, it moved into a new
building designed to house 100,000 volumes, but it took more
than a century to fill all its shelves.

    For the 18th and 19th centuries, the story of British
university libraries was one of slow but steady progress.   In
some cases the college libraries merged with those of the
university, or at least came under central direction, but in
others they retained their separate identities.   In 1715 George
I presented to Cambridge University the library of John
Moore, Bishop of Ely, including some 30,000 volumes strong
in English history and literature.   In the 1800s Lord Acton's
library of over 50,000 volumes was added.   At Oxford,
major gifts included 4800 manuscripts donated by Dr. Richard
Rawlinson in 1734 and a sum of £136,000 presented by the
Rev. Robert Mason in 1841 for the purchase of books.   Cambridge moved its library into a new building in 1755.   Oxford
University Library, after several moves, expanded into the
remodelled Radcliffe Camera building in 1860.   By 1900, each
library contained well over half a million volumes, and each
had spread into parts of several buildings.   Elsewhere in
England and Scotland, several new colleges and universities
began, each of them in time building considerable libraries:

the University of Durham (1832), the University of London
(1836), Victoria University at Manchester (1851), and the
University of Liverpool (1882).

    The national library of England, the British Museum,
has had a long and interesting history. The early rulers of
England had acquired collections of books, particularly Queen
Elizabeth I, whose library was noted for the beauty of its
bindings. In 1570, Sir Humphrey Gilbert, a favorite of
Elizabeth's, drew up a plan for a Royal Academy and Library,
and similar ideas were advanced by Roger Ascham, who was
the royal librarian. Neither of these plans was successful,
however, and the Royal Library remained simply a private
collection. Throughout the Civil War and Commonwealth period following the execution of Charles I, the Royal Library
was kept intact largely through the efforts of its librarian,
John Dury. Dury took his position seriously, and even published a booklet in 1650, entitled The Reformed Librarie
Keeper, probably the first book on library science in English.
Dury had some surprisingly modern ideas. He considered
the librarian to be an educator, rather than a mere keeper
of books, someone who would be a cultural missionary and
bring books and readers together. He called for the use of
alphabetized catalogs, preferably printed in book form, and
for the liberal use of all materials. In 1662, the Royal
Library, by act of Parliament, was allowed to claim one copy
of every book published in England, and Richard Bentley, who
became Royal librarian in 1694, enforced this act. He built
up the library considerably and made the collection at least
semi-public. To carry out his ideas for the Royal Library,
he wrote a pamphlet on A Proposal for Building a Royal Library and Establishing it by Act of Parliament. He wanted
parliamentary aid to build the Library up to at least 200,000
volumes and to support it permanently as a public institution.
His plan was good but premature, and the Royal Library remained simply the king's collection for another half century.

    Sir Hans Sloane, a physician and scientist, is the man
most directly responsible for the founding of the British Museum. During his lifetime he collected books and manuscripts
and museum pieces ranging from botanical specimens to antique
furniture. In his will, he made his collection available to the
nation on condition that it be suitably housed and displayed to
the public. In 1753, Parliament accepted this offer and
united the Sloane Collection with two others, the Cottonian
and Harleian Libraries, to form the beginnings of the British
Museum. It was finally opened to the public in Montague

House in 1759. The Cottonian Library was largely the collection of Sir Robert Bruce Cotton, whose grandson donated
the library to the government in 1701. The Harleian collection was purchased by Parliament from the heirs of Sir
Robert Harley, who had compiled it early in the 18th century.
Harley had brought together a private library of over 50,000
books and 7500 manuscripts, but only the latter were obtained
by the government, while the printed works were dispersed
through various sales. In 1760, shortly before his death,
George II donated his private library, including the remains
of the earlier royal libraries, to the Museum. George III,
who reigned from 1760 to 1820, was a noted book collector
himself, and his agents scoured England and Europe for book
treasures. After his death the library was reputed to contain more than 100,000 volumes, and most of them, along
with rare manuscripts and works of art, were later added to
the British Museum by George IV. Other notable accessions
to the Museum were the Burney Library of 13,500 volumes
purchased in 1818, the Banks collection of 16,000 volumes
on natural science donated in 1820, and the Grenville Library
of 20,000 volumes given in 1846.

Although the British Museum was the national library,
it was basically a museum, and its main purpose was to house
and display the curios and rarities collected over the years by
various donors. The major portion of the Montagu House was
the museum, while the books were shelved in rooms off the
main display hall. Would-be users of books found it difficult
to locate specific titles, and almost impossible to study them
once they were reached. Moreover, the first three directors
of the Museum were all scientists and the book and manuscript
collections did not receive the attention they deserved until well
into the 1800s. The librarian who was to transform the Museum into one of the great libraries of the world was, oddly
enough, not even an Englishman. He was Anthony Panizzi,
an Italian political refugee, who had in 1831 become an assistant in the Museum, thanks to a friendship he had formed
with a member of the Board of Trustees. While he knew
little of library work before his appointment as librarian in
1856, he was well learned in European languages and litera-
tures, and became an expert in bibliography as well.

Although he was head librarian for only ten years, to
1866, Panizzi's total of 35 years on the staff were spent in
improving the book and manuscript collections and in making
them more useful to the public. He drew up rules for cataloging the books, and began the lengthy process of organizing

and cataloging the collection. He pointed up the weaknesses
in the collection, and urged larger appropriations to fill in
the gaps. He enforced strictly the deposit laws which required
publishers to supply the library with copies of all British
publications. Probably more than anything else, Panizzi is
remembered for designing the circular reading room which
was opened to the public in 1857. It was a milestone in library architecture and served as a model for other buildings
in many countries. When Panizzi joined the staff of the Museum it was the seventh largest library in Europe, but when
he resigned it was second only to the Bibliothèque Nationale.
It was said of him that he took a book collection and made
it into a library, and it might be added that in so doing he
made of himself one of the world's great librarians. After
Panizzi's retirement, the Museum continued to grow rapidly
in size and service, and perhaps its greatest achievement
in the late 19th century was the production of the printed
British Museum catalog which was completed in 1905. It
represented book and pamphlet holdings up to 1900, and by
this date there were over 2,000,000 volumes to be included.
In addition to the printed books, there were over 5,000,000
other items in the Museum, including prints, maps, broadsides, papyri, clay tablets and other exotic book forms, pictures, art works and museum objects.

    The most important library in Scotland, and the one
that became officially the Scottish National Library after
1925, was the Advocate's Library, founded in 1682 in Edinburgh. Originally a legal library, it early began to specialize in Scottish literature and history as well. In 1709 it was
granted depository rights for all books published in Great
Britain, and under several scholarly librarians, including the
historian-philosopher David Hume, the library grew to more
than 30,000 volumes by the late 18th century. In later years
gifts of books and funds have secured steady growth, and by
1900 the Advocates Library was approaching 500,000 volumes.
Wales also has a National Library, planned as early as 1872,
but not opened until 1907 in Aberystwyth. Ireland's National
Library was originally the library of the Royal Dublin Society, founded in 1731. It became a national library when it
was purchased by the government in 1877.

    Private book collectors have played a major role in
English library history. From the small collections made
by nobles and clergymen in the 16th century through the very
large family libraries of the 19th, individuals have built valuable collections that often ended up in public holdings. Sir

Walter Raleigh, for example, had a private library of 515
volumes with him when he was imprisoned in the Tower of
London in 1604. Bishop White Kennett (1660-1728) had a library of over a thousand volumes, largely relating to the
English colonies in the New World. The historian, William
Camden, left a library of some size at his death in 1623,
and this eventually came to the British Museum. In 1678, the
Reverend James Nairne gave 2000 books to the University of
Edinburgh Library. Possibly the greatest of the 18th-century
bibliophiles was Thomas Rawlinson, who collected a library of
nearly 200,000 volumes. Several large private libraries were
increased by several generations of the same family. The
Earls of Balcarres, for example, developed the Biblioteca
Lindesiana, of which the more valuable parts were eventually
given to the John Rylands Library of Manchester. This collection comprised more than 100,000 books and 6000 manuscripts by 1900. The Dukes of Marlborough developed at
their estate, Blenheim, a library of over 20,000 volumes by
the early 1800s. George John, Lord Spencer (1758-1834),
built on a family library to develop the Biblioteca Spenceriana
which also eventually went to the John Rylands Library. This
collection was noted not only for its size but for the hundreds
of incunabula and other rare works included in it. And so the
story goes--book collectors gathering and preserving books
from vanity, scholarliness, or merely the collecting urge, but
from the standpoint of library history and the important thing is
that many of these private libraries eventually ended up in
public collections. This was not always the case, of course.
Many great libraries were sold at auction and dispersed to the
four winds, sometimes to libraries, sometimes to other collectors. Not all of them even remained in England, since
many were acquired by American buyers and others went to
European collectors, particularly French and German.

A number of English professional or "special" libraries had reached notable size and importance by the 18th century. Lincoln's Inn, a legal corporation that was noted as a
training school for young lawyers, had a professional library
dating from the early 16th century. Gray's Inn and the Inner
Temple, similar legal organizations, had large libraries by
1750, and the latter was open to the public as well as to its
own lawyers and students. The Royal Society, a scholarly
scientific organization had a library almost from its founding
around 1660. It specialized in transactions and publications
of learned societies, largely obtained in exchange for its own
publications, and by 1800 it numbered over 75,000 volumes.
The Royal College of Physicians Library dates from 1518,

being based largely on the collection formerly owned by Dr.
Thomas Linacre. In Edinburgh, the Signet (Law) Library was
founded in 1755, and in the other larger cities legal, religious
and scientific libraries were known before 1800 and were fairly common in later years. In London professional libraries
were fairly numerous in the 1800s, with large collections in
medicine, natural history, archaeology, geology, geography,
chemistry, botany, zoology and the fine arts. Some government offices had maintained small book collections, and of
course collections of public archives, but government libraries as such were largely begun in the 1800s. Particularly
notable among these were the Foreign Office Library (established in 1782), the Public Records Office Library (1838),
the Patent Office Library (1855), and the Colonial Institute
Library (1868).

There were a few early attempts to provide public
library service for the average reader, but it was not until
the late 19th century that public library service in the modern
sense was begun. A public library was established in Coven-
try in 1601, but it did not survive. A parish library was
founded at Langley Marish in Buckinghamshire for public use
in 1623, and a public library was founded in Leicester in 1632.
One established in Manchester in 1654 has survived almost intact, perhaps indicating that it was little used. The library at
Dundee, Scotland, dates from 1601, and that at Bristol,
England, from 1613. Other 17th-century "town libraries"
were established in Ipswich and Norwich, but there is some
doubt as to the public character and use of these early institutions. They were indeed public property, but their book collections were small, the caretakers were often indifferent, and
the amount of public interest and use of them is questionable.
Possibly of more use were the parish libraries founded by the
Reverend Thomas Bray and his associates around 1700. These
libraries were placed in the parish churches for the use of
ministers and church members, and were mostly religious in
nature, but they apparently had considerable use for a few
years. After Bray's death the parish library activities were
maintained by the "Associates of Dr. Bray" until well into the
1800s, but their efforts were spasmodic, and apparently the
most useful work they did was in providing small theological
collections for ministers in the poorer parishes. That there
was a wide interest in public library service in the 18th century is evidenced by a pamphlet published in Newcastle-on-
Tyne in 1769. It was hopefully entitled A Scheme for Founding
and Supporting a Public Library in Alnwick, Addressed to All
Readers in that Place and Neighbourhood.

In the latter half of the 18th century two types of semi-public libraries became fairly common in England. These were the proprietory and the subscription libraries. The former were usually connected with some organization, while the latter grew out of the earlier book clubs and were more openly commercial. An example of the proprietary type was the mechanics' library, designed to provide educational and recreational reading matter for apprentices and workers in particular locations or trades. Others were formed by cooperative societies, working-men's clubs, and trade unions, and some of them eventually formed the bases of local public libraries. They usually included trade manuals, textbooks, religious and political pamphlets, and occasionally more serious literary and historical works. They were usually open only to members. The subscription library, on the other hand, was usually open to anyone who could pay the relatively small fee. These were more in the nature of book clubs or rental book services and sometimes were connected with book stores. They may well be related to the coffee-house libraries of the 17th-century. In that era the more popular inns or coffee-houses around the universities and in the larger towns began to keep book collections for their patrons. These books could be read on the premises or borrowed for a small sum. Regular patrons paid an annual rental for the use of the books and in at least one case this rate was only a shilling for a year. The popularity of these collections stemmed from their contents: political pamphlets, poems and plays that were available nowhere else except by purchase. Needless to say, the contemporary booksellers complained of this service, arguing that it deprived them of sales.

The subscription library was a popular means of obtaining reading matter, patronized by scholar and noble along with many a worker and tradesman. By the 19th century they had become larger and more highly organized, with sizable collections of books housed in permanent quarters. Liverpool had two subscription libraries, the Lyceum, founded in 1757, and the Athenaeum, founded in 1798. Some other early ones were the Bradford Library and Literary Society (1774), and the Newcastle Library and Philosophical Society (1793). Their names indicate the broad aspirations of their founders. Probably the most famous of the subscription libraries, the London Library, was not founded until 1841, but it eventually came to own hundreds of thousands of volumes, and to have subscribers around the world. Other notable subscription libraries were those at Leeds, Birmingham, and Nottingham. Something in the way of early rural libraries were the "itinerating libraries" established in 1817 by Samuel Brown of Haddington. These small collections of 25 to 50 books, left in the homes of rural citizens for circulation in the neighborhood, met a popular need, and the system was copied in other areas to some extent. This type of library unfortunately did not long survive its founder, who related his adventures as a library promoter in his pamphlet, Some Account of Itinerating Libraries and Their Founder, published in 1856.

Although there was some free library service from endowed libraries, the development of the modern free public library service in England really dates from 1847. In that year, following requests from churchmen, social reformers, and trade union leaders, Parliament passed an act appointing a Committee on Public Libraries to consider the necessity of establishing them throughout the nation. Two years later this Committee presented a very full report on the conditions of library service then available, and the need for a tax-supported free public library service. In 1850, as a result of this and a subsequent report, the Public Libraries Act was passed, allowing cities of 10,000 or more population to levy taxes to support library service. Subsequent laws extended the Library Act to Scotland and Ireland, made the permissable rate higher, and extended permission for levies to smaller towns and rural areas. In 1870, the passage of the Gladstone-Forster School Law, which made communities responsible for the establishment and maintenance of free public schools, greatly increased the number of readers and consequently the demand for public libraries. Although there was no great rush to take advantage of the Public Libraries Acts, most of the larger towns and cities, or at least 75 of them, had begun libraries by 1877. Norwich was one of the first, adopting its tax levy in September, 1850, and opening its library officially in 1857. By 1900 there were over 300 public libraries established under the Act and many of them already had branch libraries. Generally speaking, however, public library service was poorly supported before World War I, and there was little in the way of library extension to rural areas. On the brighter side was the fact that the growth of public libraries came just as many of the great private libraries were being broken up, and some of their most valuable works found their way into public collections. For this reason, among others, the larger British public libraries compare very favorably as research centers with the university libraries and a few of them compare favorably with any but the very largest libraries in the world.

Two subjects closely connected with the history of books

and libraries are copyright and legal deposit. The first refers
to the author's or publisher's legal rights to a published work,
and the latter to the legal requirement that one or more copies of all published works be deposited in certain designated
libraries. In England the subject of copyright can be traced
at least as far back as 1557, when the Stationers' Company
was incorporated in London as an association of printers and
publishers representing all such tradesmen in England. In
effect it was a monopoly of the publishing business because
non-members were unable to get government permits for
operation. Previous to this time, what amounted to a copyright might be obtained by securing a "privilege" from the
King for printing a book. In later years, the entry of a book
title in the register of the Stationers' Company gave the publisher exclusive rights to his publication for an indefinite
term. In 1662, the first Copyright Law, in the form of a
licensing act, replaced the Stationers' Register, and this act,
revised in 1709, 1801, and later, has continued in operation
to the present. By the 19th century, British copyright was
held to be for the life of the author plus fifty years. Legal
deposit originated in 1610, when Thomas James, librarian at
Oxford, through Sir Thomas Bodley, induced the Stationers'
Company to place one copy of each book published by their
members in the Library of the University. This practice was
made legal and permanent in the Licensing Act of 1662, and
two other libraries, that at Cambridge University and the
Royal Library, were added to the deposit list. A reason for
the deposit law, in addition to adding volumes to the library
shelves, was to allow the university authorities to see if undesirable books were being published. In the 18th century,
legal deposit was extended to other English, Scottish and Irish
libraries, but in 1836 this number was curtailed considerably.
It was found that the laws were being consistently evaded, and
when a stronger copyright law was passed in 1852, deposit
was required only for the British Museum, while four other
major libraries--those at Oxford and Cambridge and the Advocates' Library in Edinburgh and Trinity College in Dublin--
could obtain free depository copies by requesting them in
writing.

     In the 1500 and 1600s, England saw but little progress
in the printing arts. After a good beginning under Caxton and
his fellows in the late 15th century, English printing felt the
burden of censorship and unsettled political and economic conditions for a century and a half. There were many printers
but their output was closely watched by both government and
religious censors and it was not until after the Restoration of

the Stuart kings in 1660 that much progress was made in
either quantity or quality of printing. Typography was a trade
and not an art in England and even the printing of the Shakespearean plays was poorly done. The types used were often
old and worn, margins were narrow, title-pages were poorly
designed, and illustrations were often so carelessly done as
to be hardly recognizable. A few fine books were printed,
such as Thomas Roycroft's excellently executed six-volume
folio Polyglot Bible of 1657. It was sold by subscription in
advance of publication, a new idea in the business of bookselling in England, and one that was to be used effectively in
later years for major publishing ventures.

After 1694 and the repeal of the censorship of the Licensing Act, printing in England took on new life, and by the
mid-18th century it was among the best in Europe. About
1720, William Caslon, a type-founder, began to develop new
type faces designed especially for the English alphabet. Taking his patterns from the better Dutch printers and improving
on them, Caslon produced a type that was clean and precise.
He employed a combination of curves and angles that was
pleasing to the eye. Later in the century, John Baskerville
took the Caslon type-forms, adapted them moderately, and
with them produced some of the most beautiful books in
English printing history. Baskerville not only improved
upon the type he used, but upon the press, paper and ink as
well. He printed some 67 different works, but probably his
best known book is his edition of the works of Virgil. Baskerville's books were expensive, even for his day, and they
were designed largely for the collector, or at least for the
appreciator of fine books. Whatever their purpose, they set
a standard of perfection and even of elegance in printing
that has influenced the book world ever since.

The output of the early English printers consisted for
the most part of religious works, political pamphlets, and
the classical authors, although the latter were never printed
as extensively in England as they were on the continent. In
the 16th century came more pamphleteering, more works by
English authors and a few government publications. Early
in the 17th century came the King James Bible, the largest
publishing venture in England to that date. Shortly after
came the first "corantos" or newspapers to be published in
England, with John Archer's first attempt in this direction
in 1621. In 1625 Charles I suppressed all news sheets, and
they were very rare throughout the century. Still later in the
same century came the first periodicals, usually folded

sheets of four to eight pages, giving the latest political or military news along with some contemporary literature and the editor's views on a variety of subjects. Usually these early journals were short-lived unless they enjoyed political or governmental support, and their fortunes varied with the political and social prestige of their publishers. By 1750, the periodical had become fairly common and newspapers, magazines and yearbooks were in general circulation among the upper classes. There were general and news magazines, such as the Gentleman's Magazine; literary periodicals, such as Richard Steele's Tatler and Joseph Addison's Spectator, and important yearbooks of current history, such as the Annual Register. Scientific and professional works joined the literary output of the English presses in the late 1700s, and in general the press of England became and remained as free and prolific as any in the world.

Although they were not printed in large numbers before the 19th century, there were a few children's books published. In 1477 Caxton published his Book of Curteseye, or a book of manners for young people, to instruct the young English how to act in church or at home, and also on what to read. The Schoole of Vertue and Book of Good Nurture for Children and Youthe to Learn Their Duty By was a similar work, written by F. S. Seager and first printed in 1577. About 1600 there appeared the horn book, the first elementary printed matter designed for the child's own reading. The horn book was really a single page, fastened to a wooden paddle and protected by a transparent cover of horn. It usually contained the alphabet and a short sentence or verse for simple reading. The World in Pictures, printed in England about 1658, has been considered the first picture book for children. About 1750 John Newbery became the first publisher to be particularly interested in children's books. He published a collection of Mother Goose Rhymes and when this proved to be popular he printed Oliver Goldsmith's History of Margery Two-Shoes, probably the first story in English written especially for children. In all, Newbery published more than 100 small books for juvenile readers, and was himself the author of many of them. He was also one of the first publishers of annual gift-books, an item which was to become very popular in the 19th century.

One other publishing development of the 18th century is worthy of note. This was the compiling and publishing of multi-volumed encyclopedias. Ephraim Chambers' Cyclopedia . . . ., published in 1728, contained only two

volumes, but it was followed by the first edition of the Encyclopedia Britannica in 1771. This work, which was to become
the standard in its field, was a major undertaking, with many
authorities contributing to it. Its three volumes appeared in
as many years. Such reference works were often sold by
subscription, and issued in numbers or parts which could be
later bound into volumes. Often two or more printers would
combine their efforts in order to print an encyclopedia or to
issue the complete works of a popular author.

In book illustrations, the wood-cut continued popular in
England until well into the 17th century, although the copper
engraving was known there as early as 1588. In the days of
Caslon and Baskerville, the copper engraving was generally
used, but in the late 18th century Thomas Bewick and William Bulmer perfected the wood engraving. Since this was a
great improvement over the wood-cut and less expensive than
the copper engraving, it was widely used for nearly a century, or until photo-engraving superseded it. The steel engraving was also widely used in the 19th century.

In bindings, English books progressed from the rather
simple leather and vellum backs of the 1500s through the more
ornate tooled and decorated leathers of the 1600 and 1700s,
down to the cloth and boards of the nineteenth. Generally
speaking, the English bindings were never quite as fancy as
those preferred by the French and Italian collectors.

Although types, illustrations and bindings progressed
noticeably over the years, the printing press itself changed
little between 1500 and the late 1700s. Perhaps the method of
intaglio printing, developed in the late 16th century might be
mentioned as a change. This involved printing from ink held
in depressions engraved on the printing surface, rather than
from raised type that had been inked. For illustrations, or
for reproducing manuscript writing, this method was widely
used for centuries, and in many respects anticipates the rotogravure of the early modern era.

Throughout the era of printing, English books and
other forms of graphic communication have played a major
role in the promotion and spread of learning. Particularly
by the late 19th century, England was a literate world and
the market for books, whether the six-penny thriller or the
20-guinea collector's item, was extensive. Moreover, as
the British Empire spread around the globe, the English
language followed, so that the product of the English presses

found a market on every continent. Both in quantity and
quality the publications of the 19th century were worthy fore-
runners of the "information explosion" of the 20th. Nowhere
is the power of the press as a vital means of education and
communication more apparent than in the England of the last
few centuries.

Bibliography

BOOKS

Aitken, W. R. History of the Public Library Movement in
     Scotland to 1955. Edinburgh, 1971. 379 p.
Altick, Richard. The English Common Reader: A Social
     History of the Mass Reading Public, 1800-1900. Chi-
     cago, 1957. 430 p.
Bennett, William. John Baskerville. Birmingham, England,
     1937-1939. 2 vols.
Blagden, C. Stationers' Company: A History, 1403-1959.
     London, 1960. 321 p.
Boulton, W. H. The Romance of the British Museum.
     London, 1931. 242 p.
Craster, H. H. E. A History of the Bodleian Library,
     1845-1945. Oxford, 1952. 372 p.
Clair, Colin. History of Printing in Britain. Oxford, 1965.
     314 p.
Dury, John. The Reformed Librarie Keeper. Chicago, 1906.
     71 p. (Original ed. 1650; reprinted 1967.)
Edwards, Edward. Free Town Libraries, Their Formation,
     Management and History in Britain, France, Germany
     and America. London, 1863. 371 p.
_____. A Statistical View of the Principal Libraries of
     Europe and America. London, 1849. 48 p.
Esdaile, A. J. K. The British Museum Library. London,
     1946. 388 p.
Great Britain, Parliament. Report from the Select Committee
     on Public Libraries. London, 1849. 317 p. (Reprinted
     1968; a second report was made in 1850.)
Greenwood, Thomas. Public Libraries; a History of the
     Movement in England. London, 1890. 586 p.
Hepworth, Philip, and Alexander, Mary. The City of Nor-
     wich Libraries: History and Treasurers. Norwich,
     1957.
Irwin, Raymond. The Heritage of the English Library. New
     York, 1964. 296 p.
_____. The Origins of the English Library. London,
     1957. 272 p.

Jayne, Sears. Library Catalogues of the English Renaissance.
    Berkeley, Calif., 1956. 226 p.
Kaufman, Paul. Borrowings from the Bristol Library, 1773-
    1784. Charlottesville, Va., 1960. 138 p.
_____. The Community Library: A Chapter in English
    Social History. Philadelphia, 1967. 67 p.
_____. Libraries and Their Users: Collected Papers in
    Library History. London, 1969. 233 p.
Kelly, Thomas. Early Public Libraries; A History of Public
    Libraries in Great Britain before 1850. London, 1966.
    281 p.
Kronick, David A. A History of Scientific and Technical Peri-
    odicals. New York, 1962. 274 p.
Lea, John Thomas. The History and Development of the
    Mechanics' Institutions. Oldham, 1968.
Library Association. A Century of Public Libraries, 1850-
    1950. London, 1950. 27 p.
McColvin, Lionel R. The Public Library System of Great
    Britain. London, 1942. 218 p.
Miller, Edward. Prince of Librarians. The Life and Times
    of Antonio Panizzi of the British Museum. London,
    1967. 356 p.
Minto, John. A History of the Public Library Movement in
    Great Britain and Ireland. London, 1932. 366 p.
Moran, John. Wynkyn de Worde, Father of Fleet Street.
    London, 1960. 56 p.
Munford, W. A. Penny Rate: Aspects of British Public
    Library History. London, 1951. 150 p.
Oldman, C. B. English Libraries, 1800-1850. London,
    1958. 78 p.
Ollé, James G. Library History. 2nd ed. London, 1971.
    131 p.
Parish, Charles. History of the Birmingham Library.
    London, 1966.
Parke, H. W. The Library of Trinity College Dublin. Dublin,
    1961.
Partridge, R. C. B. The History of Legal Deposit of Books
    Throughout the British Empire. London, 1938. 364 p.
Plomer, Henry R. A Short History of English Printing,
    1476-1898. London, 1900. 345 p.
Predeek, Albert. A History of Libraries in Great Britain and
    North America. Chicago, 1947. 177 p.
Rees, Gwendolyn. Libraries for Children: A History and Bib-
    liography. London, 1924. 260 p.
Ricci, S. de. English Collectors of Books and Manuscripts,
    1539-1930. Cambridge, Eng., 1930. 203 p. (Reprint-
    ed London, 1960.)

Savage, Ernost A. Old English Libraries. London, 1911.
298 p.
Streeter, B. H. Chained Libraries, a Survey of Four Cen-
turies in the Evolution of the English Library. London,
1931. 368 p.
Thornton, J. L. Selected Readings in the History of Librari-
anship. London, 1967. 2nd ed. 408 p.
Wiles, R. M. Serial Publication in England before 1750.
Cambridge, Eng., 1957. 391 p.
Wormald, Francis. The English Library: Studies in its
Development before 1700. London, 1958. 273 p.

PERIODICAL ARTICLES

Borden, H. K. "Libraries and Cultural Renaissance," Li-
brary Quarterly, 4 (1934), 28-35.
Collison, Robert. "Birth of a Library, 1833," Journal of
Library History, 3 (1968), 55-62.
Davis, Donald G., Jr. "Problems in the Life of a University
Librarian: Thomas James, 1600-1620," College and
Research Libraries, 31 (1970), 43-49.
Finlayson, C. P., and Simpson, S. M. "The Library of the
University of Edinburgh," Library History, 1 (1967),
2-23.
"The Foundation of Libraries," Cambridge History of English
Literature, 4, 474-497.
Garnett, Richard. "Librarianship in the 17th Century," in
his Essays in Librarianship and Bibliography, 174-190.
Hamlyn, Hilda M. "Eighteenth Century Circulating Libraries
in England," The Library, 5th ser., I (1947), 197-222.
Jackson, Sidney L. "Bodley and the Bodleian," Library
Quarterly, 39 (1969), 253-270.
Houlette, W. D. "Thomas Bray," Library Quarterly, 4
(1934), 588-609.
Joynes, Sara E. "The Sheffield Library, 1771-1907,"
Library History, 2 (1971), 91-116.
Keeling, Denis F. "British Public Library Buildings, 1850-
1870," Library History, 1 (1968), 100-126.
Ker, N. R. "Cathedral Libraries," Library History, 1
(1967), 38-45.
Lyle, Guy R. "A Royal Book-Collector, George III," Library
Quarterly, 3 (1933), 180-191.
McCue, George S. "Libraries of the London Coffee-Houses,"
Library Quarterly, 4 (1934), 624-627.
Oates, J. C. T. "The Cambridge University Library, 1400-
1600," Library Quarterly, 32 (1962), 270-286.
Russell, L. H. "A Plan for a Public Library at Church-

Langton, Leicestershire, 1760, " Library History, 1
(1968), 67-76.
Wellard, James H. "The State of Reading Among the Working Classes of England During the First Half of the
Nineteenth Century, " Library Quarterly, 5 (1935), 87-
100.

VIII

PRINTING IN COLONIAL NORTH AMERICA

The development of printing came only a half century before the discovery of America and it is not surprising that printing followed closely as European civilization spread to the New World. The Spanish were the first to secure permanent colonies, and their motives in settling them were both economic and religious. They intended to Christianize the natives, and since the printed word was an effective means of spreading and preserving Christianity, a printing press was a logical supplement to the early missionary's equipment. Thus the first printing press in the Americas was established in Mexico City sometime in the 1530s. The exact date of the first printing, and the name of the first printer are both uncertain. One student of the subject believes it was Pedro Varela in 1531, but this is not accepted by other scholars. There is a better case for Esteban Martín in 1536, but on the other hand the coming of Juan Pablos to Mexico City as a printer in 1539 is well-documented. He was an agent of Juan Cromberger, a leading printer of Seville in Spain, and from his Mexican press there came a number of works in the early 1540s. Most of his publications were religious works, but he also printed primers for children, and official publications for the colonial government. By 1550, a typefounder had joined Pablo's printing establishment, and the type and make-up of his publications improved considerably thereafter. In 1575 the first paper mill in the New World began operation in Culhuacán, near Mexico City. Printing did not thrive in Mexico and there were few presses outside Mexico City until the 1800s.

The second American country to have a printing press in operation was Peru. In 1584, Antonio Ricardo, formerly of Mexico City, opened his printshop in Lima and began his printing with a four-page royal proclamation, a copy of which still exists. Printing spread very slowly to the remainder of Latin America. Possibly, printing began in Colombia (Bogota) before 1600, but the first confirmed printing there is not until the 18th century. Argentina had a printing press around 1700, but printing had spread from Mexico to Guatemala in Central America by 1660.   Cuba had a printing press as early as 1723, but Brazil, Chile and Venezuela did not have presses until the mid-18th century.   Most of the other Latin American countries did not have printing until the late 18th or even 19th centuries.   An interesting sidelight on South America's printing history is that there were books printed from wood-blocks in the Argentine area before there was printing from movable type.   With most of the presses in the hands of religious groups, it is natural that the majority of the titles printed were religious in nature.

In the English colonies of North America the first printing was done in Massachusetts.   The Reverend Joseph Glover, who thought that a printing press in the new colony would further the causes of both the Puritan church and the new Harvard College, arranged for the shipment of a press and at least one experienced printer from Cambridge, England, to Cambridge, Massachusetts.   Although Glover died on the voyage, the Day [also, Daye] family set up the press and were in operation by early 1639, with young Matthew and possibly Stephen Day as the printer(s).   Their father, also Stephen Day, is sometimes thought to be the first American printer, but it is now considered that the elder Day was the mechanic who set up the press while at least one of his sons was the actual printer.

The first piece of printing known to have come from the Day press was a broadside, The Oath of a Free-man, and the first pamphlet was An Almanack for the Year 1639.   Not a single copy of either has survived.   The oldest known book printed in what is now the United States appeared from the Day press in 1640.   It was the celebrated "Bay Psalm Book," or The Whole Booke of Psalmes Faithfully Translated into English Metre . . . .   The Day family operated the press until 1649, when upon the death of Matthew it came under the operation of Samuel Green, who continued it until 1692.   Up to that date more than 200 books and pamphlets were published by this one press.   They included almanacs, items connected with Harvard College, and books and pamphlets of a religious nature.   In 1675 the town of Boston acquired its first printing press when John Foster set himself up as a printer there.   Foster was also a wood engraver, and he illustrated some of his books himself.   Interestingly enough, one of the earliest American printers was an Indian who took the name of James Printer.   He learned the trade at the press of Samuel Green, and his name appears as printer on at least one book.

The second of the English colonies to acquire a printing establishment was Pennsylvania, where in 1685 young William Bradford appeared as a printer sponsored by the colony's founder, William Penn. Bradford's first Pennsylvania imprint was also an almanac: America's Messenger, Being an Almanack for the Year of Grace, 1686. Bradford did not remain long in Penn's good graces, however, and in a few years he moved to New York, where in 1693 he established the first press in that colony. His first known publication there was a slap at the Pennsylvania leaders who had opposed him, and was entitled: New-England's Spirit of Persecution Transmitted to Pennsylvania. . . . Bradford remained in New York until his death in 1752, printing more than 400 books and pamphlets during his lifetime. He is noted as one of the colonial era's outstanding printers, having produced the first New York paper currency, the first American Book of Common Prayer, the first history of New York, and the first copperplate map of New York. Bradford also had a share in the establishment of the first paper mill in America, and established the first printing press in the colony of New Jersey in 1723. His sons and grandsons continued the family printing business until well into the 19th century.

The colony of Virginia had a printing press for a brief period in 1682, but the printer issued some papers of the Assembly without official permission, and was soon banned from the colony. This printer, William Nuthead, was ordered to return to London, and apparently did so, but he later came to Maryland where he operated a press at St. Mary's City, possibly as early as 1685. The earliest surviving publication of the Nuthead press is a legislative document published in 1689. Virginia did not have a permanent printing press in operation until 1730, when William Parks set up a press at Williamsburg. South Carolina followed, with printing beginning in Charleston in 1731, and from that date until the Revolution, that port city was one of the most active printing centers in the colonies. Three printers, in fact, set up shop in Charleston in 1731 and 1732, but they did not survive very long. Instead it was Lewis Timothy, a protégé of Benjamin Franklin, who became South Carolina's first important printer after his arrival there in 1733. In North Carolina, James Davis was the first printer in 1749 at New Bern, and in Delaware James Adams set up the first press in 1761 at Wilmington. Georgia, the last of the original 13 colonies, had no printer until James Johnston arrived in 1763, 125 years after printing first arrived in Anglo-America.

In Canada no printing was done until 1751, when

Bartholomew Green, Jr., a grandson of Samuel Green of
Massachusetts, set up his shop in Halifax, Nova Scotia. A
year later, John Bushell, another New Englander, began the
first Canadian newspaper, also in Halifax. Apparently there
was no printing done in the 150 years of French Canada, but
shortly after the British took over Quebec in 1763, a French-
English Quebec Gazette was published there. Also, the first
printer in French Louisiana arrived in 1764, shortly after
that colony had been turned over to the Spanish. This printer
was Denis Braud, and appropriately enough his first publication accounced the cession of Louisiana to Spain. It was not
until 1794 that Louisiana had its first newspaper, the Moniteur
de la Louisiane published by Louis Duclot. Florida had its
first publishing when in 1783 a Loyalist refugee from South
Carolina, William Wells, published briefly the East-Florida
Gazette, at St. Augustine.

Probably the most outstanding of the colonial printers
was a man who is most remembered for his other occupations. Benjamin Franklin was a statesman, philosopher, inventor and scientist, as well as a journalist and printer.
Printing was his first love, and throughout his long life he in-
sisted that his vocation was "printer." Franklin was born in
Boston and at an early age he was apprenticed to an older
brother to learn the art of printing. He worked in London as
a printer for nearly two years before setting up his shop in
Philadelphia. This work was good experience, for the materials and workmanship in the London establishments were
superior to those with which he had been acquainted in America.

At first Franklin worked for other printers, including
William Bradford, but later he entered into a partnership
with Hugh Meredith. In 1730, while Franklin was still only
23, his partnership was ended, and he set out alone as "B.
Franklin, Printer." In the next 40 years or so, this press
issued more than 700 titles, exclusive of paper money, broadsides and newspapers. In 1729, while still in partnership with
Meredith, Franklin began publishing the Pennsylvania Gazette,
the second weekly newspaper to be established in Philadelphia.
The newspaper proved fairly successful and led Franklin to
begin his second major publication, Poor Richard's Almanac.
The almanac was the colonial printer's main stock in trade,
and Franklin improved his by writing most of it himself. His
witty sayings and sensible advice made Poor Richard a house-
hold word for many generations.

The product of the American colonial printer was varied. After about 1725, the average printer published a newspaper, sometimes doubling as editor, writer, reporter, press-
man and circulation manager. Eventually he might become
editor only, while journeyman printers did the press work.
Along with the newspaper, the printer often published an annual almanac, a type of reading matter that was second only to
the Bible in the average colonial home. The almanac contained
the calendar for the year, often with elementary astronomical
information and the astrological signs. Along with this, it contained witty sayings, home remedies, and general advice on
home and farm problems. In addition, each almanac usually
gave the names of the officials of the province, and sometimes the local tax laws as well. Depending upon the ability
and popularity of the editor the almanac flourished or failed;
some lasted only an issue or two, while others survived a
half-century or more. In the case of Franklin's Poor Richard,
annual sales sometimes reached 10,000 copies or more, but
most of the almanacs were far less popular. In the latter
colonial period, the almanac was joined by the provincial
register, similar in some respects, but containing more
political and statistical information about the individual provinces.

Official government publications were important ele-
ments in most of the colonial printers' output. In fact, in
several instances the early printers were induced to come to
the colonies in order to perform the public printing, and in
at least one colony, South Carolina, a bonus was offered by
the legislature to the first printer who would locate in the
colony. The publications of the provincial governments included laws, particularly tax laws, law codes, legislative
journals, and the various legal forms needed for the transac-
tion of official business. On the other hand, early colonial
printers were quite often severely restricted by the provincial
governments and their royal governors, and the items printed
were sometimes censored. Official favoritism too sometimes
played a part and there were two or more printers in one
colony, one might be favored for political reasons, or might
win political approval by his good work, as Franklin did once
early in his printing career. Official printers in each colony were not only favored with government printing but were
often allowed more license in what they did print. A celebrated case in colonial legal history was that of Peter Zenger,
who in 1734 published some attacks against the local governor
in his newspaper, The New York Weekly Journal. For this
he was imprisoned under a charge of libel but when he finally

came to trial he was acquitted. His lawyer, Andrew Hamilton, argued that if the jury found the facts as published to be
true, then there could be no libel.   The case established a
legal precedent in similar cases of libel, providing that the
jury should be the judges of both the law and the facts in a
particular case. The Zenger case is considered a forward
step in the development of freedom of the press and of
mass communication in general.

The colonial printer, when not engaged with newspapers, almanacs and governmental publications, turned out a
wide variety of broadsides, pamphlets and books. The
numerous broadsides were usually little more than circulars
announcing new laws, giving the results of court cases, or
more often merely announcing some interesting bits of news.
They were printed on one side of a sheet only, and were designed to be posted in public places where they could be easily seen by a large number of people. In effect they were
supplements to the newspapers and sometimes they were actually called "extras." The pamphlets were usually political
or religious, and the number published by all the colonial
printers undoubtedly ran into the thousands. They were
usually hastily printed, poorly sewn, and often quickly read
and forgotten, but their numbers indicate that they served a
communication need and many of them were so popular that,
despite several known printings, no copies have survived.
Indeed, one historian estimates that for every colonial publication of which a copy has survived, at least four other publications have been lost completely.   The reason for this,
aside from poor physical condition was that in most cases
only a hundred or so of each item was printed.

In subject matter, religion led the list of publications
for most colonial printers, amounting to almost two-fifths of
all the known colonial printing. Collected sermons were
especially popular in New England, but they were widely
printed and reprinted in the colonies. Law codes, legal form
books, legislative journals and official manuals accounted for
another fifth of the printing, while literature in all its forms
was almost as extensive. Most of the literary works published were editions of the classics, with a few contemporary
European and English authors, and a very few American items.
The relatively small percentage of literary publications was
probably due to the fact that such items could be purchased
in English editions cheaper than they could be reprinted in
America. This was also true of the Bible, of which there
were few editions published by colonial printers. The social

sciences, including history, economics, education and political
science, accounted for the final fifth of the known publications
except for about three per cent of publications in the sciences
and fine arts. Among the histories were several volumes on
the development of individual colonies and many more on early
relations with the Indians, including the popular accounts of
Indian captivities.

A few books went through many editions, as for example, the New England Primer, which was printed in more
than 30 editions and thousands of copies between 1690 and
1830. On the other hand, the printer sometimes advertised
for subscribers for a work before venturing to print it.
Prince's History of New England, published in Boston in
1736, had orders for 1450 copies before it was printed, but
many other relatively large items were printed with only
250 or so subscribers. Another popular item for the colonial
printer was the handbook, The Office and Authority of the
Justice of the Peace, a legal work, went through 40 editions
between 1710 and 1800. Other similar items were The Secretary's Guide; or, Young Man's Companion, suitable for the
young man entering business, and The Compleat Housewife,
for the distaff trade. All told, at least 18,300 different
publications are known to have been issued by colonial American printers, counting a full year of a newspaper as one
item, and some estimates place the actual figure, including
items no longer in existence, as high as 80,000 separate publications.

The earliest newspaper printed in the English colonies
was an issue of Public Occurrences both Foreign and Domes-
tick, published by Benjamin Harris in Boston on September
25, 1690. The provincial government objected to the contents
of this first issue and banned further publications. Earlier
there had occasionally been published some antecedants of
the newspaper in the form of news broadsides, such as one
issued in Boston in 1689 by Samuel Green, and entitled
The Present State of the New-English Affairs, Published to
Prevent False Reports. After Harris' unsuccessful venture
it was 14 years until another printer dared to issue a newspaper, and this time it was done with the prior approval and
authority of the government. The publisher was John Campbell; the title was, appropriately enough, The Boston News-
Letter; and the first issue was dated April 24, 1704. In
size, the News-Letter was only a single sheet, about 7 by
11.5 inches, and in contents it consisted mainly of news borrowed from London newspapers, already several weeks old.

Some local news and news from other colonies was carried
in later issues, along with notices and announcements of both
the Massachusetts government and that in London. It came
out weekly or sometimes every two weeks, and it managed
not only to meet the approval of the authorities, but actually
secured a governmental subsidy on one or two occasions. It
never became financially successful and as late as 1719 the
publisher complained that he had less than 300 paying customers. Other early newspapers were the Boston Gazette
(1719; the New England Courant (1721) also of Boston; the
American Weekly Mercury (1719) and Franklin's Pennsylvania Gazette (1719), both of Philadelphia. New York's first
newspaper was the New-York Gazette, founded in 1725, while
the Maryland Gazette began in Annapolis in 1727 and the
South-Carolina Gazette at Charleston in 1732. The Virginia
Gazette, at Williamsburg, was published as early as 1736,
and the North-Carolina Gazette, at New Bern, in 1751. In all,
more than 100 different newspapers, most of them short-
lived, were published in the 13 colonies before the Revolution.

The contents of the average colonial newspaper ran
strongly to political tracts, with literary works in serial
form being also fairly common. News as such was usually
weeks or months old, often copied from English newspapers
brought over by the mail ships or "packets," Public laws and
official decrees sometimes made up most of a single issue,
particularly when the provincial legislature was in session.
Later in the 18th century advertising developed and contributed to the financial stability of the newspaper. Most of the
advertisements were of the classified type, short and to the
point, calling attention to goods for sale, a runaway slave,
or a delinquent wife who had left the advertiser's bed and
board. In the late colonial period, the larger merchants
would sometimes take a half or full column to list their
choice wares, item by item, and all "just arrived from
England." Although editorials themselves were scarce, the
editor's policies were often strong, and well known to his
readers. Rival editors often used vicious language in attack-
ing each other, usually over fictitious names. Readers contributed their ideas and opinions in long letters to the editor, often signed by pseudonyms, such as "Publius" or "Pro
Bono Publico." Social news was incidental, but sometimes
carried, particularly in the later colonial period. No daily
papers were published prior to the revolution, but exciting
news appearing between weekly issues was sometimes made
public in the form of "extras." Lists of ships arriving and
departing, schedules of stagecoaches, and similar bits of
public information were often carried, sometimes on the

front page. In format, the colonial newspaper was usually
only two to four pages, with the pages themselves being about
half the size of the modern newspaper. Subscribers were
few, usually numbered in the hundreds, even for the larger
town papers.

The first American magazine, published for about three
months in 1741 by Andrew Bradford at Philadelphia, was
appropriately enough entitled the American Magazine, but its
subtitle was more descriptive: "A Monthly View of the Political State of the Colonies." Benjamin Franklin followed
with his General Magazine and Historical Chronicle only a
few days later, and this periodical lasted six months. Both
were really little more than supplements to their publishers'
newspapers, and as such carried little appeal. In 1743,
the American Magazine and Historical Chronicle began in
Boston under the editorship of Jeremiah Gridley and survived
for about three years. Even at that it was one of the most
successful of the colonial magazines. Between 1741 and 1775
no less than 17 different magazines were started in the colonies, but most lasted only a short time, and none survived
the Revolution. The American colonial magazines lacked one
prime ingredient--writers. They could not compete with the
several good British periodicals in content, and since time-
liness was of little importance the American magazine did not
attract a stable audience.

Throughout the colonial period the printing press in
use was little changed from that developed by Gutenberg.
Most presses or their component parts were bought in England
but Christopher Sauer, a noted printer of Germantown (i.e.,
Philadelphia), built his own press and established, in 1772,
the first American type foundry. Possibly a few other printers also built their own presses in the later colonial period.
Until Sauer, and Abel Buell of Connecticut, began to cast
their own in the 1770s, type in the colonies came from
England or Germany. Jacob Bay, a native of Switzerland,
set up the first American type-founding business, also in
Philadelphia, in 1773. Paper was made in the colonies as
early as 1690 when the German William Rittenhouse and his
son Claus built a paper mill for William Bradford in Germantown. The colonial paper industry grew slowly, and the quality remained poor but by 1775 much of the paper used in the
colonies was made there, especially in Philadelphia. Benjamin Franklin was very much interested in the manufacture of
paper, and is supposed to have aided in the establishment of
no less than 18 papermaking factories from Virginia to New

Table 2

NOTABLE EARLY AMERICAN PRINTERS

This list includes only the first printers in the various colonies or states before 1800, and a few of the other important colonial printers.

Date	Printer	Location
1639	Matthew Day	Cambridge, Mass.
1649	Samuel Green	Cambridge, Mass.
1675	John Foster	Boston
1685	William Bradford	Philadelphia
1689	William Nuthead	Saint Mary's City, Md.
1693	William Bradford	New York
1709	Thomas Short	New London, Conn.
1723	William Bradford	Perth Amboy, N. J.
1727	James Franklin	Newport, R. I.
1728	Benjamin Franklin	Philadelphia
1730	William Parks	Williamsburg, Va.
1731	George Webb	Charleston, S. C.
1733	Lewis Timothy	Charleston
1738	Christopher Sauer	Germantown, Pa.
1749	James Davis	New Bern, N. C.
1751	James Parker	Woodbridge, N. J.
1756	Daniel Fowle	Portsmouth, N. H.
1761	James Adams	Wilmington, Del.
1763	James Johnston	Savannah, Ga.
1764	Denis Braud	New Orleans, La.
1783	William C. Wells	St. Augustine, Fla.
1791	George Roulstone	Rogersville, Tenn.
1787	John Bradford	Lexington, Ky.
1793	William Maxwell	Cincinnati,
1797	John McCall	Detroit
1799	Andrew Marschalk	Natchez, Miss.

York. This early American paper, like that of Europe down to the 19th century, was made of cotton and linen rags. The printing ink used was usually made of linseed oil and lamp-black, and although some ink was made in the colonies as early as the 1690s, most of it was purchased from England. Franklin and Sauer, among other printers, had facilities for making their own ink, but they too purchased much from England as surviving records show. In the early days the printer's working staff consisted largely of his wife and

128

children but as his business grew he took on apprentices and
sometimes hired extra journeymen. Most printing establishments had only one press, and the largest, such as Franklin's or Sauer's, had only three or four. Wages paid to
skilled printers were comparatively high, and they were considered to be among the most important of the "mechanicks"
of the colonial period. In addition to typesetters and press-
men, and possibly type-founders and ink-makers, the printing
trade also provided work for bookbinders. In small establishments, the printers often did much of the binding themselves, but in larger towns, the book-binder, skilled in sew-
ing, leatherwork and embossing, was a necessary addition to
the book-making trades.

The position of the printer in colonial society was
an interesting one. He was quite often an influential citizen
of his colony and sometimes grew into relative wealth as
well. Benjamin Franklin was, of course, no ordinary printer; his early successes owed at least as much to other, if
allied talents. Justus Fox of Philadelphia, besides being a
printer, practiced the professions of engraving, type-founding,
medicine, pharmacy, and surgery. William Bradford of
Pennsylvania, Samuel Green of Massachusetts, Lewis Timothy
of South Carolina, and a score or more other printers were
important leaders in their respective towns and provinces.
Part of this was due to their newspapers, which exercised
considerable influence in colonial politics, despite occasional
control or censorship. The printer was often a self-educated
man who took a place of leadership in his community. Often
a book-store was attached to the printing shop, and this attracted the more educated citizens and became a focal point
for the local leaders, whether literary, social or political.
Books could also be sold by traveling peddlers, or by the
popular book auctions held periodically in most of the larger
towns.

A number of women took an active part in the printing business. Franklin freely acknowledged the help of his
wife in the printing shop during the early days of their marriage. In Charlestown, Anne Timothy took over and operated
the press several years after the death of her husband,
Lewis Timothy (when her son, Peter Timothy, grew up, he
operated the business). Dinah Nuthead, the widow of William
Nuthead, operated a printing firm in Annapolis for a few
years after 1695, and Ann Franklin, sister-in-law of Benjamin, ran a press in Newport, Rhode Island, after 1758.
Several families included printers in several generations, and

the descendants of Samuel Green of Boston were printers and
publishers for nearly 200 years.

As the American Revolution got under way, the
colonial printer played a most important role. The Stamp Act
of 1765 directly involved the publications and forms produced
by the printer and as the differences between the colonies and
England became more pronounced it was the printer who kept
the people informed of developments through his newspapers
and broadsides. The actions of the Provincial and Continental
Congresses, and the retaliatory actions of the British Parliament were hot news events published from Maine to Georgia.
The Revolutionary Committees of Correspondence made full
use of the printing press in distributing their news from
colony to colony. The political pamphlet was particularly important in arousing the colonists to rebellion. Thomas
Paine's Common Sense, coming as it did in January, 1776,
and selling many thousand copies, did much to change an
economic and political dispute into a war for independence
simply by pointing out to the Americans that independence
was possible and that the dawn of an American empire was
at hand. It is indeed hard to imagine a successful American
Revolution without the aid of the provincial printer. And the
colonial printer, taking sides as he did with America or
England (several of them remained loyal to the King), was
worth at least a regiment to the cause he favored. Printers
on both sides suffered during the war through destruction or
seizure of their presses and from shortages of paper, ink
and labor. But in the end, the importance of the printer and
his product was fully appreciated, and when in 1789 the first
ten amendments to the new United States Constitution were
submitted, prominently placed in Article I was the firm
guarantee of freedom of the press.

Bibliography
                            BOOKS

Berthold, Arthur B. American Colonial Printing as Determined
     by Contemporary Cultural Forces, 1639-1763. New York,
     1970. 86 p. (Originally 1934.)
Green, Samuel A. John Foster, the Earliest American En-
     graver and the First Boston Printer. Boston, 1909.
     149 p.
Gundy, H. P. Early Printers and Printing in the Canadas.
     Toronto, 1957. 54 p.
Hildeburn, Charles R. Sketches of Printers and Printing in

Colonial New York. New York, 1895. 189 p.
Kaser, David. Books in America's Past; Essays Honoring
    Rudolph H. Gjelness. Charlottesville, Va., 1966.
    279 p.
Kimber, Sydney A. The Story of an Old Press; An Account
    of the . . . Stephen Day Press. Cambridge, Mass.,
    1937. 43 p.
Klapper, August. The Printer in Eighteenth-Century Wil-
    liamsburg. Williamsburg, Va., 1955. 30 p.
Lehmann-Haupt, Hellmut. The Book in America. 2nd ed.
    New York, 1952. 493 p.
Leonard, Irving A. Books of the Brave. New York, 1949.
    381 p. (On the use of books in colonial Latin America.)
Littlefield, George E. The Early Massachusetts Press,
    1638-1771. New York, 1969. 2 v. (Originally 1907.)
McMurtrie, Douglas C. The Beginnings of the American
    Newspaper. Chicago, 1935. 36 p.
_____. The Book; the Story of Printing and Bookmaking.
    New York, 1943. 676 p.
_____. A History of Printing in the United States; the
    Middle and South Atlantic States. New York, 1936.
    462 p.
Mott, Frank L. A History of American Magazines, 1741-
    1850. New York, 1930. 848 p.
Orcutt, W. D. The Magic of the Book. Boston, 1930. 315 p.
    (See p. 17-62 on early New England printing.)
Oswald, John C. Benjamin Franklin, Printer. Garden City,
    N. Y., 1917. 244 p.
_____. Printing in the Americas. New York, 1968.
    565 p. (Originally 1932.)
Richardson, L. N. A History of Early American Magazines,
    1741-1789. New York, 1931. 414 p.
Roden, Robert F. The Cambridge Press, 1638-1692. New
    York, 1905. 193 p.
Stillwell, Margaret B. Incunabula and Americana. New
    York, 1931. 483 p.
Thomas, Isaiah. History of Printing in America. New York,
    1967. 2 v. (Originally 1874.)
Thompson, L. S. Printing in Colonial Spanish America.
    Hamden, Conn., 1962. 108 p.
Weeks, Lyman H. A History of Paper Manufacturing in the
    United States, 1690-1916. New York, 1916. 352 p.
Winship, G. P. The Cambridge Press, 1638-1692. New
    York, 1968. 385 p. (Originally 1945.)
Winterich, John T. Early American Books and Printing.
    New York, 1971. 256 p. (Originally 1915.)
Wroth, Lawrence C. The Colonial Printer. Charlottesville,

Va., 1964. 368 p. (Originally 1938.)

PERIODICAL ARTICLES

Bridenbaugh, Carl. "The Press and the Book in Eighteenth
    Century Philadelphia," Pennsylvania Magazine of His-
    tory and Biography, 65 (Jan. 1941), 1-30.
Carver, Alexander B. "Esteban Martin, the First Printer
    in the Western Hemisphere," Library Quarterly, 39
    (1969), 344-352.
Harlan, Robert D. "William Strahan's American Book Trade,
    1744-1776," Library Quarterly, 31 (1961), 235-244.
Hawkins, D. L. "James Adams, the First Printer of Dela-
    ware," Papers of the Bibliographical Society of
    America, 28 (1934), 28-63.
McMurtrie, Douglas C. "The First Type-founding in
    Mexico," The Library, 4th. series, 8 (1928), 119-122.
Salley, A. S. "The First Presses of South Carolina," Papers
    of the Bibliographical Society of America, 2 (1908), 28-
    69.
Silver, Rollo. "Government Printing in Massachusetts, 1751-
    1801," Studies in Bibliography, 16 (1963), 161-200.
Winship, George P. "Spanish America," In: R. A. Peddie,
    ed., Printing, A Short History (London, 1927), 306-318.
Wroth, Lawrence C. "The First Press in Providence, a
    Stuty in Social Development," Proceedings of the Amer-
    ican Antiquarian Society, 51 (1942), 351-383.

IX

LIBRARIES IN COLONIAL AMERICA

The American colonists were largely engaged in making a living, with religious and political interests taking up
most of their free time, but a few of them were interested
enough in books and learning to form libraries--college, semi-
public and private. None of these colonial libraries reached
a large size, and the influence of any one of them may have
been limited but the sum total of them indicates a relatively
high degree of culture. Considering the time and place, their
very existence is noteworthy, and in them we see the beginnings of American library history. Although books were
scarce items for the frontiersman and the small farmer, and
almost completely unknown to the slave, they were available
to the citizens of most towns by 1750, and were present in
private and academic collections throughout the colonial period.

It is interesting to note that a college and a college
library were planned for the infant colony of Virginia along
with a school for the education of the Indians. Thomas Bergrave, a minister, left his library for the use of the proposed
college. Unfortunately, wars with the Indians in 1622 put an
end to these philanthropic and educational designs, and Virginia had to wait until the 1690s for the founding of its first
college, William and Mary. In Massachusetts, however, the
colony had a college shortly after its foundation, and that
college had a library almost before it was founded. In fact,
the college took its name from John Harvard, who in 1638
gave the college some 380 books and a small endowment.
Other gifts followed, including one of 40 books from Governor
John Winthrop in 1642, but Harvard's library grew only slowly. Its holdings were largely theological; in those days the
college was mainly a training school for Puritan ministers. In
1723, the library contained some 3500 volumes, and in 1764,
with the college more than a century and a quarter old, there
were still fewer than 5000 volumes in its library. In that
year a disastrous fire destroyed almost all of the collection,
but friends of the college came to its aid, and the Massachusetts

legislature voted £2000 to replace the burned building. In addition, a popular subscription raised almost another 1000 for books and furnishings. Many other gifts were received, so that in a few years the library was back to its former size. According to its catalog of 1790, the Harvard College library was still largely theological but it contained a variety of historical, scientific and literary works as well. In literature the English authors were fairly well represented, including Shakespeare, Milton, Spenser, Chaucer, Pope and Dryden. European works were represented by Boccaccio, Voltaire, La Fontaine, and Rabelais, among others. Needless to say, the classics were well represented, and most of them were in Greek or Latin rather than in translations.

Yale College also began with a collection of books. The 11 ministers who in 1701 organized a society for the formation of a college in New Haven each made a donation of books, and in the next decade other donations increased the collection to several hundred volumes. In 1714, a group of English gentlemen including Sir Isaac Newton made a donation of 800 volumes to the "Collegiate School" through the good offices of Jeremiah Dummer, then the agent of Connecticut in London. Then, in 1717, the Rev. Elihu Yale, for whom the college was subsequently named, began the first of several large gifts, notably 300 books, and in 1733, the Rev. Dr. George Berkeley of London sent a gift of 1000 volumes, including many valuable folios. By 1765, Yale had a library of about 4000 volumes including, besides theological works, large collections of history, classics, philosophy and mathematics. The president of the college noted in that year that the collection contained "not many authors who have wrote within these thirty years."

The College of William and Mary in Virginia was second to be founded in the colonies, in 1693. Whatever small library was achieved in its first few years was destroyed in a fire in 1705. Several gifts and bequests of books added to the rebuilding of the library in the early 1700s and in 1743 came the addition of the library of James Blair, first president of the college, upon his death. Aid from the provincial government in the form of revenue from a tax on wines and liquors helped the library grow, but this expired with independence in 1776. Even so, the library contained over 3000 volumes in 1781. Considering that the college library was intended more for the faculty than the students, this was a fairly adequate collection.

Among other colonial colleges, the library of King's

College (later Columbia University) in New York, was formed in 1754, with its earliest growth coming from a gift of books from the Rev. Dr. Bristowe of London. Oxford University Library sent a gift of duplicates from its collection and several British noblemen made gifts of books to the college library. During the Revolution this collection was destroyed by British soldiers who used its quarters as a military hospital. In 1760, the College of New Jersey (later Princeton) published its first library catalog, indicating that it contained nearly 1200 books, all gifts. This library also suffered from British troop occupation during the Revolution. The College of Rhode Island (Brown University) began its library in 1767 and had but a small library before the Revolution, as did Dartmouth College founded in New Hampshire in 1769. The only other college library of significance before the Revolution was that of the Academy at Philadelphia, begun by Benjamin Franklin in 1749. This institution, the ancestor of the University of Pennsylvania, had the benefit of Franklin's advice in the selection of its first library, and of funds from a lottery to buy its books, but it too remained small in size and limited in use. It did survive the Revolution and was even enlarged by a special gift of books from the King of France. This gift probably came through Franklin's good offices and consisted largely of scientific and mathematical works.

        In all the colonial colleges the libraries were largely reference collections, available for use only a few hours a day. Students were generally supposed to study only their text books. Since the book collections were small, arrangement was not much of a problem, and the only keys to them were manuscript accession lists and a few printed catalogs. The librarians were usually younger members of the faculty, often with little knowledge of, or interest in, the collection. In some cases the library rooms were also used for other purposes, such as board meetings, and even when open were often unheated and poorly lighted. All in all, the colonial college library must have been an uninviting place, more of a museum than a library in the modern sense of the word.

        What was probably the first attempt at a public library in the colonies came in 1656 when Captain Robert Keayne of Boston willed his library to the city for public use. In order to house the library, and also to provide a town hall and meeting place, Keayne provided funds for a building, and this was erected and in use by 1658. This first "Boston Public Library" remained small, and how much

use it had is uncertain. But it was public property and on
several occasions the town fathers took notice of its presence.
For example, in 1702, they requested John Barnard, Jr., to
prepare a catalog of its contents. In 1711, the town hall
was burned, but most of the books were saved. Another fire
in 1747, however, completely destroyed it and only one book,
Samuel Mather's A Testimony from the Scripture Against
Idolatry and Superstition, is known to have survived. This
apparently ended all attempts at public library service as
such in Boston for another century, and there was little
effort elsewhere to provide such service. However, there
were books available to the public from other sources. One
of these was the church library. The King's Chapel in Boston reportedly had a library as early as 1698, formed largely of a gift of books from the Bishop of London. Some
Congregational churches also had small libraries, probably
theological, in the early 1700s, with the First Church in
Milford, Connecticut, definitely having one by 1745.

Elsewhere in the colonies, church libraries were
established largely through the efforts of the Rev. Thomas
Bray, the religious leader who had earlier sponsored parish
libraries in England. Bray's efforts toward church libraries
in the colonies came through the Society for the Propagation
of the Gospel in Foreign Parts, an English missionary organization. This was done in the form of small theological
collections deposited in churches from New England to South
Carolina. Most of the collections were designed for the use
of the ministers, but there were also some, called "lay-
men's libraries" for the use of the general public. The
province of Maryland was particularly favored with the Bray
libraries, and in the course of a decade around 1700, some
30 parishes there obtained collections of books varying in
size from about a dozen books to 300 or more. At Annapolis there was a provincial library, not connected with the
parish libraries but still publicly available. It had begun
with a gift from Princess Anne, for whom the town was
named, and was added to by gifts and aid from the Maryland
legislature. In 1700 this library numbered about 1100 books,
and a number of them have survived to the present as a part
of the St. John's College Library.

Other parish libraries, stemming from the activities
of Bray and the Society, were formed in New York, Pennsylvania, North Carolina, and South Carolina. A collection
of books sent to Bath, North Carolina, in 1700, numbered
166 bound volumes for the use of the clergy, and some 800

books and pamphlets for the use of the general public. Oddly enough, the ministerial books were more popular in nature, including history, philosophy and travel, while those
for the public were almost entirely theological or inspirational in nature. A Bray library sent to Charleston, South
Carolina, led to the passage of a legislative act in 1700,
possibly the first library law passed in the American colonies. This act placed the minister in charge of the library
and gave detailed instructions as to its use. It did open the
use of the books to "any inhabitant" of the colony. A similar act "for Securing the Parochial Libraries of this Province" was passed in Maryland in 1704. With such an
auspicious beginning perhaps the parish libraries should have
grown to become active public services, but such was not
the case. No provisions were made for adding new books
and after the death of the Rev. Bray interest in the support
of the parish libraries subsided. Most of the books eventually disappeared but a few have survived as a part of public
or church collections, a reminder of a library venture that
came almost two centuries before the public was ready for
it.

     The first successful attempt at making books available
for general use came through the establishment of subscription libraries, of which Benjamin Franklin is usually credited with the first in America (in Philadelphia) in 1731. It
followed, in general, the pattern already familiar in England:
he and a small group of friends formed the Philadelphia Library Company and some 50 members paid £2 each for
membership, with dues of ten shillings per year. Franklin
sent to England for books and on his later visits to Europe
he personally selected and sent back volumes for the library.
At first the books were kept in the home of one of the members, but in 1740 they were removed to a room in the State
House, a public building now known as Independence Hall.
This room was opened a few hours weekly for public use,
but usually only members could remove books, and then
only after giving a note for their value to insure prompt return. Following the success of this subscription library,
others were formed in Philadelphia but by 1773 at least
three of them had joined the original one and the resulting
collection, still known as the Philadelphia Library Company,
was moved to the second floor of the newly constructed
Carpenters' Hall. There, it served the founding fathers of
the United States as virtually the only library available during the Revolution and the later Constitutional Convention.
In 1790 it moved into a building of its own and has survived

with the same name to the present.

Other colonial towns soon followed the lead of Philadelphia in establishing subscription libraries.   There were
four in Connecticut before 1740, and about 50 in all of New
England before 1780.   Some of them were merely voluntary
associations, but generally they involved some form of legal
contract, either between individuals or in the form of a
corporation chartered by the provincial government.   The
Redwood Library, in Newport, Rhode Island, was one of the
more fortunate of these early libraries.   It was operated by
the Redowdo Library Company, chartered by the provincial
assembly in 1747 and named for Abraham Redwood, a prominent merchant who was one of its organizers and benefactors.
In 1750 it moved into its own quarters, probably the first
public library building erected in the American colonies.
This library was fortunate in having as librarian between
1756 and 1778 (the year he became President of Yale College) the eminent minister, Dr. Ezra Stiles, who devoted a
few hours of his time each week in return for the privilege
of using the books.   In 1748, the Charleston Library Society
was formed in that South Carolina port city, and it received
its official charter in 1755.   One of its founders was Peter
Timothy, son of the former librarian of Franklin's Philadelphia Library Company.   The Charleston Library had some
150 members by the 1750s, and despite many trials it has
survived to the present, providing its city with a valuable
cultural asset for over 200 years.   Another surviving colonial library is that of the New York Society, founded in 1754.
Several smaller collections of books belonging to the city,
or to earlier formed and unsuccessful subscription libraries,
were eventually added to the society library, and by 1773 it
had over 1500 volumes.   It was almost ruined during the
American Revolution, but after being reorganized in 1788 it
became one of the most important of its type in the nation.

Strictly speaking, the subscription library was a private organization but it was a public library facility in the
sense that it was available to any interested reader who could
afford the relatively small membership fee.   It was sometimes available, as was the Philadelphia Library Company,
to any reader during its brief open hours.   It usually contained local and other provincial newspapers, as well as a '
few magazines from England and possibly other European
countries.   Its stock consisted of books that its members
wanted to read; sometimes the reading matter was heavily
theological or classical, but in other cases it consisted of

contemporary literature and political and economic works, depending upon the tastes of the readers.   Franklin's library, for example, contained a number of works on philosophy, history, and science, as well as practical handbooks, while that of the Charleston Library Society contained more literature, both classical and contemporary.   Ordinarily the collection was in charge of some member who devoted a small amount of time to it, or perhaps of an interested non-member who received the use of the collection for keeping it open a few hours per week.   Only rarely was there a paid librarian but usually there was a strong core of members who were interested in building up the library.   Printed catalogs were issued occasionally, but the subscription libraries were usually not large enough to require extensive classification.   All things considered, the subscription library was the nearest thing to public library service that was available in the colonial period.

Private libraries were almost as scarce in the colonial era as public collections, but there were a few notable examples of book collecting among the early leaders in the colonies.   In New England some of the best private libraries were gathered by ministers, whereas in the southern colonies it was usually the wealthy planter who had the time and means to become a bibliophile.   Government officials at times had libraries of some size, but these collections usually returned to England with their owners.

The earliest settlers of Massachusetts brought a few books with them.   Several of the Pilgrim settlers at Plymouth, including Governor William Bradford, owned small collections of books, and Governor John Winthrop of Massachusetts brought a small religious and political library with him.   William Blackstone of the Massachusetts Bay Colony claimed a collection of 186 volumes in 1630, but these were later lost in a fire that destroyed his home.   John Winthrop, Jr., later governor of Connecticut, left a library of over 1000 volumes when he died in 1676.   Increase Mather, the noted minister, collected a library of some 3000 volumes in the 1600s; his son, Cotton Mather, inherited only a part of his father's books yet built his own library to more than 4000 volumes.   Most of the books in both of these libraries were theological, including Bible commentaries, sermons, and works of the Latin theologians, but there were also works of history, geography and philosophy, and a few of science. Works of fiction, poetry and drama were conspicuously absent, but included in the son's collection was one intriguing

title: The Woman's Advocate; or, Fifteen Real Comforts of
Matrimony.   Cotton Mather wrote and published more than
400 books and pamphlets on religious and historical subjects,
making him one of the most prolific writers America has
ever produced. Thomas Prince, a minister of Boston,
formed an important library of books and manuscripts relating for the most part to New England history. He deposited
them in the Old South Church in Boston before his death in
1758 and these works later became the property of the
Boston Public Library. Samuel Sewall, a contemporary of
Cotton Mather, made frequent references in his journal to
buying and reading books. Just how many books he possessed at any one time is uncertain as he was noted for his
generosity in giving and lending them.

In the mid-Atlantic colonies, John Sharp of New York
built up a large collection of books and pamphlets and in
1713 gave it to the city for a public library. It was largely
theological and there is little record of any public use until
it became a part of the New York Society's Library in 1754.
The Rev. Alexander Innes left a sizable collection of books
at his death in 1713, and these were donated to the Anglican
churches of New Jersey and New York. Samuel Johnson,
early president of King's College in New York, built his library around English literature, the classics and history,
while the library of James Logan of Philadelphia was strong
in the sciences and mathematics. Logan had served as chief
justice and as lieutenant governor of Pennsylvania and collected over 3000 volumes before his death. A building was
erected in the 1740s to house the Loganian Library, then
containing over 2000 volumes, for public use. Upon Logan's
death an endowment was set up to preserve the library permanently, but it declined during the Revolution, and was in
1792 combined with the Philadelphia Library Company, greatly enhancing the value of that institution. Benjamin Franklin, in addition to starting the circulating library, also
gathered a personal library of several thousand volumes,
some of which he bequeathed to the Philadelphia Library
Company and to the library of the American Philosophical
Society, another of his brain-children. Thomas Chalkley,
also of Philadelphia, gathered a small library on the history
and doctrines of the Quakers and in 1742 gave it to form
the beginning of the Friends' Library which was to become
the most important library of the Religious Society of
Friends in America.

In the South the most important private library of the

colonial period was that of William Byrd II of Westover in
Virginia. His father had built up a large estate, and had
started to collect books, but it was the son who, before his
death in 1740, enlarged the library to more than 4000 volumes. The Byrd Library is interesting because of the nature
of its contents and its contrast with the New England ministerial libraries. Byrd was a planter, lawyer and public official, as well as a writer, and his library reflected the
cultural level and interests of the Virginia aristocrat. Almost a fourth of the collection was made up of works of
history, with another fourth in classical literature, and about
10 per cent each in English literature, law and science.
There were a number of volumes in French and Latin, but
theology was represented only by a few works of the church
fathers and some volumes on the Church of England. The
remainder of the collection was made up of philosophy, travel, and practical handbooks of value to the planter and his
family.

Although the Byrd Library had probably the best collection of literature in the colonies, several other Virginia
planters had libraries numbering in the hundreds of volumes.
As early as 1698 William Fitzhugh of Stafford County had a
large library which he kept in a room called his "Study of
Books," and his annual order for supplies from London always included additional books for his collection. Ralph
Wormesley of Rosegill, who died in 1701, left a library of
some 400 volumes, including much English literature.
Colonel Robert Carter, later that century, had a library of
some 700 volumes, well selected and including the classics,
law, history, travel, science and philosophy. His library
was also notable for literature, including the latest plays,
poetry and fiction from England. Other examples of early
Virginia libraries are not difficult to find, and lists of contents of a number of them have survived. In addition to
the small professional collections of the lawyers and doctors,
many other gentlemen had volumes on such practical subjects
as farming, surveying, and architecture, as well as books
on etiquette and gentlemanly conduct.

In both North and South Carolina there were several
private libraries of note, although none quite equalled those
of William Byrd or Cotton Mather. Gabriel Johnston, governor of North Carolina from 1734 to 1752, had a distinguished
library, particularly strong in biography, travel and history
but including books on medicine, economics, literature and
law as well. This library passed to his nephew, Samuel

Johnston, also a later governor of the state, and under his
attention it grew considerably. It remained in the family a
long time and at the end of the Civil War it was estimated to
contain about 4500 volumes. Edward Moseley, James Innes,
John Hodgson, and James Iredell were other colonial North
Carolinians with relatively large private libraries. In South
Carolina, plantation libraries were customary but were not
usually very large. John M'Kenzie, a Charleston lawyer and
planter, bequeathed in 1771 a "valuable library" to the
Charleston Library Society in the hope that a college could
be developed around it. Henry Laurens, merchant and
planter, had a large family library which he augmented with
books personally selected on his business trips to Europe.
Governor James Glen, in office from 1743 to 1756, made a
collection of works on history, particularly those pertaining
to South Carolina, and used them as a basis for his short
history of the colony which he published on his return to
England. A little later a Presbyterian minister, Alexander
Hewat, did much the same thing, but both carried their collections of books back to England with them. Other South
Carolina planters and ministers, including especially the
Izards, Middletons and Rutledges, had notable libraries which
remained in the same family for several generations.

Most of the colonial business, church and government
leaders had at least small collections of books in their
homes; the men who led the colonies into the Revolution
were obviously well-read. Their speeches and writings
abound with allusions to authors both classical and contemporary and most of these works were undoubtedly in their
own private libraries. Among the Revolutionary leaders who
are known to have had sizable private libraries were John
Hancock and John Adams of Massachusetts, the Livingstones
of New York, the Pinkneys and Carrolls of Maryland, Jefferson and Madison of Virginia, John Rutledge and the Pinck-
neys of South Carolina, and many others. Thomas Jefferson's first library was burned in 1770, and although he
mourned its loss, he noted that it had consisted largely of
replaceable law and text-books. He immediately began to
rebuild it and by 1783 his library totaled over 2500 volumes.
George Washington was also a book collector and he delighted
in having many books bound to his own design by a Philadelphia binder. His library is noteworthy because of his interests in essays, drama and fiction, as well as in the more
serious works so common in his day. After his marriage
to Martha Custis his purchases of books from London included those obviously selected for his wife and step-children.

Boston had several bookstores before 1700, including a fairly large one belonging to Hezekiah Usher, who died in 1676, and continued by his son, John, for many years. Bookstores spread to the smaller New England towns after 1700 and book peddlers carried them even into rural areas. Just when the first bookstore began renting books is uncertain, but by the 1760s the practice was becoming well-established. In Annapolis, Maryland, William Rind began a formal rental circulating library in 1762. He proposed to allow his customers the use of two books at a time for an annual fee of 27 shillings. Unfortunately, his reading audience in the relatively small town was too small, and his venture ended in 1764. About the same time, however, rental libraries were in operation in Boston, Philadelphia, New York and Charleston. One in Boston, operated by John Mein, was particularly successful. He published a catalog of some 1200 volumes available for rent at the rate of 28 shillings per year for all that one could read, one volume at a time. Mein was a Loyalist and as the Revolution approached he was forced to leave the city. In New York, Samuel Loudon's circulating library offered some 2000 volumes to discriminating readers in the early 1770s and some of his most popular volumes were poetry. The circulating rental library had its greatest success in the years after the Revolution.

The main business of the bookstore was, of course, selling books. Although a general merchant might offer some competition, the majority of books were usually purchased from the bookstore or, where none was available, from England. Bookstocks varied from store to store, and from colony to colony, but the basic collection included primers, prayer books and dictionaries, with almanacs and editions of the local laws being regular standbys. Aside from this, the New England bookseller would find religious books, particularly sermons, always in demand, whereas the New York or Charleston merchant might find that more mundane works would meet the usual requests of his customers. Practical handbooks on all subjects were in vogue in the later colonial period, and there was also a beginning demand for fiction and poetry then. In some of the larger towns books were available in Greek, Latin, French, and German, as well as English, and subscriptions could be placed for both English and American periodicals. When Michael Perry, bookseller of Boston, died he left a stock of over 6000 volumes, but including only 213 titles. About one-fifth of these were primers and catechisms, indicating the interest

in educating and indoctrinating the youth of the city. Other
"bestsellers" in his store included Pilgrim's Progress,
Aesop's Fables, and Cotton Mather's Folly of Sinning. Some
years later, John Mein's bookstore in the same city had a
total stock of 10,000 volumes, with over 1200 titles. The
selection was broader, but the emphasis was still theological.

In general, the average colonial American was not a
literary man, but the ministers, public officials, lawyers
and teachers were well educated and ardent readers, who
pursued their literary tastes with both mind and pocket book.
From their own private libraries, and from the book stores
and circulating libraries, they had access to almost all the
books available in England at that time. That they made
good use of them is apparent not only from their public papers, but also from the numerous journals, diaries, letters
and books that they wrote.

Bibliography

BOOKS

Abbott, G. M. A Short History of the Library Company of
    Philadelphia. Philadelphia, 1913. 26 p.
Cannon, Carl L. American Book Collectors and Collecting
    From Colonial Times to the Present. New York, 1941.
    391 p.
Clough, Wilson O., ed. Our Long Heritage: Pages from
    the Books Our Founding Fathers Read. Minneapolis,
    1955. 297 p.
Conner, Martha. Outline of the History of the Development
    of the American Public Library. Chicago, 1931. 179 p.
Gray, Austin K. Benjamin Franklin's Library. New York,
    1936. 80 p.
Harris, M. H. A Guide to Research in American Library
    History. Metuchen, N. J., 1968. 186 p.
Hughes, Howard L. Public Libraries in New Jersey, 1750-
    1850. Trenton, N. J., 1966. 87 p.
Jennings, J. M. The Library of the College of William and
    Mary in Virginia, 1693-1793. Charlottesville, Va.,
    1968. 91 p.
Johnson, E. D. History of Libraries in the Western World.
    Metuchen, N. J., 1970. 2nd ed. 521 p.
Keep, Austin B. The Library in Colonial New York. New
    York, 1909. xii, 199 p.
Lehmann-Haupt, Hellmut. The Book in America: A History
    of the Making and Selling of Books in the United States.

New York, 1939. 453 p. (Chapter on early American
libraries.)
Morison, Samuel E. The Puritan Pronaos: Studies in the
Intellectual Life of New England in the Seventeenth
Century. New York, 1936. 288 p.
Pennington, Edgar L. The Beginnings of the Library in
Charles Town, South Carolina. Worcester, Mass.,
1935. 31 p.
Potter, A. C. The Library of Harvard University.
Cambridge, Mass., 1934. 186 p. 4th ed.
Predeek, Albert. A History of Libraries in Great Britain
and North America. Chicago, 1947. 177 p.
Rantz, James. The Printed Book Catalogue in American
Libraries, 1723-1907. Chicago, 1963. 144 p.
Roberts, A. S. Two Centuries of the Redwood Library and
Athenaeum, 1747-1947. Newport, R. I., 1948. 58 p.
Shera, Jesse H. Foundations of the Public Library.
Chicago, 1949. 308 p.
Shores, Louis. Origins of the American College Library,
1638-1800. New York, 1935. 290 p. (Reprinted
1966.)
Smith, Josephine M. A Chronology of Librarianship.
Metuchen, N. J., 1968. 263 p.
Steiner, Bernard C., ed. Rev. Thomas Bray: His Life
and Selected Works Relating to Maryland. Baltimore,
1901. 252 p.
Stone, Elizabeth W. Historical Approach to American Li-
brary Development. Urbana, Ill, 1967. 233 p.
Thompson, C. S. Evolution of the American Public Li-
brary, 1653-1876. Washington, 1952. 287 p.
Tolles, Frederick B. James Logan and the Culture of Pro-
vincial America. Boston, 1957. 228 p.
Tuttle, Julius H. The Libraries of the Mathers. Wor-
cester, Mass., 1910. 90 p.
U. S. Bureau of Education: Public Libraries in the United
States of America, Their History, Condition and Management. Washington, 1876. 1187 p.
Wright, Louis B. The Cultural Life of the American Colo-
nies, 1607-1763. New York, 1957. 292 p.
Wright, Thomas G. Literary Culture in Early New England,
1620-1730. New Haven, Conn., 1920. 322 p.

PERIODICAL ARTICLES

Borden, A. K. "Seventeenth Century American Libraries,"
Library Quarterly, 2 (1932), 137-147.
Bruce, Philip A. "Libraries," in: his Institutional History

of Virginia in the 17th Century (New York, 1910), 402-
441.
"The Byrd Library at Westover, " Virginia Magazine of His-
tory and Biography, 12 (1904), 205-207.
Canavan, Michael J. "The Old Boston Public Library,
1656-1747, " Proceedings of the Colonial Society of
Massachusetts, 12 (1908), 116-133.
Fletcher, Charlotte. "The Reverend Thomas Bray, M.
Alexander Wattemore, and Library Science, " Library
Quarterly, 27 (1957), 95-99.
Houlette, William D. "Parish Libraries and the Work of
Rev. Thomas Bray, " Library Quarterly, 4 (1934), 588-
609.
Keys, Thomas E. "The Colonial Library and the Develop-
ment of Sectional Differences, " Library Quarterly, 8
(1938), 375-390.
Korty, Margaret B. "Franklin's World of Books, " Journal
of Library History, 2 (1967), 271-326.
Kraus, J. W. "Harvard Undergraduate Library of 1773, "
College and Research Libraries, 22 (1961), 247-262.
Lamberton, E. V. "Colonial Libraries of Pennsylvania, "
Pennsylvania Magazine of History and Biography, 42
(1918), 193-234.
Robinson, Charles F. "Three Early Massachusetts Librar-
ies, " Publications of the Colonial Society of Massachu-
setts, 28 (1930-1933), 107-175.
Smart, G. K. "Private Libraries in Colonial Virginia, "
American Literature, 10 (1938), 24-52.
Wallace, David H. "Reconstruction of Four Philadelphia
Eighteenth Century Libraries, " Journal of Library
History, 1 (1966), 63-65.
Weeks, Stephen B. "Libraries and Literature of North
Carolina in the Eighteenth Century, " American His-
torical Association Annual Report (1895), 171-269.
Wheeler, Joseph T. "Booksellers and Circulating Libraries
in colonial Maryland, " Maryland Historical Magazine,
34 (1939), 111-137.
Wiggin, Cynthia B. "Salem Athenaeum, " Journal of Library
History, 3 (1968), 257-260.

X

AMERICAN LIBRARIES, 1775-1850

The Revolution had a disastrous effect on many of
the early American libraries and the cultural development
of the United States in general was set back almost a generation. From Boston to Savannah, libraries were scattered,
destroyed or stolen, and only a few managed to escape un-
damaged. Aside from loss by military action, the libraries
also lacked attention and for more than a decade there was
no concerted effort to rebuild or improve them. Many
private libraries belonging to Revolutionary leaders were
destroyed by British or Tories, while those belonging to
Loyalists were confiscated or sold at auction. Following
the Peace of Paris in 1783, there was some progress, but
it was not until after 1790 that books, newspapers, magazines and libraries returned to their pre-war levels and
finally began to forge ahead once more.

Though forced to move from Cambridge to Concord
in the early part of the war, Harvard College saved its library, and even added to it with funds allocated by the state
legislature, and with books taken from the Loyalists who
fled with the British in 1776. Yale College also had its library moved for safe-keeping, but nearly 2000 volumes were
damaged or lost during the process. In 1791, Yale owned
only 2700 books, and it was not until 1805 that the collection reached its pre-Revolutionary size. Princeton's Nassau Hall, which housed the college library, was occupied by
both British and American troops at different times, and
served successively as barracks, prison, hospital and stable.
After the war, the state of New Jersey voted a sum of
money to aid in restoring the war-damaged buildings, and
the college began levying an annual library fee for the purchase of books. Most of the books in the King's College
library in New York were stolen or destroyed during the
British occupation, but a few of them were returned by
order of the British commander. The New York Society
Library was burned during the fighting in 1776, and so were

147

two subscription libraries, the Union Library and the Corporation Library. In Providence, the College of Rhode Island had its library moved to the country for safekeeping, and when it was returned only about 500 volumes were found to be usable. Fortunately, in 1784, John Brown made a gift of 1400 books to the college library, and in 1792 Nicholas Brown donated funds for the purchase of a law library. For this and other important gifts, the college was renamed Brown University. In the south, particularly along the coasts of Virginia and South Carolina, many plantation homes were burned or ransacked by raiding British troops and their libraries were destroyed. Bookstores and circulating libraries also suffered during the war years and a few of the subscription libraries survived. With the coming of peace and independence, however, new types of library and literary activities were begun on a larger scale than ever before.

Harvard's library was one of the first to revive and it soon achieved and maintained a position of pre-eminence among libraries in the nation. By 1790, it contained more than 12,000 volumes, and its printed catalog of that year indicates that more than half of its collection consisted of theological works. However, there was a good collection of English literature and the classics, and a few titles of recent European authors. History and travel were present, but titles in the sciences were scarce, and periodicals, with the exception of the Gentleman's Magazine, were almost entirely absent. By 1827 there were 25,000 volumes in the Harvard Library, and by 1850, after it had moved into a new building, the book stock was over 50,000, exclusive of pamphlets. Yale's library grew slowly after the Revolution, but after some notable gifts it contained some 6500 volumes by 1823, moved into its own building in 1846, and reached a bookstock of about 21,000 by 1850. Princeton suffered another disastrous fire in its library in 1802, but by 1812 its collection had again reached 4000 volumes. In 1850, it had only about 15,000 volumes in its main library. Columbia College, which grew out of the pre-Revolutionary King's College in New York City, also had a slow growth and possessed only a few more than 10,000 volumes by mid-century. Brown University was about the same size, and in the South, William and Mary had grown even slower, having fewer than 5000 volumes as late as 1850. For all of the colleges, acquisitions were largely in the form of gifts, but fortunately these were relatively plentiful. Harvard alone listed more than 1000 donors in the period from 1780 to 1840. Funds from other sources were scarce and student library fees made up most of the amount available for book purchases.

The early 19th century saw the founding of many new colleges, both public and private. In almost every case, a library was begun as soon as the college doors were opened to students, and sometimes even before. Bowdoin College in Maine began with a small collection of books in 1802, but in 1811 it received a gift of 4000 volumes from its main benefactor, James Bowdoin. Amherst College, in Massachusetts, began in 1821 with a single case of books, but after a drive for donations by 1832 its library reached 3000 volumes, suitably housed in a room in the chapel building. By 1855 it could boast 12,000 books and a building of its own. Wesleyan University, at Middletown, Connecticut, began with a ready-made library of 2000 volumes purchased from Thomas Chapman of New Jersey. Hamilton College, founded in 1812 in Clinton, New York, inherited a small library from an earlier academy but a campaign for more books was disappointing and the library numbered only 1600 books in 1826. Another small college library, that of Dickinson College in Pennsylvania, began in 1783, but with insufficient funds and no large donations it grew so slowly that in 1850 it still numbered only about 5000 volumes. Eight colleges in Pennsylvania, including the University in Philadelphia, averaged only a little over 3000 volumes each, while 18 major colleges in the southern states averaged about the same. West of the Appalachian mountains colleges were beginning to appear in the early 1800s, but their libraries were even smaller than those in the east. A notable exception was Transylvania University, founded before 1800 in Lexington, Kentucky, which had a library of some 12,000 volumes by 1850 and boasted of it as one of the largest west of the mountains.

Before 1850 publicly-owned colleges took the form of state universities for the most part, and these were established in almost every state. North Carolina's University Library at Chapel Hill began in 1795 with a small collection including 14 volumes donated by the governor of the state, William R. Davie. Other donations followed, and in the 1820s, the president of the university sent to England to purchase almost a 1000 volumes for the college library. In 1850, the library was moved into a separate building, and at that time it numbered just fewer than 7000 volumes. The University of South Carolina's Library opened in 1805 with an appropriation for books of $3,000 from the state legislature. It continued to receive support from the state,

moved into its own building in 1841, and by mid-century contained some 15,000 volumes, forming the largest and most
important library south of Virginia.   Not only was it impressive in numbers, but its contents were well selected,
and many of its works were rare and valuable.   The University of Virginia, opening in 1825, had the benefit of the
advice of ex-President Thomas Jefferson in selecting and
organizing its library.   Although Jefferson's own library had
been sold to the Library of Congress, President James Madison donated his library of 2500 volumes to the University of
Virginia along with a gift of $1,500.   Many other gifts came
from Virginia's planter families, and by 1850 its university
library contained upwards of 30,000 volumes, making it one
of the best in the nation.   The University of Georgia, opening in 1800, had a small collection of books in the New
College building which was destroyed by fire in 1830.   A
serious effort to build a useful college library began after
this date, and by 1840 Georgia had the third largest college
library in the South.   Other state universities with libraries
founded before 1850 included Vermont (1800), Tennessee
(1807), Indiana (1828), Alabama (1831), Missouri (1840),
Michigan (1841), and Wisconsin (1849).

     Although Harvard, Yale and possibly one or two other
college libraries reached a point where assistant librarians
were employed, most of them had only one staff member.
As in the colonial days, the librarians were usually either
junior members of the faculty, or retired teachers.   Organization of the collections varied; some were arranged by
language, some by size of books, some by donors, and
probably most by loose subject collections.   Most were
shelved by a permanent location basis, noted by symbols
such as "Alcove 5, Shelf B, Book 2."   Catalogs were either
manuscripts or printed lists, usually arranged alphabetically.   The hours of opening were very limited, sometimes an
hour or so per day, and circulation rules were quite strict.
In some cases, only faculty, and possibly upper classmen
could remove books from the library, and in other cases
students could use the library only on the recommendation
of a faculty member.   The library was usually housed in
a room or wing of a building, often in the same building as
the college chapel or auditorium.   By 1850, the larger university libraries were being housed in separate buildings,
but they were still more often austere and forbidding than
open and inviting, and they were little used by the average
student.   Their purpose was still more that of preserving
books than that of making them available for use, and the

person in charge was a keeper of the books rather than a librarian.

In content, the college library of the early nineteenth century remained largely theological and/or classical. Books in foreign languages were usually in Greek or Latin, although French and German titles were becoming more usual. Philosophy was well represented; recent works of literature somewhat less so. In the social sciences, law predominated, with history fairly well represented, and geography making a beginning. In the sciences, often loosely grouped under "natural philosophy," the fewest books would be found. Current periodicals and newspapers were almost entirely absent, and no self-respecting college library would have allowed popular fiction or "light literature" on its shelves. Needless to say, the contents, as well as the hours and the general atmosphere of the mid-19th-century college library, were hardly designed to entice students through its portals.

In addition to the regular college library, there was usually another type of library on the college campus. This was the literary society collection. The Linonia Society at Yale had formed a student library as early as 1768, and by the early 19th century most colleges had one or more student society libraries. With such names as the Cliosophic or the Athenaen or the Calliopean, these groups combined debating or declaiming with library service, and with small subscriptions collected from members they built up serviceable book collections designed to meet the immediate needs of the students. In time, many of these literary society libraries grew to be almost as large as the college libraries, and even scholarly collections. They had student librarians, were open reasonable hours, and usually met the needs of the students far better than the regular college libraries. In the later 1800s student society libraries usually merged with the central collections, although they sometimes kept their identity in special rooms. In a few cases, particularly at Harvard, departmental libraries also had their beginnings before 1850. Harvard had separate libraries at the medical school, the divinity school, and the Philips Observatory, while Yale had collections for its law school and its medical school before 1850.

Somewhat akin to the college library and even more important from the reference point of view were the scientific society libraries that developed in the larger cities during the early 19th century. The oldest of these was the

American Philosophical Society Library, founded in Philadelphia in 1743.   By 1850 it had over 15,000 books and nearly
as many pamphlets.   The Franklin Institute, also in Philadelphia, was founded in 1824 as a scientific society particularly interested in the physical sciences and its library was
nearly as large as that of the Philosophical Society.   At
mid-century in Boston, the American Academy of Arts and
Sciences (founded in 1780) and the Boston Society of Natural
History (1831) each had libraries of more than 10,000 volumes, while the Massachusetts Horticultural Society Library
(1829) had about 2500.   The New York Academy of Sciences
(1818) and the Albany Institute of Science (1824) each had respectable libraries of their own, and throughout New
England, the Middle Atlantic and Middle Western states,
the major cities usually supported one or more scientific
societies by 1850.   Historical societies were also plentiful, with those of New England and the eastern states
having the better libraries.   The Massachusetts Historical
Society (1791), the American Antiquarian Society of
Worcester, Massachusetts (1812), and the Historical Society
of Pennsylvania (1824) were among the largest and most important as far as their libraries were concerned.

Almost in a class by itself was the Boston Athenaeum
library, founded as a subscription library in 1807.   Through
wise purchases, valuable gifts, and the deposit of several
important collections, the Athenaeum rapidly became one of
the most important libraries in the nation.   By 1814 it contained over 8000 volumes, and by 1827 more than 21,000.
Moving into a new building in 1849, it had passed the 50,000
mark and ranked along with Harvard and the Library of
Congress as the largest libraries in the United States.
Strictly speaking, scientific and historical society libraries
were for the use of members only, but in general practice a
serious applicant could usually obtain access to them.

Elsewhere in the special library field, there were
theological, medical and legal libraries, as well as a few in
prisons and reformatories before 1850.   Most of the theological collections were connected with colleges and semi-
naries, and so resembled those usually found in academic
institutions.   On the other hand, the medical libraries included those belonging to medical societies and those located
in hospitals.   The Pennsylvania Hospital Library in Philadelphia was probably the first medical library in the nation,
beginning in 1763.   Five other professional medical libraries were begun before 1800, and 23 before 1860.   Their

collections were usually numbered in the few thousands.
Among the medical society libraries, those of the Massachusetts Medical Society and the Boston Society for Medical Improvement were the largest in 1850. Legal libraries came
after 1800, with Philadelphia's Law Association Library beginning in 1802, and Boston's Social Law Library in 1804.
County law libraries, semi-public in nature, were established in New York and other Northeastern states by the
1840s, sometimes by state legislation, and at other times
by local law associations. A library at the state penitenti-
ary in Philadelphia was begun in 1829, and another at Sing
Sing in New York in 1840. To further indicate that special
libraries were off to a good start there was at least one
newspaper library before 1850, that of the New York
Tribune.

The period after the American Revolution saw rapid
development of the social library in all its phases. In its
simplest form, the social library was a subscription library,
containing popular reading available to all who cared to pay
a small fee, and as such it had been known before the
Revolution. But after 1800, the social library took on other
forms, with book collections built along specific lines and
serving specific groups of readers. Some of those forms
were lyceum libraries, mechanics' libraries, mercantile libraries, apprentices' libraries, young men's association libraries, and even factory workers' libraries. Best known
in New England and the middle states, they spread gradually
into the Middle West and even to the larger towns in the
southern states. In New England alone, more than 1000
social libraries were established between 1776 and 1850 and
many of them survived for long periods.

Almost every small town had at least one collection
of books available on some terms and the larger towns often
had several. A few of them were connected with local societies and hence directed their collections along subject
lines such as theology, history, agriculture or medicine.
Most of them were general in nature, however, and were
designed to meet or improve the reading interests of members. In book stock, the libraries ranged from fewer than
100 up to 10,000 or so, and in a few cases they were even
larger. Some completely excluded fiction and some collected a great deal of it. Science, economics, agriculture,
sociology and law made up only a small percentage of the
titles in most social libraries, but literature, travel, history and religion were well represented. Many added to

their holdings of books and pamphlets by supplying the latest
English and American periodicals.

The organization of the social library was usually
very simple. In the smaller ones there was little or no attempt at arrangement or classification, but in the larger collections books were usually divided by larger subjects, or
even by locally invented systems of classification. Catalogs
ranged from none through simple manuscript accession records to printed alphabetical or classed lists. Housing might
be a member's home or business, rented rooms, a public
building, or in the case of larger collections, separate buildings. Hours of opening varied according to size and use, but
were usually few, and a voluntary or paid assistant charged
books and checked their return. As early as 1793 a pamphlet had been written to advise the book selectors for social
libraries on the best methods of obtaining books and the
best books to be selected. This was entitled: The Selected
Catalog of Some of the Most Esteemed Publications in the
English Language Proper to Form a Social Library. Its
author was Thaddeus Mason Harris, a young man who had
served for a short time as a librarian at Harvard. His
pamphlet was one of the earliest American works on book
selection. He divided all books into three classes: memory,
reason, and imagination. The first class included all
phases of history, biography and travel; the second, science,
philosophy, and religion; and the third, poetry, drama,
fiction and art. The smaller social libraries bought only a
few titles a year on the average, but collectively they made
up an important book market, so that book publishers and
dealers soon came to offer them special discounts in order
to secure their trade.

One popular type of social library was that designed
for the use of workers or apprentices. These were intended primarily for the younger employees in the factories and
trades, and though there were a few factory libraries for
the girls of the New England cotton mills, most of them
were for men. They provided popular reading, manuals on
the various trades, textbooks, books of manners, and inspirational or popular religious works. Educational materials were
thus provided for young people who could not attend school
and they were apparently well used. In some cases the expenses of the apprentices' library were born by the company
or some community philanthropist, but ordinarily they were
paid by small subscriptions from the workers. Similar to
the apprentices' libraries, but designed for young men in

stores and business offices, were the mercantile libraries.
These latter often grew to considerable size and served
management and owners as well as workers, in time tending
to become professional business libraries. In New York,
the Apprentices' Library was founded in 1820; its services
were free to apprentices but a subscription fee was charged
to other users. It grew rapidly and neared 50,000 volumes
by 1850. In Philadelphia, an Apprentices' Library Company
was formed in 1820, and a Mercantile Library in 1821. The
idea spread rapidly and by mid-century most of the larger
cities of the nations had such libraries in one form or another. Being designed for popular reading rather than research,
they had liberal hours of opening and went far toward meeting the library needs of their particular clienteles.

Thus, until about the mid-19th century the nearest
approach to public library service generally available was
the social library. Although privately owned, the membership fees were usually low enough for anyone who was likely
to be seriously interested in reading. The quantity and quality
of reading matter could be varied to suit the demands of the
reading public, and was probably more in tune with popular
reading tastes than a public library would have been. The
majority of the library users were men but women were becoming more accustomed to use them also and they were
even encouraged to do so in some cases. The social libraries served their purpose for more than a century, giving
way only after regular public library service became widely
available. A small percentage of them survived into the 20th
century, a few in their original form, but most of them as
public libraries or as parts of public collections.

As the settlers from New England and the eastern
states poured into the Middle West in the early 1800s they
soon established the same type of towns and villages they had
known back home. As soon as towns were established libraries followed, usually social libraries of one type or other.
St. Louis had a subscription library as early as 1811, and a
St. Louis Library Association after 1824. The latter began
with about 50 subscribers and 1000 books. Even earlier but
smaller collections were noted in Marietta, Ohio, and Vincennes,
Indiana. Cincinnati had an active circulating library in 1814,
and Detroit in 1817. Chicago had a Sunday School library in
1832, a Lyceum library in 1834, and a Young Men's Association library in 1841, among others. If newspaper notices can
be believed, there were a variety of "reading rooms" in almost every midwestern town, with St. Louis boasting, at

at different times, one in a hotel, one in a newspaper office,
and a combined "reading room and punch house" which must
have been very popular. The New Harmony, Indiana, Working Men's Institute Library of 1847 consisted of about 1000
volumes, including 250 titles of history, 105 of science, 95
of fiction and 60 of sociology, but only 12 of poetry and
seven of religion. In all, there were more than 160 social
libraries chartered in Ohio before 1850, and though there
we re considerably fewer in Indiana, Illinois and Missouri,
the coverage in those states was fairly general for the larger
towns.

     In the South the Charleston Library Society remained
the most successful of the subscription libraries, having about
4500 volumes in 1808 and about 18,000 in 1850. It was not
alone, however, since there were three other library societies in Charleston and about 30 in other parts of South Carolina for shorter or longer periods of time before 1850. One
that is particularly worthy of notice was the Georgetown Library Society, formed by a group of planters in that coastal
South Carolina town in 1800. It never grew large in size,
but it was well used and as a combination of a popular library
and an agricultural collection it existed down until the Civil
War. It is interesting to note that the local printer was the
librarian for a time and did much to insure the library's success.

     New Orleans in 1820 contained a Library Society, a
Law Library, a subscription library with a public reading
room, and a "free library at the Presbyterian Church. " The
Library Society collection was burned in 1828, but re-opened
later as a Commercial Library which by 1837 contained over
5000 volumes. In 1847, New Orleans also held a State Library, a Merchants' Exchange Library, and a Young Men's
Society Library. Elsewhere in the South, there were subscription libraries in Natchez, Mississippi; Mobile, Alabama;
Savannah and Augusta, Georgia; Knoxville, Tennessee; Lexington, Kentucky; Wilmington and New Bern, North Carolina,
and several towns of Virginia and Maryland. Otherwise in the
South the scarcity of large towns kept down the number of opportunities for social libraries, and library development
along with education in general made only slight progress before the Civil War.

     The purely commercial circulating library also in-
creased in numbers and popularity after the Revolution but
its cultural importance was negligible when compared to the

social libraries. It depended upon a public slightly different
from that of the social library--more the casual reader than
the serious one. It was usually small but a few old, established stores sometimes offered several thousand volumes.
Caritat's Circulating Library in New York City, opened in
1797, had several thousand volumes in its catalog of 1804,
including more than 1000 books of fiction. Even more than
a social library, the circulating library reflected popular reading tastes but unfortunately there are few if any records of
the bookstocks of these commercial ventures much less any
counts of actual use. Suffice it to say that they were less important than the social library in the ultimate creation of public libraries but that they did provide a needed public service.
They may be considered as the ancestor of the public library
pay collection or the drug-store rental shelf.

If we define the public library as being a book collection that is publicly owned and supported, publicly controlled,
and for general public use, then there were very few public
libraries in the United States before 1850. However, those few
were important and deserve recognition. In Salisbury, Connecticut, a collection of books donated in 1803 by Caleb Bing-
ham was preserved and made available by the town as the Bing-
ham Library for Youth. It survived to become a part of the
present Scoville Memorial Library. In Lexington, Massachusetts, in 1827, the town meeting voted to purchase a library
for the youth of the town and to employ a librarian to manage
it. The collection was deposited in the town church, but so
small was the public support and use that it went out of existence in 1839. Other examples of small public collections
such as those might be found, but the town usually considered
to be the pioneer of permanent public library service in the
United States was Peterborough, New Hampshire. There, in
1833, it was decided by the town meeting that a part of the
State Literary Fund, usually applied to the support of schools,
should be used for the purchase of books for a free public library. Other donations added to the size of the book collection, and it was kept for public use in the store that housed
the local post-office, with the postmaster acting as librarian.
By 1837, the collection numbered 465 titles, made up largely
of religion, history and biography. The Peterborough Public
Library provided a prototype for the future public libraries
of the nation. Only in the late 1840s was there a definite
movement toward real public libraries, and this came in the
passages of laws in Massachusetts and other New England
states allowing for the levying of taxes to support them.

One widespread attempt at public library service before the Civil War was the school district library. This type
of publicly supported book collection apparently originated in
New York, but it spread rapidly throughout New England and
the Middle West. Governor Dewitt Clinton of New York is
credited with first proposing the school district library in a
message to the state legislature in 1827, but it was not until
1835 that an act was passed implementing his suggestion.
This law, allowing school districts to levy small taxes for
local libraries, brought little response, but a second one in
1838 that provided state funds to match local book levies was
more successful. In three years the school district libraries of New York state contained more than 400,000 books, and
by 1850 there were more than 10,000 school districts with
over 1,500,000 books in their libraries. However, each district collection was merely a small bookcase with a hundred
or so books, and without proper care or quarters the volumes
were lost or allowed to deteriorate. Interest in the books
soon declined, and state laws allowed the book funds to be
diverted to other purposes, including even the payment of
teachers' salaries. However, the idea was popular at first,
and other states followed New York's example and founded
similar collections. Massachusetts passed a school library
law in 1837, and by 1850 that state reported 2084 libraries
in its schools, but the average size was only about 50 books.
Connecticut followed Massachusetts in 1839, and Rhode Island
in 1840. In these states the school district library program
was slower in getting under way, but a little more successful
in the long run. The Indiana state constitution in 1817 called
for publicly supported school libraries as did that of Michigan in 1835, but in actual practice few such libraries were
started until after the Civil War.

The school district libraries were apparently intended more for the teachers and parents than for the children if
the nature of their contents is considered-- textbooks,
general works, and a smattering of inspirational books, of
which most were above the reading level of all but the older
children. Several publishing firms took advantage of the
school district library laws and hastily compiled poorly selected, printed, and bound sets of works, which were sold
through local representatives. These sets often took up
most of the funds available, and their drab appearance and
dry content did little to promote the school library movement.
For lack of suitable quarters in the schools themselves, the
library books were often stored in the homes of teachers or
school board members and an investigation of the New York

school district libraries in the 1850s found many of the books
molding in closets, cellars and attics. The school district
library movement was premature and unsuccessful but it did
serve to establish the precedent of public support for library
service, and in this respect to pave the way for genuine public libraries in a later era.

Probably the most numerous and least known of all libraries of the 19th century were the Sunday school libraries.
Practically every church, particularly in the North and West,
had a small collection of books designated as the "Sunday
School Library." Sometimes they were rather general in content, but usually they contained religious and inspirational
works. Where other sources of reading matter were not
available, they were well-used, but in time many of them
came to include works of such maudlin sentimentality that
their use declined. The term "Sunday school book" came to
be used almost as a term of derision when other types of
literature became available. In the larger cities, several
churches of the same denomination were sometimes able to
combine their efforts and provide a larger collection of
books, complete with a library room and at least a part-
time librarian. Even circulating collections were tried,
rotating boxes of 50 to 100 volumes between several churches
of the same denomination in a given area.

Most of the school libraries prior to the Civil War
were found in the private schools and academies. These collections were usually poor, but in some cases they approached
the level of the smaller college libraries. They often consisted
of gift books rather than purchases and their contents were
not well selected. Private libraries of the teachers were
usually available to augment the school-owned collections and
often there were literary societies with libraries even in the
academies. In the smaller towns of the South and West the
academy library was often the best available and the only one
that the average student ever knew.

Along with the other types of libraries that were developing with difficulty in the early 19th century, several important government libraries were established. Of these, the
one destined to become the greatest in the western hemisphere was the national library in Washington, D. C. , the
Library of Congress. The government of the United States,
in its earliest formative period, made use of several book
collections in Philadelphia and New York, and a proposal was
made for a formal "Library of Congress" as early as 1790.

However, it was not until 1800, after the capital had been
moved to its new site on the Potomac, that the library was
actually begun. In that year Congress appropriated funds for
a library, and in 1802 the books were placed in a room in the
new Capitol with a printed catalog arranged by size. President Thomas Jefferson appointed the first librarian, John
James Beckley, who also served as Clerk of the House of
Representatives. In its early days the Library of Congress
was almost wholly a legal reference collection for the use of
the members, and by 1814 it had only about 3000 volumes. In
that year, while the United States was at war with Great
Britain, the Capitol was burned by the invading British, and
the library was lost. After the war, ex-President Jefferson
offered to sell his magnificent library at cost to the government to replace the destroyed one and after much debate in
Congress, the offer was accepted. In 1815, a total of 6700
books were purchased from Jefferson for $23,950 and this
collection made up a library actually superior to the one
that was lost. George Watterson was appointed librarian and
temporary quarters for the new library were found in the
Post Office Building until 1824 when it was removed to the
new Capitol building. By that time Congress was appropriating
$5000 per year for the national library, and it was growing
rapidly. At mid-century, the Library of Congress had reached
50,000 volumes, but it was still largely a legislative reference library and could boast but one librarian and one assistant
as its staff. In 1832, part of the legal works in the library
had been removed to a room for the use of the Supreme Court,
but it was still under the jurisdiction of the librarian of
Congress. In addition, both the House and Senate had libraries or at least collections of official documents for their own
use.

     The various government departments also developed li-
braries of their own almost from the time they were founded.
The State Department, for example, was instructed by law to
collect the laws of the various states from 1789 on, and
these together with the publications of the federal government
formed the beginning of the State Department Library. By
1825, the department had added to this core the legal publications of other major countries plus books on history, international law, and diplomacy, to a total of more than 3000 volumes. Newspapers, both American and foreign, were also
collected in the State Department Library and by 1850 the
number of volumes totalled over 15,000. The Treasury Department Library was begun in 1803 but it was not of significant size until after the Civil War. This was also true of the

collection in the War Department, formed in 1832, but some of
the military agencies of the nation, such as the Military Academy at West Point, had important libraries. The Academy
Library began in 1812 and had some 20,000 volumes by 1850.
The U. S. Naval Academy at Annapolis was organized in
1845, and its library had reached only about 3000 volumes by
the mid-century. The Bureau of Ordnance Library was begun
in 1838, and the Artillery School Library at Fortress Monroe,
Virginia, was formed in 1824. Each of these libraries had
about 2000 volumes in 1850. The forerunner of the National
Library of Medicine was begun in 1836 as a small collection
of medical works in the office of the Surgeon General. In the
same year a library was begun in the Patent Office, and this
collection grew rapidly to reach some 20,000 volumes by
1850, but the few other federal libraries begun before that
date were relatively insignificant.

In addition to the libraries of the federal government,
most of the states also had libraries in their capitols. Even
before the Revolution there were usually collections of legal
works available in most of the provincial legislative halls.
Virginia had a small provincial library as early as 1661 and
a few of the books from this era have survived. Pennsylvania had a "State House Library" as early as 1752 and
Benjamin Franklin, during his years in England, purchased
books for it. New Hampshire also had a pre-Revolutionary
State library, and it is probable that the other provinces also
had small collections of legal and historical works available
for their legislators. However, it was not until after 1800
that most of the states established state libraries by law and
made specific provisions for their maintenance and growth.
South Carolina passed state library laws as early as 1814,
Pennsylvania by 1816, New York and New Hampshire by 1818,
and most of the other states in the next few years. The newly formed western states often provided for state libraries in
their first constitutions and these, like their eastern neighbors, were largely legal and historical. Their acquisitions
came largely from exchange of state publications with other
libraries and through receipt of Federal documents through
acts of Congress. Gradually either the legal works came to
be maintained separately from the historical ones or separate state law libraries or supreme court libraries were established. The state libraries themselves tended to become historical and general reference libraries, designed for the use
of state officials and legislators but open to the general public for reference use. On the other hand, where historical
societies maintained libraries of note in the state capitals,

then the state library usually remained a strictly legal collection. In either case, growth of the state libraries was slow
before 1850 and by that date the total of volumes in all of them
was scarcely 200, 000. Closely related to the state libraries
were theterritorial libraries established by the federal government in several of the western territories before they became
states.

The period between the Revolution and the Civil War
saw the development of many important private book collections. It was a period when a few major fortunes were being made and a larger number of business and professional men
were wealthy enough to afford libraries. Among the Presidents, the libraries of Washington, Jefferson and Madison
have already been mentioned, but most of the other early
Presidents had fairly large book collections as well. John
Adams had one of the largest private libraries in the nation
and it was a fairly well-rounded collection. It was weak in
literature and science, but strong in theology, the classics
and history, particularly Americana. In the 1820s he gave
most of it, some 2750 volumes in all, to the town of Quincy,
Massachusetts. Although his grandson, John Quincy Adams,
gave away many of his books during his lifetime, still he left
a library of about 8000 volumes at his death. President Monroe left a small private library as did also President Jackson, although the latter lost many of his books in a fire that
destroyed his home in 1834. President Van Buren's collection was largely that of a prosperous lawyer but President
Tyler had an extensive library at his home in Virginia, particularly strong in the classics and English literature.

When Benjamin Franklin died in 1790 he left a library
of over 4000 volumes consisting of books on a wide range of
subjects. It was rather weak in literature, but strong in
science and included a few finely printed books as evidence of
his lifelong interest in typography. Peter Force, the editor
and historian, began collecting books in the 1820s and became
such an avid collector that he often borrowed money on his
home in order to add more volumes to his library. Center-
ing his interest on American history he collected books,
pamphlets, newspapers, periodicals and manuscripts until he
owned more than 60, 000 items in all. In 1867 his heirs sold
this collection to the Library of Congress, thereby doubling
its holdings in American history. George Ticknor of Boston
collected more than 3000 volumes of Spanish history and literature, which, after his death in 1871, went to the Boston
Public Library. John Carter Brown of Rhode Island was also

a great collector of Americana and in the first half of the 19th
century he began the accumulation of literary treasures that
was to eventually become the John Carter Brown Library on
the campus of Brown University. In Philadelphia, Stephen
Colwell, lawyer and economist, bequeathed his library of
some 6000 books and pamphlets on politics and economics to
the University of Pennsylvania Library. In Cincinnati, W. H.
Mussey gave his collection of history and classics to the
public library. Even in relatively out-of-the-way places,
leading citizens often had private libraries of several hundred
volumes. For example, Zebulon Baird Vance, growing up in
the mountains of western North Carolina in the 1830s, had the
advantage of using a library collected by his uncle Robert
Vance. Also, David Caldwell, Presbyterian minister and
teacher of piedmont North Carolina, owned a library that
was well used by his students and neighbors. A few libraries
that were to become famous in later years were begun in this
era, as for example the James Lenox collection that was later
to become an important part of the New York Public Library.
Throughout the nation, ministers, educators, merchants and
planters acquired collections of books, large or small, for
their personal and professional use, while a few could actually be classed as bibliophiles with serious interests in their
libraries. Unfortunately most of these small private libraries were scattered upon the death of their owners, only a few
of them finding permanent homes in public or academic libraries.

    In the Constitution of the United States, Congress was
given the power to pass copyright laws. Such a law was
passed in 1790, giving any author who was a citizen of the
United States the sole right to print or sell his copyrighted
work for a period of 14 years, renewable for an additional
14-year period. In 1831, this act was replaced by one extending the copyright period to 18 years, renewable for 14
years. In 1846, a deposit law was passed, requiring that
one copy of each copyrighted work should be placed in the
Library of Congress and one copy in the newly established
Smithsonian Institution Library. The combination of copyright
and depository laws promoted the growth of government libraries while at the same time encouraging the writing and
publishing of books.

    Another series of laws designed to help the growth
of libraries were those relating to the distribution of public
documents. It was understood, of course, that copies of all
federal documents should be placed in the Library of

Congress and also in all official libraries requiring them but in
1813, Congress ordered that copies of all Congressional
journals and documents should be placed in the libraries of
all colleges, universities and historical societies in the United
States. During the next quarter century almost every session of Congress directed that copies of public documents,
including census reports and historical works published at
government expense, should be distributed to the institutional
libraries. This aided considerably in building up early libraries. Where they have been preserved they constitute
valuable holdings today. In return, many of the states passed
laws sending copies of their public documents to the Library
of Congress and the State Department Library and made copies
available for exchange with other states. The idea of exchange was even carried to the international level and in
1840 Congress directed that 50 copies of all Federal Publications be set aside for international exchange.

Generally speaking, the period from 1775 to 1850 was
not only one of growth and expansion in American libraries,
but also one of experimentation. Various types of privately
supported semi-public libraries were tried with lesser or
greater degrees of success. Libraries in educational institutions lagged and a change in the philosophy and methods of
teaching were necessary before much improvement could be
made. Tentative steps were taken in the direction of true
public libraries but definite progress in this respect was
still in the future. A number of great private libraries were
in the making, but, public or private, school or college, all
collections were small. 50,000 volumes was a major achievement, and only half a dozen libraries had reached this size
by 1850 while not more than 100 had even 5000 volumes. But
the seeds of progress were there and the foundations of
most of the great libraries of the present day had been laid.

Bibliography
                              BOOKS

Bestor, Arthur E., ed. Three Presidents and Their Books:
     the Reading of Jefferson, Lincoln and Franklin D.
     Roosevelt. Champaign, Ill, 1955. 129 p.
Bidlack, Russell E. The Nucleus of a Library: A Study of
     the Book Collection of the University of Michigan
     . . . 1837-1845. Ann Arbor, 1962. 106 p.
Boston Athenaeum. The Athenaeum Centenary, the Influence
     of the Boston Athenaeum from 1807 to 1907. . . .

Boston, 1907. 236 p.
Cole, George W. Early Library Development in New York
     State. New York, 1927. 19 p.
Conner, Martha. Outline of the History of the Development of
     the American Public Library. Chicago, 1931. 179 p.
Eaton, Thelma, ed. Contributions to American Library His-
     tory. Champaign, Ill, 1961. 277 p.
Edwards, Edward. A Statistical View of the Principal Public
     Libraries of Europe and America. London, 1848. 48 p.
Harris, Michael H. A Guide to Research in American
     Library History. Metuchen, N. J., 1968. 186 p.
Harris, Thaddeus M. A Selected Catalog of Some of the Most
     Esteemed Publications in the English Language Proper
     to Form a Social Library. . . . Boston, 1793.
Hughes, Howard L. Public Libraries in New Jersey, 1750-
     1850. Trenton, 1965. 87 p.
Jefferson, Thomas. Jefferson's Ideas on a University Library,
     ed. by Elizabeth Cometti. Charlottesville, Va., 1950.
     49 p.
Johnson, Elmer D. A History of Libraries in the Western
     World. 2nd. ed. Metuchen, N. J., 1970. 521 p.
Johnston, W. D. History of the Library of Congress. Wash-
     ington, 1904. 535 p.
Keep, Austin B. History of the New York Society Library.
     New York, 1908. 607 p.
Kruzas, Anthony T. Business and Industrial Libraries in
     the United States, 1820-1940. New York, 1965. 144 p.
Lewis, John F. History of the Apprentices' Library of
     Philadelphia, 1820-1920. Philadelphia, 1924. 101 p.
McMullen, Haynes. The Founding of Social and Public Li-
     braries in Ohio, Indiana and Illinois through 1850.
     Urbana, 1958. 18 p.
Quincy, Josiah. The History of the Boston Athenaeum.
     Cambridge, Mass., 1851. 104 p.
Raddin, George G. An Early New York Library of Fiction.
     New York, 1940. 113 p.
Rhees, William J. A Manual of Public Libraries, Institutes,
     and Societies in the United States. . . . Philadelphia,
     1859. 687 p. (Rep. 1968.)
Shera, Jesse H. Foundations of the Public Library. Chicago,
     1949. 308 p.
Shores, Louis. Origins of the American College Library,
     1638-1800. New York, 1935. 290 p.
Smith, Josephine M. A Chronology of Librarianship.
     Metuchen, N. J., 1968. 263 p.
Stone, Elizabeth W. Historical Approach to American Library
     Development: a Chronological Chart. Champaign, Ill.,

1967. 233 p.
Thompson, C. S. Evolution of the American Public Library, 1638-1876. Washington, 1952. 287 p.
U. S. Bureau of Education. Public Libraries in the United States of America. Washington, 1876. 1187 p.

PERIODICAL ARTICLES

Borden, Arnold K. "Sociological beginnings of the Library Movement," Library Quarterly, 1 (1930), 278-282.
Clark, Thomas D. "Building Libraries in the Early Ohio Valley," Journal of Library History, 6 (1971), 101-119.
Clayton, Howard. "The American College Library, 1800-1860." Journal of Library History, 3 (1968), 120-137).
Davis, Richard B. "Jefferson as a Collector of Virginiana," Studies in Bibliography, 14 (1961), 117-144.
Ditzion, Sidney. "The District School Library, 1835-1855," Library Quarterly, X (1940), 545-577.
_____. "Mechanics and Mercantile Libraries," Library Quarterly, 10 (1940), 192-219.
Everhart, Francis B. "The South Carolina College Library: Background and Beginnings," Journal of Library History, 3 (1968), 221-241.
Gilchrist, D. B. "The Evolution of College and University Libraries," A.L.A. Bulletin, 20 (1926), 293-299.
Harding, Thomas S. "College Literary Societies: Their Contribution to the Development of Academic Librar- ies, 1815-1870," Library Quarterly, 29 (1959), 1-26.
Houlette, William D. "Books of the Virginia Dynasty," Library Quarterly, 24 (1954), 226-239.
Kaplan, Louis. "Peter Force, Collector," Library Quarter- ly, 14 (1944) 234-238.
Lowell, M. H. "Indiana University Libraries, 1829-1942," College and Research Libraries, 22 (1961), 423-429.
McDermott, John F. "Public Libraries in St. Louis, 1811- 1839," Library Quarterly, 14 (1944), 9-27.
Stewart, Nathaniel. "Sources for a Study of American College Library History, 1800-1876," Library Quarterly, 13 (1943), 227-231.
Storie, Catherine P. "The American College Society Library and the College Library," College and Research Librar- ies, 6 (1945), 240-248.
Stott, C. A. "Schools and School Libraries over Two Cen- turies," School Libraries, 19 (1971), 15-23.
Walter, Frank K. "A Poor But Respectable Relation--the Sunday School Library," Library Quarterly, 12 (1942), 731-739.

Wellard, J. H. "Popular Reading and the Origins of the
Public Library in America," Library Journal, 60 (March
1, 1935), 185-187.

XI

A PERIOD OF LIBRARY PROGRESS
1850-1900

Although the foundation of the American Library Association in 1876 is often considered the beginning of the
modern library movement in the United States, its beginnings
can be traced to the decade around 1850. In 1845, Massachusetts passed legislation allowing the city of Boston to establish a public library and to appropriate municipal funds for its
support, thus making that city the first major municipality in
the United States to have publicly supported free library service. Three years later this authorization was extended to
other towns in the state by "An Act to authorize Cities and
Towns to establish and maintain Public Libraries." New
Hampshire had passed similar legislation in 1849, and Maine
followed in 1854. It is interesting to note that the New
Hampshire act saw the public library as more than a collection of books; it authorized the acquisition of maps, charts,
periodicals and other publications as well as books. Eight
other states had legislated public library service by 1875 and
of these all were in New England or the Middle West except
Texas. Of the 11, however, only Massachusetts had made
real progress in this early quarter century of development
of public libraries and that state easily led the nation in
1875, both in number of public libraries and in number of books
in them.

Another event that marked the beginning of the modern
library era came with the first meeting of librarians on a national level in 1853. This conference, 82 strong, met in New
York at the call of Charles Jewett, then the librarian of the
Smithsonian Library. Participants came largely from the
Northeast, but there was one representative from New Orleans
and another from San Francisco. Not all of them were active
librarians but all were interested in the field and they met
"for the purpose of conferring together upon the means for ad-
vancing the prosperity and usefulness of public libraries and
for the suggestion and discussion of topics of importance to

book collectors and readers. " Among those present were Seth
Hastings Grant, librarian of the New York Mercantile Library;
Reuben Aldridge Guild, librarian of Brown University; Lloyd
Pearsall Smith, librarian of the Philadelphia Library Company;
and William F. Poole, Librarian of the Boston Mercantile
Library. Almost all of them were outstanding men, and at
least a third of them are included in the Dictionary of American Biography. It is interesting to note that most of the men
present also had other professions in addition to their library
interests and duties. They included ministers, college professors, historians and lawyers as well as a physician or
and an astronomer.

The topics for discussion at the conference were mainly
subjects familiar to the librarian of today. They included cataloging and classification, public reading rooms, circulating
books versus reference books, and the distribution of government documents. The best methods of establishing popular
libraries throughout the country were discussed and the need
for strong public support for them was emphasized. A central national library was proposed, preferably built around
the Smithsonian Institution Library, and some form of national
cumulative bibliography was encouraged. Charles Folsom,
librarian of the Boston Athenaeum, presented a scheme for
arranging punched cards on a string that sounds remarkably
like a card catalog, but his cards were really slips of paper
nine inches long and two inches wide, and they were merely
steps in the preparation of a printed library catalog. Before
adjourning, the members resolved "that this Convention be
regarded as preliminary to the formation of a permanent
Librarians' Association, " but such was not to be the case. The
members of the Committee appointed for that purpose soon had
other interests and with the coming of the Civil War and Reconstruction, it was not until 1876 that a permanent national
organization of librarians was finally achieved.

Although proprietary and subscription libraries continued to operate during the latter half of the 19th century,
the general trend was toward the development of free public
libraries in their stead. The value of public library services
as a complement to public education was rapidly being realized as was also the general cultural and social value of having
good reading matter readily available to persons in all walks
of life. Several of the larger mercantile and mechanics' libraries grew larger and more important as the years passed but
others, particularly the smaller ones, were either dissolved or
converted into free publicly-supported institutions. The New

York Mercantile Library, for example, was still growing and
owned over 250,000 volumes in 1900, but this was a notable
exception from the general trend. For the most part, only
the endowed library could compete with the free public one
after the latter was able to offer the same or similar services
at no immediate cost to the borrower.

The growth of public libraries was slow but steady.
New England and the Middle West led the way, with Massachusetts claiming 127 free public collections by 1875. Some
of the Middle Western states had library laws that permitted
townships and counties to provide library service and steps
were taken in this direction, particularly in Ohio and Indiana.
Eleven county libraries were reported in Indiana in 1875, but
altogether they contained only 13,000 volumes and their use
was apparently small. Illinois passed a free public library
law in 1872, and 14 town libraries had been established by
1876. Van Wert County, Ohio, went even further in 1897 and
began what is usually considered to be the first successful
rural library service with a traveling book van. Hamilton
County, Ohio, and Washington County, Maryland, also established effective rural library service before 1900. Another
significant step in the promotion of general public library
service was the establishment of state library commissions.
The first of these was established in Massachusetts in 1890
and by 1900 sixteen other states had formed similar bodies
to encourage and support public libraries. For the most part
these state agencies sided in the establishment of public libraries, advised their personnel, and provided a clearing
house for library and book information, but did not provide
financial aid. In Massachusetts, however, direct state aid
was a part of the library laws, and the disbursing of such
aid was directed by the state library commission.

A good example of the foundation and growth of a large
municipal library can be found in Boston. The Boston Public
Library was authorized in 1848, supported by city ordinance
in 1851, and opened in 1854. Various gifts aided this new
library from the beginning. Mayor John P. Bigelow of Boston gave $1000 and Edward Everett gave a collection of over
1000 books, including many valuable government publications.
Joshua Bates gave an endowment of $50,000, the proceeds
from which could be used for the purchase of books. In
1857, Charles Coffin Jewett came from the Smithsonian Library to head the Boston Public and in 1858 it moved into
its own building. Mr. Bates later gave a large collection
of reference works which, together with other volumes, was

opened to the public in 1861 as the main reference room, or
Upper Hall. Under Jewett's direction, printed catalogs of
both the circulating library and the reference library were issued and the library grew rapidly in size and use. By 1877
it contained nearly 300,000 volumes, was circulating over a
million volumes a year, had several branches in operation,
and was easily the most important public library in the nation.
Numerous gifts of money and books, including the Prince Library collected before 1758, the Bowditch Library of mathematics and science, and the George Ticknor collection of
Spanish history and literature were added to further the
scholarly development of the library.

In contrast to Boston, New York City did not develop
a free public library until the end of the 1800s, although it did
have a valuable public reference collection much earlier. In
1848, the will of John Jacob Astor provided funds for a free
reference library for the city, including the cost of books,
building and maintenance. Later his son and grandson added
other gifts to form one of the most important libraries in the
nation. The Astor Library was opened for use in 1854 with
80,000 volumes, largely the result of buying expeditions made
by the first librarian, Joseph C. Cogswell. By 1875, it contained over 150,000 works, of which, according to the librarian,
could be classed neither as "light nor ephemeral." Another
important private collection in New York City was the Lenox
Library, collected and endowed by James Lenox, and destined
to become a part of the New York Public Library. It was particularly strong in American history and Shakespearean literature. Still a third collection, the Samuel Tilden library, was
left to the city in 1866, along with a fund for the establishment of a public library. When this fund became available in
the 1890s, the city fathers decided to combine all their libraries into one centrally controlled system, and this was
done in 1895 with the creation of the New York Public Library. Dr. John Shaw Billings, formerly librarian of the
Surgeon General's Library in Washington, became its first
librarian. Although it lacked a public circulating library for
most of the 19th century, New York was relatively well supplied with important private and semi-public collections, including the New York Society Library, the New York Historical Society Library, the Mercantile Library and the Apprentices' Library, to name only a few. These, together
with professional, society and commercial circulating libraries made New York one of the book centers of the nation.

Elsewhere in the nation, the other major cities were

developing public libraries in the latter half of the century,
although none of them quite equalled those of New York and
Boston. Baltimore, for example, had the Peabody Institute
Library, founded in 1857, and the Library Company of Baltimore, dating back to 1795, but its first real public library
was the Enoch Pratt Free Library, opened in 1886. Cincinnati Public Library was established in 1833, but its early
period of growth was a troubled one and it was not firmly
established until the 1870s. It moved into a permanent building in 1870 and by 1875 contained a well-used 70,000 volumes.
It was one of the first public libraries in the nation to be
opened for Sunday use, beginning this service in 1871. Chicago's Public Library was created by act of the state legislature in 1873 and it opened a year later. Part of its first
collection was a group of books donated by English gentlemen
in sympathy for the city that had lost so much in the great
fire of 1871. Chicago was fortunate in having William F.
Poole as one of its first librarians and under his wise guidance, the library soon assumed a position second to that of
Boston in size and importance. Philadelphia's Free Library
was not established until 1891, but of course that city had
many fine libraries of the private and semi-public nature,
including that of the Philadelphia Library Company, the Mercantile Library, and some 50 others of over 1000 volumes.

    In the South, many libraries were destroyed in the
course of the Civil War, particularly in Georgia, South
Carolina and Virginia. The Charleston Library Society building was ransacked in 1865 but most of the valuable books
had been removed earlier and were saved. The Winyah Indigo
Society Library in Georgetown, South Carolina, was almost
completely destroyed. In Virginia, the library of Washington
college (later Washington and Lee University) was also destroyed or carried off by raiding soldiers as was the neighboring library of Virginia Military Institute. Many Southern private libraries were destroyed, as for example that of ex-
President John Tyler. After the war, public library service
was slow to develop in the South and it was not until around
the turn of the century that much progress was made. There
were, of course, social libraries in the larger towns, as
well as a few historical society collections. "Library Associations" operated semi-public collections in Petersburg,
Virginia; Augusta and Atlanta, Georgia; New Orleans, Little
Rock, and several other cities. Galveston, Texas, opened
a "free public library" in 1874 by a city ordinance taking
over a former mercantile library. On the other hand, in
the rapidly growing Pacific coast states of Washington,

Oregon and California, library service followed close on the
heels of the earliest settlement. San Francisco had a mercantile library as early as 1853, and Portland, Oregon, a
"library association" in 1874. These and other major western cities began free public library service before 1900.

The late 19th century was also a period of strong development of college and university libraries. Many new
colleges were established after the Civil War, including colleges for Negroes in the South, state and private institutions
in the newly settled West, and the state agricultural and mechanical colleges established with federal aid under the Mor-
rill Land-Grant College Act of 1862. These new colleges
all had to establish libraries and in many cases the going was
slow and the funds were scarce. Donations from private
benefactors often helped and in other cases whole libraries
were acquired from academies or societies by gift or purchase. The older colleges also had problems, particularly
as student enrolments increased and as graduate work came
to be offered. College curricula changed, with the development
of new disciplines in the social and physical sciences, and
the output of books and periodicals increased rapidly. Bookstocks had to be greatly increased, departmental and specialized libraries were formed, and trained or experienced
libraries were employed. Most of the literary society libraries were amalgamated with their main library collections
and in a few cases training classes were started for young
librarians. Harvard University still had the largest college
library and its growth and development during this half century was to serve as an example to other larger university
libraries. In 1866 Harvard had some 40,000 books and
30,000 pamphlets; in 1875 it had in its main and departmental
collections together nearly 250,000 volumes. By 1900 it had
passed the half million mark, and included, besides the main
library still in Gore Hall, a number of special libraries in
various fields.

Among the other university libraries, Yale had some
78,000 books in 1875, with an additional 25,000 pamphlets;
at the end of the century its collection reached nearly 300,000
volumes. The two literary society libraries, totaling together about 20,000 volumes, were placed under the management of the college librarian in 1871 but they continued to be
shelved separately for many years. Princeton University
moved its library into a new building in 1873 and gave its
total bookstock as 126,000 in 1900. Columbia University
Library reached 250,000 volumes by 1900 in all of its col-

lections, while Brown University Library was about half as
large. Among the newer state and land-grant universities,
some of the larger were: University of Illinois, founded in
1867, with 42, 000 volumes in 1900; University of Nebraska
(1859), 47, 000; University of Missouri (1843), 34, 000; University of Michigan (1841), 145, 000; University of Minnesota (1868), 65, 000; and the University of California (1869),
80, 000. Among the important new private and endowed universities, Cornell, founded in 1868 had 225, 000 volumes in
1900, while the even newer University of Chicago had 300, 000
volumes when less than ten years old. Stanford University
in California, founded in 1892, had 35, 000 volumes by 1900,
while the older Vanderbilt University in Tennessee had 32, 000.
The Southern university libraries lagged behind those of the
remainder of the nation despite slow and steady growth. By
1900, the University of Virginia Library bookstock was 49, 000;
the University of North Carolina, 31, 000; South Carolina,
32, 000; Georgia, 24, 000; Louisiana, 21, 500; and Texas,
34, 000. Smaller denominational colleges, teachers' colleges,
and some of the land-grant colleges struggled along with only
a few thousand volumes, often housed in a single room and
staffed with inexperienced "librarians. "

     Although the school district libraries had preceded
public libraries and spread throughout much of the nation except for the South, they were fast losing their popularity
before 1875. Various reasons were advanced for this failure
but it seems that the major causes were lack of experienced
and interested personnel to handle them and lack of adequate
quarters to house them. As public libraries were organized,
many of the remaining school district books came into their
hands and the general trend was toward allowing the public
librarian to take care of the reading needs of school children
and teachers as well. There were exceptions, of course, in
some of the better secondary schools and in the larger cities.
St. Louis, for example, was noted for its excellent system of
school library service, as was also Buffalo, New York. In
this latter city, the school libraries were taken over in the
1890s by the public library, which made deposits of selected
books in the various schools. These deposits rotated from
classroom to classroom and in the summers they were returned to the public library for mending, sorting and general
preparations f or the coming year. Generally speaking,
good school libraries, both elementary and secondary, had to
wait for the 20th century, although several states added school
library supervisors to their state departments of education
and a number of public libraries opened special rooms for

children before 1900. Of course, one of the reasons for lack
of library service for children was the lack of good literature
written on the child's level. As more books became available and as more women entered the field of library service,
the promotion of library work with children became an accepted part of the general library program. Both the National
Education Association and the American Library Association
became interested in the problem of library service for children in the 1890s and in 1896 a joint A.L.A.-N.E.A. committee was formed to study the possibilities of getting books to
children both in and out of school. In that same year the
N.E.A. formed its school library section and in the next
year the A.L.A. devoted a special conference in Atlantic City
to a study of the relationship between schools and libraries.

Among government libraries, the Library of Congress
remained preeminent. By mid-century, it had passed the
50,000 volume mark, but on December 24, 1851, it suffered
a disastrous fire, and only 20,000 volumes were saved.
These, however, were among the more valuable in the collection and formed a nucleus from which a new and more permanent library emerged. The library hall in the Capital was
rebuilt of fireproof materials and $75,000 was appropirated
by Congress for the replacement of books. By the end of the
Civil War the Library had passed its original high mark in
size and was once more growing rapidly. For a while there
had actually been two national libraries. One of these was
the library of the Smithsonian Institution, donated to the
government by the will of the British philanthropist, James
Smithson, in 1846. Charles Coffin Jewett became librarian
of the Smithsonian library in 1849, and proceeded to build it
up into a collection of more than 40,000 volumes, particularly strong in the scientific fields. He had plans of building
it into a real national library, which he felt the Library of
Congress was not, and of making it into the bibliographical
center of the United States, with a national union catalog to
reflect the holdings of all its major libraries. Congress did
not agree with these plans and in 1866 the Smithsonian Library was added to the Library of Congress, while Jewett
transferred his abilities to the new Boston Public Library.
In 1867, the Library of Congress added still another valuable
library in its purchases of the Peter Force collection of
early Americana. This library contained over 60,000 books,
pamphlets, maps and manuscripts, and made the Library
outstanding in the field of American history. The policy of
collecting virtually all American newspapers and periodicals
added considerably to the Library's holdings, while the

Copyright Act of 1870 brought in two copies of every book or
printed item published in the nation or protected by its copyright.   By 1875, the Library of Congress was overflowing its
quarters with more than 300,000 volumes.

When Ainsworth R. Spofford became Librarian of
Congress in 1864, the library entered upon a long period of
growth and progress, both in size and in service to the nation. As early as 1871, Spofford suggested the need for a library building designed solely for the collection and in 1874
Congress appointed a committee to look into the possibilities
for building a national library structure. The wheels of
government grind slowly and the building was not begun until
1887 nor completed until 1897. This new structure, still the
main building of the Library, was capable of holding nearly
three million volumes.   It was equipped with the latest in
library equipment from reading rooms and stacks to book con-
veyors and inter-office speaking tubes. Though Spofford had
begun with a staff of five in 1864, this new building was manned
by a staff of 185 in 1900, with an additional 45 employees in
the copyright office. An immense reclassifying and recataloging project was begun and this called for a large staff, as did
also the new and notable services of printing and distributing
catalog cards and providing book services for the nation's
blind.   Though the Library of Congress was still essentially
what its name implied, a collection of books designed to aid
the Congress in the performance of its duties, it had by 1900
come a long way toward being a truly national library.

The other government agencies in Washington continued
to develop their specialized libraries. The Department of
Interior Library opened in 1850, that of the Attorney General's
Office in 1852, one in the Department of Agriculture in 1860,
and one in the Bureau of Education in 1870. These and other
governmental libraries remained rather small down to 1900,
but one of them in particular, the Library of the Surgeon
General's Office did attain considerable prominence. Under
the librarianship of Dr. John Shaw Billings, an army officer,
physician, bibliographer and scholar, this collection grew from
a miscellaneous group of some 1800 books in 1865 to a well-
organized library of 50,000 books and 60,000 pamphlets in
1880. Dr. Billings made it one of the best medical collections
in the world, developed a subject card catalog for it, began
indexing medical journals, and published a bibliography of
medical literature.   In addition to his many other notable accomplishments, both in the library world and in the fields of
public health and hospital architecture, Dr. Billings is

remembered and honored by the library profession as one of the first and best special librarians.

There were many other specialized libraries that were started or improved during this period. The various state libraries, whether historical or legal or both, continued to improve slowly, with their acquisitions coming from small appropriations, gifts and exchanges with other states. In size these collections varied from the New York State Library, with well over 100,000 volumes, down to some of the smaller ones which had fewer than 3000 even as late as 1900. The state historical society libraries gained in size and importance as research centers, particularly in the North and West. The New York State Historical Society Library had over 60,000 volumes in 1875, while that of Wisconsin had 33,000. Wisconsin also had the benefit of the collecting activities of the historian, Lyman C. Draper, who gathered in print and manuscript one of the best historical collections in the nation. It was strong in local history materials for both the South and New England as well as for the Middle West. Specialized medical libraries developed around the medical schools and hospitals and in the headquarters of medical societies. The New York City Hospital Library had about 10,000 volumes in 1875 while that of the Philadelphia College of Physicians was almost as big. Scientific society libraries continued to expand in numbers, and several of them reaching considerable size. The Academy of Natural Sciences in Philadelphia had nearly 65,000 books and pamphlets in its library in 1875, while the Essex Institute Library in Salem, Massachusetts, claimed over 100,000. The older societies were joined by similar ones in the western states and by newer groups devoted to agriculture and natural history. In addition to these were numerous smaller legal, historical and scientific libraries, ranging from those of county professional and patriotic societies to those of specialized university departmental collections.

The growth of libraries set the stage for the development of a library profession. Although most of the outstanding librarians of this period were members of other professions as well, they devoted a major portion of their time to library service, developed special skills in that field, and came to consider themselves professional librarians. A few of them were librarians only, including Ainsworth R. Spoffard and Melvil Dewey and they, among others, began the systematic training of assistants who in turn became librarians. Along with the growth of the profession came the

organization of the American Library Association in 1876.   Its
first meeting was held in the hall of the Philadelphia Historical
Society, with 104 persons present, including 13 women.   Justin Winsor, librarian of the Boston Public Library and a distinguished historian, was elected first president and Melvil
Dewey, then still a young man, became the first secretary.
A constitution was drawn up in 1877 and the purposes of the
association were given as the promotion of public libraries,
the encouragement of public interest in and the financial support of libraries, and the elevation of librarianship to a rank
equal to other professions.   At the early meetings of the association, papers were presented on practical subjects:
cataloging, indexing, bibliography, book sizes, copyrights, the
qualifications of a librarian, and the reading interests of the
general public.   Growth in membership was slow, but the A. L. A.
ranked high professionally and its meeting called forth speak-
ers of the first rank in the educational field.   The needs of
different types of libraries were recognized and in 1889 a
section for College and Reference Librarians was formed, with
another for Library Trustees following in 1890.   By 1900
A. L. A. had nearly 1000 members, with the proportion of
women members steadily increasing.   The association was
truly representative of all phases of library work and all
parts of the nation.

        Closely associated with the growth of the A. L. A. and
with the library profession in general was the problem of
training librarians.   Several of the larger public libraries
began training classes for their assistants in the late 19th
century but with the exception of the Astor Library in New
York none of these assumed the form of a regular school.
In 1887, Melvil Dewey started classes in "library economy"
at Columbia University as a regular part of the college
curriculum.   Though students were not lacking, the university
administration was far from enthusiastic about this new department and in 1889 Dewey took his school of library science
with him when he moved to Albany as librarian of the New
York State Library.   There it prospered and became a model
for succeeding library schools.   In 1925 it returned to
Columbia as the School of Library Service.   Library training
courses were also developed before 1900 at Drexel Institute in
Philadelphia and at Pratt Institute in Brooklyn.   In 1893,
Katherine Sharp began a library course at the Armour Insti-
ute in Chicago and four years later moved on to the University of Illinois to inaugurate the first school of library science
in the West (and the first to be a recognized department in a
state university).   By 1903 this school had six instructors

and more than 40 students. Other universities offered courses
in "bibliography" before 1900, and most of the teachers' colleges offered training in a small way for school teacher-
librarians. For the most part early library training was
very practical and approached the subject from the point of
view of method rather than theory. Dewey developed a curriculum at Albany which included book buying, cataloging,
classification, card writing, book lettering, library record
keeping, and similar practical subjects. He also strongly
recommended for future librarians a sound knowledge of literature and a general education as well as training in library
methods. At Illinois the two-year course was a little more
advanced, combining most of the library techniques into one
course, "library economy, " while separate courses were offered in reference, bibliography, book selection, and the history of books and libraries.

Rounding out the professional library field were the
state and local library association which also had their beginnings in the 1890s. New York State Library Association was
the first, organized on July 11, 1890, and similar groups
were formed soon after in Iowa, New Hampshire, Massachusetts and New Jersey. By 1900 state library organizations
were quite general, and they were already being joined by
library "clubs" in the larger cities. These local library
groups worked with the American Library Association and the
National Education Association in promoting library service
of all types at all levels.

The growth of the library profession was closely paralleled by the development of a professional library literature.
In 1852, Charles C. Jewett issued from the Smithsonian
Library his plan On The Construction of Catalogs for Libraries . . . with Rules and Examples. Jewett was mostly interested of course in printed catalogs and in the possibility of
a national union catalog, but his rules were useful to all
catalogers. William Frederick Poole began indexing periodicals in 1848 while he was student librarian of the Brothers in
Unity Society Library at Yale. He continued this activity
soon after becoming librarian of the Athenaeum Library in
Boston, and in 1853 his "Index to Periodical Literature" appeared. This index, with his later supplements, is still a
standard reference tool for 19th-century periodical literature.
The first American general work on librarianship was Reuben
A. Guild's Librarian's Manual, issued in 1858--one of the few
concrete results to come from the Librarians' Conference of
1853. In 1876, the U. S. Bureau of Education published its

compendium of the American library world entitled Public
Libraries in the United States. This was at once a history
and a handbook of libraries in the United States. Its chapters
included such practical topics as "library buildings" and
"organization and management of public libraries" and these,
together with a supplementary volume which was Charles A.
Cutter's Rules for the Printed Dictionary Catalog, contributed a manual for the working librarian. Cutter's rules pointed
the way toward the dictionary arrangement for library catalogs, as compared to the generally used method of a classified or topical arrangement, with or without an author index.
Previous to 1850, library catalogs had almost always been
printed in book form or kept in handwritten sheets or note-
books. After this date many of the major libraries still issued
printed catalogs, but more of them began to keep supplements
on slips or cards arranged in trays, and eventually the card
catalog replaced the book catalog for most libraries.

The first edition of Melvil Dewey's Decimal Classification System appeared in 1876 and in the same year the
first professional library periodical, the Library Journal,
was begun with Dewey as editor. Before the appearance of
Dewey's classification every library had its own system;
these varied widely. The new system was simple and practical and although it did not gain immediate approval, it was
gradually adopted, particularly by the newer public and school
libraries. Dewey was not the only librarian to be working
on a classification system, however, for Charles A. Cutter
was also developing one, and before he died in 1903 the major
part of his Expansive Classification System had been completed. Although it was not widely used in the United States
at first, it did meet with some favor abroad. Moreover,
in a form greatly revised and adapted it became the basis for
the Library of Congress Classification System which was
developed after Herbert Putnam became Librarian of Congress in 1899. The need for a library materials supply
house was felt by the members of the profession and for a
time after 1876 a "Supply Department of the American Library Association" under Dewey's direction attempted to
meet this demand. This venture was not successful and a
private company, the Library Bureau, took over as a national vendor of special library supplies in 1888. Another
library need, that for a national index of books in print,
was met in 1880 by Frederick Leypoldt with his American
Catalog of Books in Print and for Sale. Begun in 1876 and
issued in parts even before the first full edition appeared,
this bibliographical masterpiece was continued down to 1910.

One other outstanding service for libraries came just at the
end of the century when the Library of Congress began
printing its catalog cards and selling them to other libraries
of the nation. Thus, in one form or another, most of the
library services so well known to the 20th century librarians
had begun by 1900.

Private book collectors were no rarity in 19th-century
America and private libraries of considerable size were developed in all parts of the country. Many of these libraries
were later donated to public and college collections and
others were endowed to become cultural monuments to their
founders. More importantly, many wealthy men who themselves never found time to collect books made up for this by
leaving funds for use in building or enlarging libraries. One
of the first major library gifts was Enoch Pratt's endowment
of the Free Library in Baltimore in 1886. This library under
his name but with later support from the city has become one
of the outstanding public libraries of the nation. In 1889 the
Howard Memorial Library in New Orleans was opened as an
endowed reference collection for public use. In 1895 the
New York Public Library was formed with funds from the
Tilden Trust and libraries bequeathed to the city by the Astor
and Lenox families. In Chicago a bequest from Walter L.
Newberry formed the basis of the Newberry Reference Library which was opened in 1887. This library, largely in the
humanities, was balanced in 1895 by the gift by John Crerar
of the science reference library which bears his name. The
Caleb Fiske Harris Collection of American poetry and drama
was given to Brown University in 1885. Elsewhere over the
nation other individuals gave collections of varying sizes to
both college and public libraries. It is difficult to assess the
total significance of private collectors in the building of the
nation's great libraries; hardly a single one of our major
collections would have reached their present importance
without them.

The greatest benefactor of American libraries, however, was not himself a book collector but merely a lover
of books and the information contained in them. This was
Andrew Carnegie, the immigrant from Scotland who made
millions in the United States and repaid both his native and
adopted countries with gifts of millions of dollars for the
construction of library buildings. He theorized that if the
building was there, the public would support the library with
necessary funds for books and staff. As early as 1881 he
began to aid in the construction of free public libraries and in

40 years provided financial encouragement for the construction of no less than 2500 buildings for libraries in the
United States, Canada and Great Britain. The Carnegie
buildings provided a tremendous stimulus to the public library movement for several decades and it is difficult to
imagine how American library history would have developed
without them.

In 1900, according to the U. S. Bureau of Education
reports, there were 5383 libraries in the nation containing
300 volumes or more and open to the public in one way or
another. Together, these "libraries" contained over
45,000,000 volumes, but it is interesting to note that nearly
half the libraries and over half the books were in the nine
North Atlantic States between Maine and Pennsylvania. Another interesting fact is that as many books were added to
American libraries in the years between 1895 and 1900 as had
been contained in all American libraries in 1875. This ac-
celeration of library growth, together with the development of
professional attitudes and tools, indicated that the library was
taking its rightful place in the broad field of cultural communication. More than ever before it was serving as a connecting link between the knowledge of the past and the needs
of the present.

Bibliography
                                     BOOKS

Adams, Herbert H. Public Libraries and Popular Education.
     Albany, N. Y., 1900. 49-271 p.
Bay, J. Christian. The John Crerar Library, 1895-1944:
     An Historical Report. Chicago, 1945, 188 p.
Borome, Joseph A. Charles Coffin Jewett. Chicago, 1951.
     173 p.
Cannon, Carl L. American Book Collectors and Collecting
     from Colonial Times to the Present. New York, 1941.
     xi, 391 p.
Clemons, Harry. The University of Virginia Library, 1825-
     1950. Charlottesville, Va., 1954. 231 p.
Columbia University. The School of Library Economy at
     Columbia University, 1887-1889. New York, 1937.
     272 p.
Conner, Martha. Outline of the History of the Development
     of the American Public Library. Chicago, 1931. 179 p.
Danton, Emily M., ed. Pioneering Leaders in Librarianship.
     Chicago, 1953. 202 p.

Library Progress, 1850-1900   183

Ditzion, Sidney. Arsenals of a Democratic Culture; A Social
    History of the American Public Library Movement in
    New England and the Middle States from 1850 to 1900.
    Chicago, 1947. 263 p.
Dunglison, Richard. History and Condition of the Medical
    Libraries of Philadelphia. Philadelphia, 1871. 46 p.
Eaton, Thelma, ed. Contributions to American Library
    History. Champaign, Ill., 1961. 277 p.
_____., ed. Contributions to Mid-West Library History.
    Champaign, Ill, 1964. 180 p.
Fletcher, W. I. Public Libraries in America. Boston,
    1894. 164 p.
Green, Samuel S. The Public Library Movement in the Unit-
    ed States, 1853-1893. Boston, 1913. 336 p.
Hadley, Chalmers. John Cotton Dana. Chicago, 1943. 105 p.
Hassenforder, Jean. Developpment comparé des Bibliothèques
    Publiques en France, en Grande-Brétagne, et aux Etats-
    Unis dans la Seconde Moitie du XIXᵉ siècle, 1850-1914.
    Paris, 1967. 211 p.
Held, R. E. Public Libraries in California, 1849-1878.
    Berkeley, Calif., 1963. 193 p.
Jewett, Charles C. Notices of Public Libraries in the United
    States of America. Washington, 1851. 207 p. (Re-
    printed 1968.)
Johnston, W. D. History of the Library of Congress. Wash-
    ington, 1904. 535 p.
Kalisch, Philip A. The Enoch Pratt Free Library: A Social
    History. Metuchen, N. J., 1969. 264 p.
Kilgour, Frederick G. The Library of the Medical Institution
    of Yale College and Its Catalogue of 1865. New Haven,
    1960. 74 p.
Lee, Robert Ellis. Continuing Education for Adults Through
    the American Public Library, 1833-1964. Chicago,
    1966. 158 p.
Lydenberg, Harry M. John Shaw Billings. Chicago, 1924.
    95 p.
_____. History of the New York Public Library. New
    York, 1923. 643 p.
Oliphant, J. O. The Library of Bucknell University.
    Lewisburg, Pa., 1962. 154 p.
Ranz, Jim. The Printed Book Catalogue in American Li-
    braries, 1723-1900. Chicago, 1964. 144 p.
Rider, R. K. Samuel Swett Green. Chicago, 1926. 92 p.
Roseberry, C. R. For the Government and the People of
    This State: A History of the New York State Library.
    Albany, 1970. 126 p.
Shera, J. H. Foundations of the Public Library. Chicago,
    1949. 308 p.

184   Communication

Spencer, Gwladys. The Chicago Public Library: Origins and
    Backgrounds. Chicago, 1943. 473 p.
Spofford, Ainsworth R. A Book for All Readers. . . . New
    York, 1900. 509 p.
Thompson, C. S. Evolution of the American Public Library,
    1653-1876. Washington, 1952. 287 p.
U. S. Bureau of Education. Public Libraries in the United
    States of America. Washington, 1876. 1187 p.
Utley, George B. The Librarians' Conference of 1853.
    Chicago, 1853. 189 p.
Whitehill, Walter M. Boston Public Library: A Centennial
    History. Cambridge, Mass., 1956. 274 p.
Williamson, William A. William Frederick Poole and the
    Modern Library Movement. New York, 1963. 240 p.
Woodford, Frank B. Parnassus on Main Street: A History
    of the Detroit Public Library. Detroit, 1965. 487 p.

PERIODICAL ARTICLES

Bishop, W. W. "A Decade of Library Progress in America,"
    Popular Science, 64 (Dec., 1904), 131-138.
Briggs, F. A. "The Sunday School Library in the Nine-
    teenth Century," Library Quarterly, 31 (1961), 166-177.
Carnegie, Andrew. "The Best Fields for Philanthropy,"
    North American Review, 149 (1889), 682-698.
Cole, George W. "Book-Collectors as Benefactors of Public
    Libraries," Bibliographical Society of America Papers,
    9 (1915), 47-110.
Ditzion, Sidney. "Social Reform, Education and the Library,"
    Library Quarterly, 9 (1939), 156-184.
Fletcher, W. I. "The Public Library Movement," Cosmo-
    politan, 17 (1894), 99-106.
Grotzinger, Laurel. "The University of Illinois Library
    School, 1893-1942," Journal of Library History, 2 (1967),
    129-141.
Harrison, J. L. "The Movement for Public Libraries in the
    United States," New England Magazine, 10 (1894), 709-
    722.
Kilgour, Fredrick G. "Justin Winsor," College and Research
    Libraries, 3 (Dec., 1941), 64-66.
Lacy, Dan. "The Library of Congress: A Sesquicentenary
    Review," Library Quarterly, 20 (1950), 157-179.
Leidecker, Kurt F. "The Debt of Melvil Dewey to William
    Torrey Harris," Library Quarterly, 15 (1945), 139-
    142.
Mead, Theodore H. "A Free Lending Library for New York,"
    Scribners' Monthly, 20 (1880), 929-935.

Library Progress, 1850-1900   185

Norton, Frank H. "The Astor Library," Galaxy, 7 (1869), 527-37.

Rayward, W. B. "Melvil Dewey and Education for Librarianship," Journal of Library History, 3 (1968), 297-312.

Spofford, Ainsworth R. "The Public Library of the United States," Journal of Social Science, 2 (1870), 92-114.

Thurber, Evangeline. "American Agricultural College Libraries, 1862-1900," College and Research Libraries, (1945), 346-52.

Vandemark, P. "Cleveland Public Library, 1869-1969," Wilson Library Bulletin, 43(1969), 728-33.

Walter, Frank K. "The Sunday School Library," Library Quarterly, 12 (1942), 731-739.

Wright, Thomas. "Possible Culture Through Libraries." Contemporary Review, 40 (1881), 25-44.

XII

BOOKS AND PRINTING SINCE 1775

From the days of Gutenberg until the late 18th century there were improvements in typography and illustrations, but the printing process itself was relatively unchanged. The type was set in a wooden form and locked in and placed in the "bed" of the press. The type was then inked by hand, the press was raised by means of a turning screw, a sheet of paper was inserted over the type and then the press was lowered to make an impression from the inked type onto the paper. Each printed sheet meant a laborious raising and lowering of the screw press by hand, and the amount of printing that could be done in a day was very limited. On the other hand, with every step of the process under hand control, very fine work could be done by skilled and conscientious workers.

In 1798, Charles, the Third Earl Stanhope (1753-1816), brought out an iron press in England that added the power of a lever to the screw process of raising and lowering the press, and this speeded up printing considerably. The Columbian press, developed in the United States about 1810 by George Clymer, did away with the screw press and used levers and springs to provide the proper pressure. The Columbian press remained popular for more than a half century, and was probably the best of the Gutenberg-style flat-bed presses. In 1813, Friedrich König, a German printer, introduced the first press to make use of the cylinder. In his press the type bed remained flat but the paper was pressed upon the type by means of a revolving cylinder moving from one end to the other. The London Times adopted the König press and powered it with a steam engine in 1814, producing a press that printed 1100 sheets per hour. Along with these improvements in the press came the use of stereotype plates. This process used movable types to make molds from which solid plates were cast. These solid plates had the advantage of being easily handled and were so durable that thousands of impressions could be made from them.

To the cylinder press, stereotypes and steam power, the 1830s saw the addition of the assembly-line method of printing, folding, stitching and binding, making possible the production of books and pamphlets at much higher speed. In the 1840s, Richard M. Hoe developed the Hoe Rotary Press, which locked the type itself into a cylinder, and produced up to 8000 impressions per hour. Some 20 years later, William A. Bullock further perfected this press by replacing the type with a stereotype cylinder (actually two half-cylinders locked onto a roller) and by providing for the continuous feeding of paper from a roll to the press. This type of press met with immediate approval by the producers of newspapers and magazines and it was continually enlarged and improved until the largest newspapers in the country could be printed and folded at the rate of many thousands per hour. For the printing of books and pamphlets, however, the flat-bed presses continued to be used throughout the 19th century and in many cases for small jobs or fine work down to the present.

A rival for the stereotype plate came after 1840 with the development of electrotype. Whereas the stereotype plate was made from a papier-mâché mold impressed by the original type, the electrotype plate was produced by taking an impression in wax from the original type, depositing a thin shell of copper on the wax by an electrolytic process, and then filling in the copper shell with type-metal alloy. Both processes achieved the same result, a stable plate capable of being continuously used for long runs, but the electrotype plate gradually displaced the stereotype except for the production of newspapers. The electrotype had the additional advantage of being able to reproduce pictures from woodcuts or engravings much better than could the stereotype.

Despite the improvement in printing methods, typesetting by hand continued throughout much of the century. In the 1820s, William Church, a native of Vermont then living in England, designed and constructed a machine for casting and composing type mechanically, with the type sorted into appropriate bins and then set up for printing by means of a hand-operated keyboard. Church received a patent for his device in 1822, but it was not immediately accepted by the printing profession, and it was some 30 years before a similar machine was put into wide commercial use. This successful type-setting machine was patented by William H. Mitchell and first used in the John F. Trow printing office in New York in 1853. It was a considerable improvement over all previous methods and made type-setting a comparatively easy

task. Type-casting machines were also developed separately,
so that there was a plentiful production of type for either hand-
or machine-setting. To round out the development of these
forms of printing equipment came the development of the Linotype in 1885. Ottmar Merganthaler (1854-1899) designed and
build this keyboard composing machine which cast a complete
line of type in one piece, properly spaced and ready for the
press or the making of plates. This was a boon to the newspaper printing industry, and the New York Herald Tribune
was the first to use it in 1886. The Linotype soon took its
place as standard equipment in the larger newspaper and book
publishing firms.

The new high-speed printing processes required strong
paper in the form of rolls so that a continuous stream of
paper could be fed into the rapidly rotating presses. Moreover, as more and more books, newspapers and magazines
were published, paper had to be plentiful as well as economical, strong and durable. Up to about 1800, the paper-making process, which resulted in flat sheets of good quality rag
paper, had been little changed for 300 years. In 1803,
Henry and Sealy Fourdrinier, two brothers who were stationers in London, set up operation of a paper-making machine
originally designed and patented in 1798 and then brought to
England by a Frenchman, Nicolas Louis Robert. This paper-
making process centered around a revolving wire band that
passed through a vat of paper pulp, picking up a layer of
pulp which was then removed from the wires and fed in a
continuous stream along a conveyor belt. On this belt the
pulp was carried through a process of pressing and drying,
producing rolls of paper in almost any needed length. A
similar device was produced by John Dickinson of England in
1809, and a variation of this, patented by John and Thomas
Gilpin of Delaware in 1817, brought a revolution to the paper-
making industry in the United States. The Gilpin machine was
capable of turning out a continuous sheet of paper, 30 inches
wide, at the rate of 60 feet per minute. With many improvements, the Fourdrinier and Gilpin machines remain the basis
for most paper-making equipment in modern use.

The other great innovations in paper-making in the 19th
century came in the discovery of new paper-making materials.
Linen and cotton rags, the source of most paper through the
1700s, were too scarce and expensive for the large quantities
of paper needed in the 1800s. A new, cheaper source of
paper was needed, and after much experimentation with various vegetable fibers a process was developed for making

paper from wood pulp. At first the pulp was prepared by macerating wood chips by mechanical means but this was both slow and unsatisfactory, and it produced only a coarse paper. In the 1850s a method was developed for reducing the wood to pulp by chemical means, particularly sodas and sulphites which reduced the solid wood to a liquid, fibrous solution that could be handled in the paper-making machines. Since there was a seemingly endless supply of wood in the United States, these developments in the making of paper made America the center of the industry for the modern world. So important was the industry and so rapid its growth that by 1880 there were 742 paper mills in 29 states. In the present century, the demand for paper rapidly caught up with the supply and several steps have been taken to insure a constant source of pulp materials. New forests of quick-growing soft woods are being continuously planted and experiments are being made with new paper sources such as rice straw and hulls, peanut hulls and the remains of sugar cane after the juice has been removed. Even so, much of the paper being used in the United States today must be imported.

Illustrations in American books of the 17th and 18th centuries were produced either from wood-cuts or from copperplate engravings. Excellent work was produced in a few cases, but for the most part American printers did not equal the Europeans in the quality of their book illustrations. By 1800 and shortly after, however, American publishers were using many illustrations, including portraits, maps, architectural drawings, cartoons, prints and views of cities. Even color prints were beginning to be used, and the works of outstanding artists were employed in book illustrations. The American edition of Rees' Encyclopedia, published in Philadelphia in 1797, was a particularly fine example of the copperplate engraver's art. Steelplate engravings were introduced after 1810, and although the resulting prints were not of the quality of copperplate engravings, the steel could be used almost indefinitely, producing many more copies than copper. Another new method of reproducing illustrations was introduced early in the 1800s, but did not become popular for many years. This was lithography, a process of reproducing pictures from a flat surface, originally smooth stone, but later zinc or other metals. Aloys Senefelder of Germany had developed a lithographic process as early as 1803, and published a book on the subject in 1818, but for many years lithography was largely used in the reproduction of art works, with a separate plate for each color. By the mid-19th century color lithography had reached a state of near-perfection and the

excellent prints of Currier and Ives, so illustrative of America and American life of that period, attest to this fact.

     The next great step in book illustration came with the
development of photo-mechanical processes, particularly
photo-engraving. This process employed chemical means to
transfer pictures from the photographic film to the engraver's
plate, permitting any photograph to be readily reproduced in
print. Photography had been invented or developed before
1840, and was fairly common by 1860, but it was not until
1873 that the first photograph was printed lithographically in
the New York Daily Graphic. The half-tone process, which
enabled a photograph to be reproduced by regular printing,
was developed in the 1870s, and from about 1880 on the
photograph was an accepted feature in most newspapers and
magazines. Color printing, rotogravure, and off-set printing
were all coming into use by 1900, or were well beyond the
experimental stages. Rotogravure was photo-engraving adapted to the high-speed rotary presses for newspapers, while
off-set/was a process of lithography also adapted to a cylinder
rather than a plate. In off-set, the picture is transferred
from the original plate to a rubber covered cylinder and from
this to paper revolving around a third cylinder. The off-set
process has the advantages of reproducing both picture and
text at the same time and also of printing on cheaper paper
than that required for regular lithography. In the 20th
century, chemistry, photography, electronics, and space
satellite technology have combined to produce various methods
of transmitting pictures or texts over vast distances and
printing them almost simultaneously with reception.

     In the book-making process the final step is the bind-
ing. In this field the changes have not been so radical but
there have been many developments in the last century. Before 1800, the printed sheets of four, eight or 12 leaves were
folded, stitched in signatures, then sewn together in volumes,
and finally bound in boards covered with leather or vellum.
Thus the early printed books simply followed the binding
methods of the later medieval manuscript volumes and although the book-binder became an artist in the 15th to 18th
centuries his artistry lay more in the technique of decorating
the leather covers than in departures from earlier binding
methods. The 19th century saw the replacement of leather
by cloth or paper as the outside book covering and the wooden
or stiff leather boards by heavy cardboard. Machine stitching took the place of hand-sewing, and stronger glues were
used to strengthen the spine. As the printing presses be-

came more mechanized and their output more prolific, the
process of binding also began to be done by machinery and
by the 1860s the handbound edition became a rarity. The late
1800s saw the introduction of wire-stapling for pamphlets and
smaller books, and in the present era appeared the paper-
backed, non-sewn book that relied entirely upon glues or
plastics for its binding. Finally, plastic-impregnated fabrics
are being used to form an attractive and durable type of book
cover that can be printed as easily as paper yet has the lasting
qualities of the finest leather.

One of the results of the change from leather-bound
books to cloth bindings was the necessity for a protective
cover over the cloth to prevent its becoming soiled before the
book was sold. A solution was found in the paper book jacket,
or dust cover, which was introduced in England in 1833, but
which did not come into common use until the 1890s. It was
not until 1906 that the thought arose to use the paper jacket
as a place for advertising. Some book jackets have been
quite artistic, but most have been more advertising than art.
With the coming of the paper-bound book, the jacket merged with
the binding boards, resulting in a stiff cover, often brightly
illustrated in several colors.

The early 19th-century printing firm was often a partnership or family-owned corporation and it often combined
under one roof both printing and binding processes. Gradually, however, publishing became a business distinct from
printing, with the latter often being performed on contract by
other firms. Printing workers were among the first to or-
ganize into labor unions and by the late 1800s were a powerful force in the industry. Also, the printing industry tended
to specialize, with some doing only job printing, others only
books, and still others magazines or newspapers. Book publishers too, of course, tended to specialize, particularly in
the 20th century. A distinctly new kind of publisher appeared, the university press, which by the mid-20th century
were producing a large proportion of published scholarly
works. Newspaper runs increased until they were numbered
in the thousands and some of the larger metropolitan dailies
published nearly a million copies daily. Magazines also increased in numbers, from a bare half-dozen around 1800 to
several score by 1850, several hundred by 1900, and over
12,000 by 1970. The illustrated weekly appeared in the 1860s
and proved very popular, while monthly magazines appeared
for all interests from the juvenile to the professional and
technical, with circulations ranging from a few hundred to

to several million. Print runs for books went from a few
hundred in the early 19th century to several thousand for a
popular work before 1900, and even into the millions for a
best-seller today. The broadside largely disappeared in the
1800s, but the almanac held its own and the pamphlet became
more versatile and plentiful than ever. Cartoons appeared
early in the 1800s, became popular by 1900, and in the form
of comic books reached mass distribution by the 1930s.

Most of the early literature printed in the United
States was borrowed from European or classical authors, but
by the 19th century the trend was toward the production of
works by American authors. Particularly after 1840,
writers of American birth, whether in literature, history or
science, far outnumbered those of European origin in the
output of the American press. New types of publications,
including encyclopedias in many volumes, collected works,
and the illustrated gift book or annual, entered the field and
the book-seller, long associated with the printer, emerged
as a separate profession. Not content with waiting for the
customer, both publisher and bookseller sent salesmen
throughout the country to advertise their products and increase their sales. Many books continued to be published
on a subscription basis, with orders being taken in advance
of publication. By mid-century, the publication of textbooks
for schools and colleges became a major business, as those
institutions of learning increased in number and size. Books
written and designed especially for children also appeared in
larger numbers after 1850, and by 1900 the illustrated children's book was an accepted stock in trade for both publisher and bookseller. For popular reading, the paper-backed
"dime novel" appeared after the Civil War, and in the form
of westerns, adventure stories and mystery thrillers they
were sold by the hundreds of thousands. In the output of
the 19th-century presses, quality may have been lacking to
a large extent, but quantity was there and the literate American could scarcely complain of a lack of reading matter.

Among the larger and better known publishers of the
early 19th century were a few that survive in present-day
firms. Matthew Carey and Sons, for example, was a firm
founded and directed by an economist and politician. When the
father withdrew from the company in 1822, it became the
firm of Carey and Lea, which has lasted and survives today
as Lea and Febiger, Inc. D. Appleton and Company, founded
as a publishing house in New York in 1831, survives today in
Appleton-Century-Crofts. J. and J. Harper, beginning in

1817, later became Harper and Brothers, and survives after a century and a half as Harper and Row. By the 1830s, Harper's had introduced the assembly line into the printing and binding of books and employed over 300 workers in one building, a very large undertaking for that time. In the same decade, Harper's began publishing its "Family Library," a series of popular books on many subjects, low in price and wide in appeal. It was one of the first of many such series.

Some of the larger publishers in the later 19th century experimented with the publication of both books and magazines. Harper's, for example, published not only Harper's Monthly, but at different times, Harper's Weekly, Harper's Young People, and Harper's Bazaar. D. Appleton and Company not only published a periodical, but added the New American Encyclopedia to its list, and for a long time issued an annual supplementary volume. Charles Scribner and Sons, another pre-Civil War publishing firm, began issuing Scribner's Monthly in 1870 and made it one of the most important periodicals of its day. Other publishers turned to the reprint as a major specialty, issuing what are essentially two different types of reprints. One is the inexpensive re-issue of popular fiction and non-fiction, designed for the general reader, while the other, usually by photo-offset, is of out-of-print but still needed scholarly works for the specialist. Since the 1930s the reprint field has been supplemented by the micro-publisher, who reproduces in micro-film, micro-fiche, micro-card or micro-print those rare and lengthy works needed in only a relatively few copies. Micro-publications are a boon to the scholar and librarian, but form only a small portion of the total publication field. Bibliographic control over the thousands of items issued from the nation's presses each year is a vital matter, and various indexes and bibliographies attempt this. The publications of the H. W. Wilson Company, such as the Cumulative Book Index, and of the R. R. Bowker Company, with its Books in Print, go a long way toward making this bibliographic control possible.

The vital link between the publisher and the buyer of books is, of course, the bookseller. This occupation is little appreciated in the American economic and cultural scene, but it is important and remains an important part of the general field of graphic communication. In the 20th century, booksellers have been faced with a major competitor in the form of book clubs which, with national advertising and direct mail service, have taken over a large portion of sales. There

were no less than 122 different book clubs in 1968, selling
everything from children's books to limited editions, and offering low prices or premium books in return for continued
buying. This has undoubtedly resulted in a wider distribution
of books to the reading public, but it has cut down on the
sales of the average retail bookstore. Many small bookstores have found that they must rely on the sale of greeting
cards, toys or other non-book merchandise in order to remain in business, while others have found that the rapid
turnover of sales in the paperback field allow them to continue stocking the slower-moving trade volumes. The larger
towns can usually support one or more good bookstores, but
the smaller towns and most rural areas of the United States
are without the benefits of a good bookstore. Some bookstores are able to deal largely in rare books and fine editions,
but most of them must depend on the "best-sellers" for
much of their business. Yet bestsellers are few and many
well-reviewed books sell only a few thousand copies. Fortunately, better sales methods, more advertising, and a
larger book-buying public are continuing to improve the lot
of the bookseller in the 1970s.

        For both book publisher and bookseller two topics of
continuing interest are censorship and fair trade laws.
American publishers have been relatively free of government
intervention since the trial of Peter Zenger in the 18th century, yet they have had to be constantly on the alert, particularly in times of war and national stress. Local governments have also attempted to suppress or control the press
at various times, for example the Comstock Acts in New
York state in the 1870s. These laws, directed against alleged obscenity in print, gave a private society the power
to seize questionable publications and arrest their owners.
In addition, federal post office and customs officials have
at times seized publications under charges of obscenity or
pornography. Fortunately, in the 20th century the Supreme
Court has generally been liberal in its interpretation of such
laws, and although there are still some points in question,
the American press is today freer than ever before. The
question of fair trade concerns the attempt on the part of
the publishers, aided in some cases by laws, to protect the
bookseller from unfair competition from those who would
sell books at less than the publisher's announced price.
Fair trade laws have been generally upheld in the courts, although there are still attempts by "discount houses" as well
as by some department stores to get around them.

From a few scattered printers in the 13 colonies in 1775, the American publishing industry has become by the 1970s a gigantic business, employing thousands of workers and producing over a billion copies of books per year. General trade books alone, not including textbooks and paperbacks, accounted for over one billion in sales in 1968. If the typewriter and the linotype revolutionized the graphic communications of the 19th century, the various electronic devices have provided constant change in the 20th. The teletype added electronics to the printing processes by making it possible to transmit information in written form almost instantaneously. Electrostatic printing does away with both type and press, and reproduces directly anything in graphic form. Type-setting can be controlled from previously prepared tapes. Finally, by wireless transmission of electronic impulses, copy can be set up in one city and the actual printing done in another hundreds of miles away. Rapid, computer-controlled presses can print books, magazines or newspapers at speeds unbelievable a quarter century ago. With these advances in the field of graphic communication have come others equally amazing in the area of instantaneous communication, such as radio and television. Television signals have been received from astronauts on the moon, while even their heart-beats were recorded electronically back on earth. By means of communications satellites radio and television programs can be sent to any spot on earth, as well as telephone and telegraph messages; sometimes hundred of messages can pass at the same time. The videophone, long a science-fiction specialty, has become a fact, and it is possible to develop a radio-newspaper that for the price of a television set would produce newspapers in the home directly from a central news room if there were sufficient demand for it. Moreover, any and all of this instantaneous communication can be preserved in print, on film, disk or tape for use tomorrow or 100 years from now. Electronic tape, for example, has many uses--it can give the television viewer an "instant replay" of a crucial moment in a sports event, but it can also give us oral and visual history libraries that will make this generation's history the most well-preserved since time began. True, electronic marvels have also brought about such unpleasant results as wire-tapping and electronic surveillance of private activities, but these are things man must learn to control.

Despite all the remarkable developments in all methods of communication in the 20th century, the book remains a basic means of preserving and disseminating information.

Other means may embellish or supplement the book, but for
the foreseeable future its presence seems to be assured, and
the roles of printer, publisher and bookseller will continue
to be important ones in the society of men.

Bibliography

BOOKS

Bailey, Herbert S., Jr. The Art and Science of Book Pub-
    lishing. New York, 1970. 216 p.
Bland, David. A History of Book Illustration. 2nd ed.
    Berkeley, Calif., 1969.
Bennett, Paul A. Books and Printing. New York, 1951.
    258 p.
Clair, Colin. A Chronology of Printing. New York, 1969.
    228 p.
Day, Kenneth, ed. Book Typography, 1815-1965, in Europe
    and the United States of America. Chicago, 1966.
    401 p.
Fabey, Herbert. Early Printing in California. San Francis-
    co, 1956. 141 p.
Green, Ralph. The Iron Hand Press in America. Rowayton,
    Conn., 1948. 40 p.
Greenhood, David. Chronology of Books and Printing. New
    York, 1936. 186 p.
Halsey, R. V. Forgotten Books of the American Nursery:
    A History of the Development of the American Story
    Book. Boston, 1911. 245 p.
Hunter, Dard. Papermaking; the History and Technique of
    an Ancient Craft. New York, 1947. 680 p.
Klemin, Diana. The Illustrated Book, Its Art and Craft.
    New York, 1970. 159 p.
Lehmann-Haupt, Helmut. The Book in America: A History
    of the Making and Selling of Books in the United States.
    2nd ed. New York, 1964. 512 p.
Levarie, Norma. The Art and History of Books. London,
    1968. 315 p.
McMurtrie, Douglas C. The Book. New York, 1943. 676 p.
Madison, C. A. Book Publishing in America. New York,
    1966. 638 p.
Marianaccio, Anthony. Exploring the Graphic Arts. Scran-
    ton, Pa., 1946. 275 p.
Morison, Stanley. Four Centuries of Fine Printing. London,
    1924. 243 p.
Mott, Frank Luther. A History of American Magazines.
    Cambridge, Mass., 1930. 4 v.

Mumby, Frank A. Publishing and Bookselling; A History
from the Earliest Times to the Present Day. 4th ed.
New York, 1956. 500 p.
Pitz, Henry C. A Treasury of Book Illustration. New York,
1945. 255 p.
Pottinger, David. Printers and Printing. Cambridge,
Mass., 1941. 143 p.
Reiner, Imre. Modern and Historical Topography. New
York, 1946. 125 p.
Rosner, C. Printers Progress, 1851-1951. Cambridge,
Mass., 1951. 119 p.
Schick, Frank L. The Paperbound Book in America and Its
European Antecedents. New York, 1958. 262 p.
Sheehan, Donald. This was Publishing. Bloomington, Ind.,
1952. 288 p.
Shove, R. H. Cheap Book Production in the United States,
1870-1891. Urbana, Ill., 1937. 155 p.
Silver, Rollo G. The American Printer, 1787-1825. Char-
lottesville, Va., 1967. 189 p.
Stern, Madeleine B. Imprints on History: Book Publishing
and American Frontiers. Bloomington, Ind., 1956.
492 p.
Thompson, Ralph. American Literary Annuals and Gift
Books, 1825-1865. New York, 1936. 183 p.
Weeks, Lyman H. A History of Paper Manufacturing in the
United States, 1690-1916. New York, 1969. 352 p.
(Originally 1916.)
Wentz, Roby. Eleven Western Presses; An Account of How
the First Printing Press Came to Each of the Eleven
Western States. Los Angeles, 1956. 57 p.

PERIODICAL ARTICLES

Green, Ralph. "Early American Power Printing Presses,"
Studies in Bibliography, 4 (1951-52), 143-154.
Hagedorn, Leo H. M. "The First Century of Photo-Engrav-
ing," Penrose's Annual, 19 (1917), 189-197.
Morison, Stanley. "Towards an Ideal Type," The Fleuron,
2 (1924), 57-75.
"Printing--Ancient Craft Is Stirring with Technological Inno-
vations," Fortune, 40 (Oct., 1949), 100-109.
Rollins, Carl P. "A Survey of the Making of Books in
Recent Years," The Dolphin, 1 (1933), 288-301.
Tanselle, G. T. "The Historiography of American Literary
Publishing," Studies in Bibliography, 18 (1965), 3-40.

XIII

MODERN FOREIGN LIBRARIES

Library service in other countries varies considerably from that which we consider normal in the United States. In many countries individual libraries and library service in general approach and even surpass ours, but in others and in most of the world, great steps must still be taken to reach even minimum standards of acceptable library service. Generally speaking, library services are best in northern Europe and in most British Commonwealth nations and poorest in other former colonial areas and in the tropics. The value of books and libraries is becoming more highly appreciated, however, particularly in the Communist nations, and great strides are being made in library progress all around the world. Thus any generalization about library service in any particular area may well need to be changed in a few short years.

Canada

As one might expect, library service in Canada has developed in much the same way that it has in the United States. There are records of a few private libraries and even book collections in religious institutions in the 17th and 18th centuries, but there was little effort toward school and public libraries until the 19th. As early as 1791, the provincial legislature of Ontario (then known as Upper Canada) established a government library and the early 1800s saw the formation of social and academy libraries similar to those in the United States. School district libraries, and mechanics' institute libraries with some public support were also tried. Most library progress in Canada, however, has come since 1875, with the passage of provincial public and school library acts, such as that of Ontario in 1882. In the present century, library progress has accelerated, particularly since World War II. In the school libraries, centralized libraries have dominated the secondary schools, while

classroom collections remain popular in many elementary
institutions. Trends toward the use of audio-visual aids and
toward the development of teaching materials centers have
in recent years paralleled those in the United States. In
the public library field, the larger cities have developed major collections, with numerous branches, while in the sparse-
ly settled areas regional libraries, bookmobiles, and even
packaged libraries are necessary to bring books to readers.

On the governmental level, the National Library Act
of 1953 established for Canada a National Library in addition
to its Parliamentary Library, founded in 1815. The National
Library in Ottawa serves as a bibliographic center for the
nation, with a national union catalog, a clearing-house for
inter-library lending, and other services available to libraries and citizens throughout the nation. After moving into a
new and modern building in 1966, its collection had grown to
some 450, 000 volumes by 1970. The Library of Parliament
also in Ottawa, with some 350, 000 volumes, serves as a legislative and legal collection and also as a national reference library. A score or more additional governmental libraries
are to be found in the capital also, ranging downward in size
from that of the Department of Agriculture's 300, 000 volumes. Still other national agencies have libraries, or
branches, scattered throughout Canada.

Each of the provinces also has a library; that of
Quebec is probably the largest, with about 375, 000 volumes.
Each province also has its specialized governmental libraries, making each provincial capital something of a book
center. Public libraries in Canada are present in almost
all cities and towns, but still the number of people without
immediate library services varies from one-fourth to one-
third in several provinces. Toronto's Public Library, with
23 branches and over 700, 000 volumes, and Montreal's with
15 branches and 775, 000 volumes, are among the largest,
but other notable municipal collections are to be found in
Quebec, Winnipeg, Vancouver, Edmonton and Calgary. Prince
Edward Island claims the distinction of providing library
service for 100 per cent of its population through a regional
library, branches and mail service. Regional libraries are
also popular in Western Canada, where the Fraser Valley
Library, one of the oldest, serves nearly 300, 000 population
with more than as many books, 28 branches and two bookmobiles. In Eastern Canada, the province of Quebec has
also turned to regional libraries to serve its rural areas
and small towns. The Quebec "Service des Bibliothèques
Publiques" has been formed eventually to serve 23 regional

libraries in the province. Even the Yukon territory in the
near-Arctic Canadian Northwest, has a regional library with
65, 000 volumes serving a scattered population of 18, 000.

The largest Canadian University Library is that of
the University of Toronto, with over 3, 000, 000 volumes in
all of its campus collections, but several others, including
McGill University, Carleton University, Queen's University,
and the universities of Manitoba, Saskatchewan, and British
Columbia have collections in the hundreds of thousands. Two
universities, Laval University and the University of Montreal,
and several colleges serve the French-speaking Canadians and
Laval in particular is known for its outstanding collection of
French language and literature. Several new colleges and
universities have been established in recent years, such as
the Sir George Williams University in Montreal, whose library had 270, 000 volumes in 1970, and the University of
Prince Edward Island, founded in 1969, but with a library
of 70, 000 volumes almost as soon as it opened. The best
known schools of library and information science in Canada
are probably those at McGill University and the University
of Toronto, but other approved schools are at the universities of Montreal, British Columbia, and Western Ontario,
while another dozen or so Canadian institutions offer some
form of library training. Many Canadian librarians belong
to the American Library Association, but since 1946 the
Canadian Library Association has also been very active and
there are in addition several regional and specialized library
organizations. Generally speaking, Canadian libraries and
library service are progressing rapidly, with public support
and encouragement from national, provincial and municipal
sources.

Mexico

The library picture in our southern neighbor, Mexico,
is not so favorable as that in Canada. The National Library
in Mexico City was formed from collections dating back to
the 1830s, but it was not opened to the public until the
1860s. Its growth was slow and it was often neglected by
the government, but it now numbers some 800, 000 volumes,
including more than 100, 000 manuscripts relating to the history and development of the nation. Since 1929, the National Library has been under the direction of the University
of Mexico and it is now housed on the new university campus. There it constitutes the core of the library materials

available to the university, supplemented by the central university library and many departmental collections to form a research center of over a million volumes. Elsewhere in Mexico there are a number of college and university libraries, some old and hallowed with tradition, while others are modern and progressive. The older ones often have valuable and rare volumes, while the newer ones may be turning to micro-materials, but all, generally speaking, are small in comparison to their needs.

Public libraries as such were virtually unknown in Mexico prior to the 20th century, but since the 1920s there has been in the Federal Ministry of Public Education a Bureau of Libraries which has encouraged the development of public libraries throughout the country. Many small collections have been formed but outside of the Federal District, which includes Mexico City, very few of them approach anything like adequate service. Libraries especially for children are available in some of the Mexico City suburbs. Since 1943 the United States has operated the Benjamin Franklin Library in Mexico City, which serves both information needs and as something of a model library illustrating American methods in librarianship. It contained some 45,000 volumes in 1970, while a similar British institution, the British Council Library, contained about half as many. Other types of libraries in Mexico include church libraries, many including old and rare volumes; special libraries, almost all in Mexico City; and a few notable private libraries. Among some of the specialized collections would be the National Library of Anthropology and History, with some 280,000 volumes; the library of the Society of Geography and statistics, with about 100,000 items; and the National Academy of Science Library and the library of the National Teachers College, each with well over 100,000 volumes. School libraries are being encouraged, but still most of Mexico's public schools lack adequate library services, although in the larger towns the public libraries sometimes provide and emphasize books for children.

Elsewhere in Latin America, the library picture is similar to that in Mexico, with some outstanding individual libraries, but with library service in general quite backward. Each country has a national library of some size, but few public or institutional libraries of note. Library service is hampered by the generally poor educational facilities, the low economic status of the majority of the population, and

the lack of trained personnel. Too often the general philosophy of library service tends toward protection and preservation of books rather than encouragement of their use. However, this picture is gradually and in many cases rapidly
changing, with the jump being made from virtually no libraries to computer-controlled information centers. To help in
the training of librarians, the Interamerican School of Library Science was founded in Medellín, Colombia, in 1956,
and since that date it has not only graduated many skilled
librarians, but it has served as a model for other library
schools in South America. In addition to formal library
schools, many Latin American librarians receive training
in short courses and institutes held in colleges and in some
of the larger libraries, while others still receive their
training in the United States and other countries.

Brazil

        In recent years, Brazil, Argentina and Chile have
taken the lead among South American countries in the field
of library service. Brazil in particular has many outstanding libraries, including federal, provincial, municipal,
school, institutional, and special. The National Library at
Rio de Janeiro contains over a million and a half items,
including bound periodicals and over 600,000 manuscripts.
The National Library also provides such services as printed
catalog cards, national bibliographical publications, and a
national legal depository. It also contains the national copyright office and maintains a school of librarianship. At the
national capital of Brasília, a new city built in the interior
of Brazil, there are several government libraries, including
that of the Chamber of Deputies, with 200,000 volumes.
Another new library, or system of libraries, is that being
established at the National University at Brasília, which
will have a school of library and information science, in
addition to the usual professional schools and colleges.

        Brazil's larger cities have municipal libraries that
are relatively modern, but in other parts of the nation library service is a function of the province or state, with
libraries in the smaller towns usually being branches of
the state system. Many areas are still unserved. In São
Paulo the municipal library, which contains nearly a million volumes, has a central library housed in a 24-story
building completed in 1942. It and a few other public library systems in Brazil are thoroughly modern, with book-

mobiles, branches and collections of circulating non-book materials. University libraries, both public and private, vary
considerably in size and usefulness, and most of them follow
the European system of having several departmental or institute libraries in addition to, or in place of, a central library.
These range in size from a few hundred to many thousand
volumes, but they usually are handicapped by lack of uniform
cataloging, a union catalog, and centralized controls. The
University of São Paulo, for example, has over a million
volumes in its campus libraries, while some of the smaller
colleges, such as the University of Parana, have only a few
thousand volumes. On the whole, Brazil's libraries are progressive, with improved library standards, pilot school and
public libraries, special workshops for librarians and library
employees, and sponsored translation and publications of
texts in library science. In 1965 a census of libraries in
Brazil showed 514 college and university libraries, 3035 public libraries, 5407 school libraries, and 186 special libraries, with the latter figure admittedly inaccurate since it included only the more important collections. A National Foundation of Brazilian Library Associations helps to bring together
the many smaller associations of librarians, and coordinates
the drive to improve library service throughout the country.

Argentina

The largest and most important library in Argentina
is the National Library in Buenos Aires, with its more than
800,000 volumes and over 50,000 manuscripts. It was founded in 1810, and preserves some of the rarest historical materials in any of the Latin American countries. Public library service in Argentina is directed from a national Commission for the Promotion of Popular Libraries, which encourages library service through 115 major public libraries
and some 2000 branches and stations. Altogether these public
collections contain some ten million volumes and to these
are added another seven million in over 24,000 public school
libraries. The latter are controlled through a National
School Library Service which attempts to place at least a
small reference library in every school. The libraries at
the University of Buenos Aires, including the main library
and those of the various faculties, contain over 1,150,000
volumes, while the National University of Córdoba, the oldest university in Argentina, has a bookstock of some 200,000.
The National University of the Littoral in Santa Fé has over
a million volumes and there are seven other public universi-

ties and five private ones with libraries of smaller size. There is a school of library science in Buenos Aires, a national library association, and several regional library associations. In the cities and towns popular subscription libraries, often associated with bookstores, provide a supplement to public library service, much of which is non-circulating. There are a number of growing special and technical libraries, particularly in Buenos Aires. Among these are the law library of the university, with over 250,000 volumes, and National Academy of Medicine library, with nearly 100,000. One interesting feature of Latin American libraries, particularly noticeable in Argentina, is that banks and newspapers often have libraries that are open for public use. For example, the newspaper La Prensa, has a library of about 75,000 volumes. Generally speaking, Argentina has a number of excellent libraries, but it lags in popular and school library service.

Chile

The National Library at Santiago de Chile has nearly a million volumes, and there are over 500 other public and institutional libraries in that country. With the exception of some of the larger municipal libraries, all public library services in the nation are under the National Library Service. The University of Chile, also at Santiago, has a central library and about 40 faculty and institute libraries, containing in all some half million volumes. The University of Concepción Library has about 180,000 volumes, while the Southern University at Valdivia, established in 1954, has for its library a rapidly growing "documentation center." Public libraries especially for children are associated with the national school system, and 180 secondary schools throughout the nation are provided with their own libraries. There is a national library association and it has been very active in helping Chile to maintain one of the better library systems in Latin America.

Peru

The National Library of Peru burned down in 1943 but it was reopened in 1947, and rapidly grew back to some 700,000 volumes by 1970. Peru has, in the library of the San Marcos National University, what is probably the oldest library in the western hemisphere. It was founded sometime

before 1600, probably as early as 1575. Its central library
has some 125,000 volumes, while some of its faculty libraries are almost as large. Public libraries are to be found in
the larger cities, but most of them are small and school libraries are generally poor. There is a national school of
library science in Lima, connected with the National Library.

Colombia and Venezuela

In Medellín, Colombia, there is a pilot project in public library service for all Latin America. Operated as a joint
project between the Colombian government and Unesco from
1954 to 1959, this library has since been locally supported.
In 1970 it contained about 45,000 volumes, and similar publicly supported libraries have been established in other Colombian towns. In neighboring Venezuela there are modern cities
with good public libraries, but also there are large rural
areas with little or no library service for either public or
schools. The Venezuelan National Library in Caracas has
over 400,000 volumes, while the Central University of Venezuela in the same city has about 100,000 volumes in its main
library.

Cuba

In the Caribbean area Cuba took the lead in librarianship in the early 20th century with strong collections in the
National Library, founded in 1901, and in the Havana University Library. Before 1959, Cuba's libraries were patterned
on those of the United States, but since the Fidel Castro re-
gime came into power, the libraries have developed more
along the lines of those in the Communist countries. More
attention is being paid to school libraries, and to collections
for workers in the various areas. The library of the University of Havana has been reported as suffering from lack of
materials formerly received from non-Communist countries,
but the National Library has grown to some 840,000 volumes,
and the internationally known library of the "Economic Society
of the Friends of Peace" had by 1970 about 250,000 volumes.

Panama

Panama is taking the lead among the Central American countries in planning a regional library system to cover

the entire country. When completed the regional library will
comprise ten systems, each with its own central library,
branches, bookmobiles and book stations, all directed from
the National Library under the direction of the Ministry of
Education. There are excellent libraries in the Panama Canal
Zone, including school, junior college, and public collections.
The public library in Balboa Heights, for example, has nearly 150,000 volumes.

Elsewhere in Latin America, each country usually has
a national library, a national university with several faculty
libraries, and public libraries, often non-circulating, in the
larger cities. Many of the more important libraries are simply
repositories of valuable but poorly organized and seldom used
volumes, while popular circulating libraries are few, under-
staffed, and lacking in funds. Since World War II a number
of outside forces have been felt in the development of Latin
American libraries, including those stemming from Unesco,
from the Organization of American States, and from other
nations individually. The United Nations Educational, Scientific and Cultural Organization (Unesco) has been particularly active, sponsoring inter-American library conferences,
seminars on library training, inter-library co-operation, and
other topics, as well as cooperating in the Pilot Library
program and the international library school in Colombia.
The organization of American States has been active, through
the Pan-American Union and its library in Washington,
D. C., in gathering and disseminating information on the status of Latin American libraries and in promoting library progress in general. Foreign countries, the United States and
Great Britain particularly, but also France, Spain, Germany,
and even some of the Communist nations, have maintained information libraries in most of the Latin American countries.
Although obviously propaganda-oriented, these libraries also
serve as model collections, and often provide the latest foreign literature available in their particular locations. In
many cases, Latin American libraries are jumping from almost no service to automated information centers without
passing through the intermediate stages, and this rapidity of
advance has its drawbacks as well as its obvious benefits.

United Kingdom

The West European countries have, as one might expect from history, some of the largest and most important

libraries in the world, and the United Kingdom is no exception. In England, the most important single collection is that of the British Museum in London. It is one of the largest libraries in the world with more than 8,000,000 printed volumes, including some 10,000 incunabula, and over 75,000 manuscripts. Its holdings in many fields, ranging from Anglo-Saxon manuscripts to Egyptian papyri, are among the best in the world. In recent years its use has been restricted to serious scholars due to crowded conditions and lack of reader space. Other great English libraries include those at Oxford and Cambridge Universities, the former with the Bodleian and various college libraries together totalling nearly 5,000,000 volumes, and the latter almost as large. Cambridge University's central library moved into a new building in 1934, with what was then a revolutionary development in the form of a "skyscraper" book tower. The universities at Edinburgh, Manchester, Liverpool, Aberdeen and London all have sizeable libraries, ranging from 300,000 to a million volumes, while the newer and smaller municipal, technical and liberal arts colleges have libraries in the 100,000 range. The University of York, founded in 1963, is one of the more recent of these. Its library is housed in an ultra-modern building, with open stacks, a book store in the building, and closed-circuit television for transmitting material from the library to classrooms and offices.

The National Library of Scotland in Edinburgh has some 2,500,000 volumes, while the National Library of Wales which also serves as the University Library at Aberystwyth, is somewhat smaller. Scotland's national collection grew out of the Faculty of Advocates' Library, founded before 1684 and turned over to the government in the 1920s. There are several hundred government, institutional and special libraries in London alone, many of them quite large and containing valuable collections. For example, the Royal Botanical Gardens Library at Kew has over 100,000 volumes, almost entirely restricted to horticulture and related fields. The India Office Library is one of the finest collections in the world relating to the history and culture of India. The National Library for the Blind provides talking books and books in Braille for blind readers throughout the United Kingdom. One of the most interesting of England's libraries has been the London Library, a subscription collection that survived from the pre-public library days. At its height it owned more than 500,000 volumes and served readers by the thousands, both from its main library and by mail throughout the world.

Since 1916 the National Central Library in London has
provided a very useful service for English readers. Beginning as a national students' library it has come to serve as
a national clearing-house for inter-library loans and as a
center for cooperative library and bibliographic projects.
It also houses a union catalog of the holdings of all major
London libraries to supplement its own 300,000 volume collection. A National Lending Library for Science and Technology was opened near London in 1962 and serves as a national bibliographic and documentation center for the sciences.
National library planning for the 1970s includes a "British
Library" to include the British Museum, the National Central
Library, and the National Lending Library under one supervision. The reference and bibliographic services will be retained in London, but the circulating and readers' services will
be moved to Yorkshire.

England's Public Libraries Act of 1850 resulted in the
formation of public libraries in more than 200 of the larger
urban areas by 1915, but the great majority of rural residents
were still without library service at that time. In 1919 a new
libraries Act allowed the county councils to provide library
services for rural areas and since that date service has been
gradually extended until it is nationwide. Since the Public Libraries and Museums Act of 1964 two types of public libraries
have emerged, one serving cities and the other, counties.
The Devon County Library, for example, serves in addition to
central library and branches, some 500 schools, 43 welfare
homes, 26 hospitals and five prisons. The larger cities are
decentralizing services from their public libraries, concentrating on metropolitan districts. London has no less than 32
library systems, one in each borough, but a city-wide library
borrower's card makes them equally available to any citizen.
In the nation as a whole, library service is available to 100
per cent of the population through some 562 central public libraries, 1750 branches, and over 30,000 other outlets. In
round numbers there are over 80 million books in English
public libraries to serve some 50 million people, and with
union catalogs and wide-spread inter-library lending, virtually every one of these books is available to every citizen.

The libraries of Great Britain suffered heavy losses
during World War II. The British Museum lost a wing which
housed some 150,000 books and 30,000 volumes of bound
newspapers, many of which could not be duplicated. Some 60
British libraries were completely destroyed in air raids and
the public libraries in several major cities were severely

damaged. The total book loss of the war, including libraries,
bookstores, and publishers' stocks, was estimated at over
20 million volumes. Since the war, British libraries have
not only replaced their war losses, but have grown rapidly
and have extended their services both quantitatively and quali-
tatively. With the Library Association as their professional
organization, British librarians have taken a lead in many in-
novative library procedures and have given their country one
of the best library systems in the world. This association,
founded in 1877, has since 1924 been supplemented by the
Association of Special Libraries and Information Bureaux.
Professional library education courses are given at the school
of Librarianship and Archives at University College, London,
and at several technical schools throughout the country.

France

        The great national library of France, the Bibliothèque
Nationale, is another of the world's outstanding cultural
treasures. Having developed over a period of some 500
years, it has received books by virtually every possible
means, including gift, purchase, copyright law, expropriation
and military conquest. Together with four other great libraries of Paris--the Bibliothèque Mazarine, the Bibliothèque
Ste -Geneviòvc, the Bibliothèque de l'Arsenal, and those of
the University of Paris--the national library rounds out a
research center of over 12,000,000 volumes. In addition to
books these libraries contain hundreds of thousands of manuscripts, engravings, periodicals, prints and newspapers.
Elsewhere in Paris there are at least 33 other libraries of
over 100,000 volumes each, along with a "phonothèque" containing over 250,000 recordings. The public library service
in Paris is decentralized with each of the 20 political sub-
divisions or "arrondissements" of the city having its own
public library. Counting all school, government, special,
institutional and large private collections, there were over
1200 libraries in Paris in 1970.

        Outside of Paris there are many other important uni-
versity and municipal libraries. The universities at
Grenoble, Bordeaux, Lille, Lyon, and Toulouse, to name
but a few, have collections numbering from 300,000 to a million volumes, while the combined national and university
library at Strasbourg has nearly 3,000,000 volumes. The
cities and towns of France have a wide variety of public libraries, ranging from large and ancient collections, filled

with incunabula and manuscripts, to small and modern collections that rival the rental libraries in popularity. The "Bibliothèque de la Ville" in Lyon, for example, has over
750,000 volumes, while many of the smaller towns with their
"bibliothèques communales" have only a few thousand. Regional library service is being tried in some more rural areas,
with the Departement of Haute-Vienne serving a large area
with 65,000 volumes and 295 branches and stations. Public
library service in France is still hampered, however, by
small collections, small staffs, and inadequate quarters.
Rental collections, operated by private agencies, provide
reading materials for a large proportion of the younger population. School libraries are also inadequate, although they
have improved considerably since 1945. In that year a library
division was established in the National ministry of Education
to coordinate and improve library service in the schools, with
particular emphasis on the small towns and rural areas.

Germany

        In the mid-19th century, Germany was probably the
most advanced area in the world in library service. Not only
in the size of its book collections and in the number of its
libraries but in its library methods and general philosophy of
librarianship it was far ahead of both England and the United
States. The outstanding municipal and university libraries
of the world patterned themselves after the German libraries
in the late 1800s. This was true, however, only for the
scholarly libraries since free circulating public libraries were
not widely developed in Germany until the present century
and even then they lagged considerably behind those of the
United States. Prior to World War II, the major German
libraries were the National Library in Berlin, with 2,850,000
volumes, including one of the largest collections of incunabula
in the world; the State Library of Bavaria at Munich, almost
as large; and the State Libraries at Dresden and Breslau
[now Wrocław, Poland] with about 750,000 volumes each.

        University libraries at Munich, Heidelberg and Göt-
tingen contained about 1,000,000 volumes each while several
others were around the half million mark. Some of the German municipal libraries, particularly in the larger cities,
had better research collections than most American universities but many of them were non-circulating and available only
a few hours daily. Public circulating libraries, sometimes
charging small fees to borrowers, were developed in many

cities after 1900, but they were usually small, poorly housed and
served only a small percentage of the potential reading public.
Much popular reading came from commercial rental libraries.
The Deutsche Bücherei at Leipzig, founded in 1912, was
unique in the way of libraries since it was a non-circulating
copyright collection which attempted to obtain a copy of every
book published in Germany or in the German language. It
contained nearly 2,000,000 volumes before World War II, but
about a fifth of these were lost when the building was largely
destroyed in 1943.

     When the Nazis came to power in Germany the develop-
ment of libraries was seriously curtailed, except for a few
favored institutions. All public libraries, whether popular or
research, were placed under strict government control and
censorship over their contents was rigidly maintained. Many
books were ordered destroyed or restricted from circulation,
andacquisitions were hampered, particularly in the case of
non-German publications. The popular circulating libraries
were used as propaganda outlets by the Nazis. During the
military action of World War II, many German libraries
were wholly or partially destroyed. Of 14 million books in
31 major German libraries, nearly 8,000,000 were destroyed
during the war and damage to buildings ran to millions of
dollars. Since 1945, however, remarkable results have been
achieved in rebuilding German libraries and in developing new
ones, particularly in the public library field. The American
Memorial Library was opened in West Berlin in 1954, as a
model public library patterned after American practice and
built largely with American funds. In 1970 it had about
350,000 volumes and was one of the most popular collections
in West Germany. American aid has also been extended to
the new Free University of West Berlin and U. S. Information Service libraries in the major German cities have demonstrated the American public library service. With this stimulus, Germany has been developing more public libraries with
openstacks, free circulation and service for children. As an
example, the city of Hamburg now has, in addition to its
scholarly libraries, a public circulating library of some 800,000
volumes. It has over 75 branches and other outlets in the
suburban areas. However, public library service still lags
in Germany and there is still a different approach to library
service in the sense that research libraries and public libraries are considered to be entirely separate institutions, even
to the extent of having separate training programs and library
associations for the personnel of the two services. In the
special library field, Germany has hundreds, ranging from the

small to the very large in almost all conceivable subject
areas.

  The division of Germany after World War II into two
separate countries of West Germany and East Germany, with
Berlin itself divided, brought about a number of changes in
the German library world. Part of the former National Library in Berlin had been damaged during the war, but much
of its more valuable contents had been sent into western Germany for safekeeping. After 1945, these books located in
Western Germany were used to form the West German Library
in Marburg, while the remainder of the National Library, now
located in East Berlin, became the national library of East
Germany. The West German Library at Marburg had about
2,000,000 volumes in the mid-1960s, when a decision was
reached to reconstitute a national library in West Berlin. By
1970 a new and modern building was completed for this collection, and a new institution, now known as the National
Library of Prussian Cultural Heritage (Staats bibliothek
Preussischer Kulturbesitz), shares a single director but has
a dual location in Marburg and Berlin. Elsewhere in West
Berlin there are large public libraries (Stadtbücherei) of
100,000 volumes or more in each of the municipal divisions,
plus scores of special and academic collections of all kinds.

  In East Germany, the National Library now has about
3,500,000 volumes and serves along with the Deutsche Bücherei
in Leipzig as the national bibliographic center. The latter
institution is a national depository library and reference collection, and also houses over 3,000,000 volumes. Under the
pretense of removing pro-Nazi books, the libraries of East
Germany were thoroughly purged after World War II of any
literature not acceptable to Communist authorities. Thousands
of books were confiscated or destroyed. Many of them were
replaced by pro-Communist works and their reading by the
public was made practically compulsory. Many private and
institutional libraries were expropriated by the Russians on
one pretext or other and either taken to Russia or turned over
to the new workers' libraries. At Potsdam, outside Berlin,
a new Communist university was opened and its library was
selected to conform to the new political philosophy. Several
other universities in East Germany, including some ancient
and honorable institutions, have libraries of over a million
volumes each. Throughout East Germany, as in most of the
Communist-dominated world, books are considered a major
part of the social and cultural scene. The publication and
dissemination of printed material in all forms is widely

encouraged, but unfortunately it is strictly controlled. There
is little or no freedom of either speech or press and the librarian is at once a tool and a victim of the government
propaganda machine. A Central Bureau for Scholarly Literature controls purchases for technical and reference libraries,
particularly for materials coming from outside East Germany. Similarly, the Central Institute for Librarianship ad-
vises the public libraries and coordinates their activities
through a system of administrative district libraries. There
is an advanced School of Librarianship in East Berlin, a professional library organization, and an active professional library press.

Italy

        The library situation in 20th-century Italy has been
somewhat similar to that in Germany. As of 1900, some of
the finest libraries in the world were in Italy, but two world
wars and two decades of dictatorship have taken their toll,
and although war damage as such has been small, deterioration
due to lack of proper care has been almost as destructive.
Although the larger reference and research libraries of Italy
contain some of the most valuable books and manuscripts in
the world, popular library service has not been widely developed and public libraries as known in the United States
do not exist in most Italian towns and cities. Italian libraries suffered some damage during World War II, but much of
their most valuable possessions were sent to the Vatican Library for safekeeping.

        Of all the libraries in Italy, the Vatican Library
(strictly speaking, not in Italy but in Vatican City) is the
most outstanding. With more than 900,000 printed books,
including 7,000 incunabula, and nearly 100,000 valuable
manuscripts, it is a treasure house of knowledge concerning
the history and culture of the western world. However,
down to the 1920s, it was just that, a treasure house, largely unorganized and almost entirely unavailable to any but the
most important scholar. During the decades after World
War I, a major effort was made to modernize the Vatican
Library. American and other experts in library services
were invited in to advise, and in 1926 the Carnegie Corporation sent William Warner Bishop to survey the Library and
to make recommendations for its future growth and development. Dr. Bishop's visit came while Pius XI was Pope and
since he himself was a former librarian, his interest and

influence favored modernization.   Book stacks were installed,
new quarters were added, cataloging and classifying were in-
tensified, and the purposes and aims of the Library were re-
defined to make it not only more useful, but more used.
Since then, thousands of new books and manuscripts have
been added and scholars from all over the world have made
use of its facilities.   Printed catalogs of books and manuscripts in several areas have been prepared and the Vatican
Library is becoming noted as a bibliographic center as well
as a research collection.   Many of its rarest treasures are
now available in photocopies or microform, and well-prepared
bibliographies make the Vatican Library useful to almost
anyone in the world.

     The major public libraries of Italy are all controlled
by the National Library Service, including the National Central Libraries at Rome and Florence and some 30 other
state libraries, many of which were formerly important private or ecclesiastical collections.   In 1875, the majority of
the monastery libraries in Italy were taken over by the government and these formed the basis of the present state library
system.   The National Central Library of Rome has some
2, 200, 000 volumes, while the one at Florence is even larger,
with nearly 4, 000, 000 items.   Among university libraries,
the Alexandrine Library at the University of Rome has almost a million volumes, while there are other large collections at the universities of Bologna, Padua, Naples, Pisa and
about 20 others.   The Biblioteca Casanatense at Rome and
the Mediceo-Laurenziane Library at Florence are now under
government control.   The former is a strong reference library containing some 310, 000 volumes in literature, religion,
law, economics, social sciences and history, while the latter
was formed from the collections of the Medici princes of
the 16th century.   Although it contains only about 75, 000 volumes, almost all of them are rare.   Among its treasures are
over 10, 000 manuscripts, more than 700 of which date from
before A.D. 1000.   The Biblioteca Ambrosiana at Milan, also
a great rare book collection, has about 800, 000 printed volumes and about 25, 000 manuscripts, including holographs of
Petrarch and Leonardo da Vinci.

     Most of the libraries noted above are strictly refer-
ence collections, or at least have restricted circulation.
Popular circulating libraries have developed rather slowly in
this century but in the past two decades there have been
great improvements.   Public libraries, known variously as
"biblioteca communale, " "biblioteca civica, " or "biblioteca

circolante" are to be found in most Italian towns and cities.
Milan's public library, for example, has over 750,000 volumes
and 30 branches. Popular reading rooms, and even "reading
gardens" are to be found in villages and suburbs. There is
some experimentation with library extension services and bookmobiles in some of the more rural areas, but public library
service in Italy is still not as advanced as that in northern
Europe. School library service, as known in northern Europe
and the United States, is also lacking in much of Italy although the government is encouraging the development of school
and children's libraries. On the other hand, special libraries
are growing rapidly in the larger Italian cities, with several
dozen of them in Rome. They range, for example, from small
technical collections of societies or firms, up to the library
of the national senate, with 700,000 volumes, or the United
Nations Agricultural Library of about 600,000 books. In the
industrial centers of northern Italy, reading rooms for workers
are to be found; some of them are sponsored by the industries
themselves, others by the labor unions or by political parties.

Denmark

        Probably the best public library service of any country
of Europe is in Denmark. The Royal Library in Copenhagen
has over 1,700,000 volumes and it is only one of several large
government libraries. The University Library at Aarhus,
with some 900,000 volumes, also serves as a national public
library, and is a part of a library system that serves every
citizen of Denmark. Copenhagen has a central public library
of some 900,000 volumes, several branch libraries with over
100,000 volumes each, and a university library, with nearly
1,500,000 volumes in its two major parts and associated libraries. The university library has a major collection for
liberal arts and general reference and another for the sciences. School and public library service throughout Denmark
is excellent, and there are many special libraries in the
capital city and larger towns. A Royal School of Librarianship in Copenhagen supplements library science courses in
the teachers' colleges and provides the nation with a steady
flow of trained librarians.

Sweden

        Sweden has a strong public library system, with major
research libraries in the Royal Library in Stockholm and in

the universities of Lund, Goteborg, and Uppsala. Each of
these contains over a million volumes, supplemented particularly in the Royal Library and at Uppsala with strong manuscript collections. In addition, Uppsala University has nearly
the richest yearly book buying budget of any university library
in Europe. Public library service in Sweden is comprehensive,
with town libraries, county libraries, separate children's libraries in many cases, and library service by mail to isolated
fishing villages and other outposts. There are many special
libraries, particularly in Stockholm, including for example
The Royal Musical Academy Library with some 700,000 books
and scores.

Norway and Finland

          These two Scandinavian countries suffered considerable
library damage during World War II, but their library services have improved considerably since 1945. In both countries the national libraries are also the libraries of major national universities--in Oslo and Helsinki respectively. The
national-university library of Norway has about 1,750,000
volumes, while that of Finland has about 1,200,000. There
are large public libraries in the major cities, such as the
Bergen Public Library in Norway with 275,000 volumes and
the Turku Public Library in Finland with 325,000. There are
smaller libraries in all towns, and, as in Sweden, mail library service is also available. In the northern Norway fishing ports there are packages of public library books available
for carrying on the fishing boats that go out for long voyages.
In Oslo is the unusual Deichman Library, an endowed institution with government support which serves as the city's public
library. It now has over 700,000 volumes. One of the largest special libraries in the two countries is that of the Technical University at Trondheim, Norway, with over 300,000
volumes in the natural and applied sciences.

Switzerland, Belgium, and the Netherlands

          Switzerland has a somewhat complicated system of
local, cantonal and national libraries, further confused by
the four national languages, but it nevertheless provides excellent library service for its entire population. The National Library at Bern contains over 1,200,000 volumes,
while the University of Geneva Library is almost as large.
The library of the University of Basel is one of the largest

libraries in the nation, with 1, 700, 000 volumes. This university library (along with those of Uppsala, Hamburg, Göttingen, and Oxford) is among the richest in Europe in acquisitions budget. There are many special libraries in Switzerland,
including industrial, bank, academic and international. The
League of Nations Library at Geneva is now the European
branch of the United Nations Library, and contains some
700, 000 items.

In Belgium and the Netherlands, library service is also
quite modern, with Belgium having the problem of two national languages, French and Flemish, and the Netherlands library
scene being enhanced with church-owned libraries. Among
the larger libraries in the two countries are the national libraries and several outstanding university collections. The
Royal Library in Brussels has over two million volumes,
while that in The Hague has nearly a million. University libraries at Leiden and Amsterdam in the Netherlands, and at
Ghent, Liège and Louvain in Belgium each have well over a
million volumes. There are excellent public reference libraries in the large cities, but circulating libraries at public expense leave something to be desired in both countries. Both
Catholic and Protestant groups provide local public reading
rooms in the Netherlands, while labor unions and privately
endowed institutions supplement public libraries for popular
use in both countries.

Spain and Portugal

        The Spanish National Library in Madrid has over
2, 000, 000 volumes, while the combined libraries of the University of Madrid contain at least half as many. There are
strong university libraries at Barcelona (over a half million
volumes), Granada, Salamanca, Santiago, Seville and Valla-
dolid. The many special libraries in the larger cities include
the Royal Academy of History in Madrid with its library of
over 200, 000 volumes. The historic library of San Lorenzo
del Escorial, founded in the 16th century, has only about
40, 000 books, but its many thousand valuable manuscripts
make it one of the nation's treasures. The establishment
of school libraries and popular circulating collections has been
encouraged by the government since 1945, but outside of the
larger cities most of these collections are small and poorly
supported.

        In Portugal, the National Library in Lisbon has about

a million volumes. The University of Coimbra, with its central and faculty libraries together, has about 1,500,000.
Oporto has a large municipal library, but it is mainly a reference collection. There are small public libraries in most of
the towns, but as in Spain, both public and school library service in Portugal leave much to be desired.

Greece and Yugoslavia

        In the Balkans, the Greek National Library in Athens
contains over 1,000,000 books and pamphlets, and there are
several academic collections of respectable size. Public
library service outside of Athens and Salonika is slow in
developing and there are few publicly supplied books available
for the average reader, particularly for children. There are
some special libraries in the larger cities that are quite
modern, but library service on the whole is backward. The
same is true also in neighboring Albania, but here the Com-
munist-inspired leadership has provided reading rooms
throughout the small nation and the major handicap is the
relatively small amount of literature available in the Albanian
dialects.

        Yugoslavia has a "national" library for each of its six
major states, and these are sometimes combined state and
university libraries. The largest, as of 1970, was that at
Ljubljana, serving the Slovene Republic, but others at Bel-
grade (Serbia) and Zagreb (Croatia) were almost as large.
The larger cities have sizable public libraries, many of them
descended from church-related collections several centuries
old. These are supplemented by district or regional libraries, with outlets in virtually all inhabited areas, often
manned by volunteer workers. Libraries in schools are
strongly emphasized, although several languages and the two
scripts in use (Roman and Cyrillic) mean that there are often
few suitable books for children. There are many special libraries in the cities, but one of the most interesting in
Yugoslavia is the Gazi Husrev Beg Library in Sarajevo, a
survival from the years of Turkish domination. Founded in
1537, this library has been in its own building since 1850,
and contains thousands of books, manuscripts, periodicals and
government publications in Turkish, Arabic, Persian and
other languages relating to the history and culture of the
Balkans and the Near East.

Austria

Austria, a land-locked nation in South Central Europe, has some of the last surviving monastery libraries. Well-preserved, and often more used now than ever, these collections range from a few hundred in size up to the library of the monastery at Klosterneuberg with more than 150,000 volumes. Otherwise, Austria has a national library in Vienna with about 2,000,000 volumes, major university libraries at Graz, Innsbruck, Salzburg and Vienna, and dozens of special libraries in the capital city. The public reference libraries in the larger cities have excellent collections, but popular public library service has largely been developed only since 1945.

Soviet Union

In Eastern Europe, library service is entirely a government function and is both heavily emphasized and controlled. Recognizing the power of the printed word and the importance placed on it by the Communists, the Soviet Union claims to have the largest library in the world in the National Library in Leningrad (the Saltykov-Shchedrin Library, founded in 1795 and opened to readers in 1814), the largest number of libraries of any country in the world, and the largest number of library books in use. With the former Russian Imperial Library as a base, the Saltykov-Shchedrin Library has been built up since 1917, absorbing many private, government and church libraries in the 1920s. It is now reported to contain over 15 million volumes. Another gigantic Russian library is the Lenin State Library in Moscow, founded in 1862, with some 13 million volumes, but with nearly 25 million cataloged items including periodical issues, pamphlets, prints, scores, etc. It contains not only 11th-century manuscripts but modern books in 96 foreign languages as well as the 89 languages of the peoples of the Soviet Union. The Gorky Library at the University of Moscow contains over 6,000,000 volumes, and the library of the Russian Academy of Science at Leningrad almost 5,000,000. Elsewhere in Russia there are some 30 other national, republic and university libraries of over a million volumes each.

Generally speaking, the libraries of the Soviet Union may be divided into four types. First there are the large state or national libraries headed up by the one in Leningrad, but including others in the capitals of the constituent

republics of the USSR, such as those in Kiev, Minsk or Alma
Ata. Next there are the public or "mass" libraries ranging
from large city libraries and tremendous regional deposi-
tories down to small collections of books in factories and
collective farms. The third group of libraries consists of
the special or research libraries, ranging from national central subject libraries such as the All-Union State Library of
Foreign Literature, with 3,000,000 volumes, down to small
research shelves in individual laboratories. Finally, there
are the libraries of educational institutions, from nursery
schools to universities. From the Caspian to the Arctic and
from White Russia to Kamchatka, Russia is dotted with libraries, with 110 million "registered borrowers." All told
there were reported in Russia in 1970 more than 124,000
public libraries; 190,000 school libraries; 51,000 special libraries; and 500 special children's libraries: a total of
370,000. To supplement these, more than 300,000 rotating
library units circulated among housing developments, industrial plants, collective farms and similar locations.

There are library schools at the larger universities,
particularly at Moscow, Leningrad and Kharkov. School
librarians are trained at teachers' colleges, where there are
also courses for library clerical and sub-professional workers, and in-service training for minor library positions.
Several bibliographic and library journals are published and
there are national, regional and local library associations.
Advanced work is being done in the field of documentation, with
national offices handling such matters as periodical indexing,
printed catalog cards, and centralized cataloging. Although
books are considered as ideological tools in the Communist
countries, and freedom of the press is far from a reality
there, Russia has demonstrated to the world what can be done
with books and libraries when the full support ofgovernment
and people is applied.

Poland

Many Polish libraries were destroyed during World
War II, but by the 1950s library reconstruction was well
under way. A National Library Law, passed in 1946, laid
the foundations for wide-spread public library services. Poland obtained two library centers from Germany after World
War II. These cities, Danzig [now Gdansk] and Breslau
[Wrocław] contained numerous libraries, both ancient and
modern. The University of Wrocław contains over a million

volumes. The National Library at Warsaw contains 2,100,000
volumes, while the public library in the same city has 121
branches and over two million volumes in all. Among university libraries in Poland, that at Warsaw is the largest
with 2,300,000 volumes, while there are other major universities at Kraków (Jagellonian University, 1,200,000 volumes)
and Toruń (Copernicus University, one million volumes). The
public library system is well organized, with central public
libraries, branch libraries, and book deposits in industrial
plants. Overall there are more than 30,000 public library
service points in the nation and virtually every citizen is
reached by one or more of the library units. Some 27,000
school libraries supplement the public library system, and
in addition there are a number of excellent government and
special libraries, particularly in Warsaw. Poland has library
schools in its main universities and there are also training
classes for library workers in the larger public libraries.

Rumania and Bulgaria

          Libraries in these two countries are almost entirely
under control of the national governments. There were a few
important reference collections but little popular library service prior to World War II. Since then, under Communist
domination, library service in the best Russian traditions
has been introduced. The largest library in Rumania is the
library of the Rumanian People's Academy in Bucharest, with
nearly 4,000,000 volumes and many rare manuscripts. This
serves as a national research library, while the Central
State Library, also in Bucharest, heads up a national public
library system. There are public libraries in the larger
towns and reading rooms on the village level. Important
university libraries are to be found in Bucharest, Iasi, and
Cluj, each with over a million volumes. There are several
large special libraries in the capital city, such as the Lenin
Institute of Economic Sciences, with a library of over 400,000
volumes. The two largest libraries in Bulgaria are both in
Sofia: The Kolarov State Library with over 750,000 volumes
and the Sofia State University Library of about 700,000. There
is a special children's library in Sofia with nearly 50,000
volumes as a part of a public library system of over 250,000.
District libraries of 50,000 to 100,000 volumes serve large
regional areas, with popular libraries and reading rooms
throughout the nation. There are several other colleges and
institutes, and also governmental and special libraries in the
capital. In both Rumania and Bulgaria there is a strong

222 Communication

emphasis on providing library services, and both popular and
technical libraries are growing rapidly.

Czechoslovakia and Hungary

    In Czechoslovakia, much library progress had been
made in the period between the country's independence in 1919
and World War II. A public library organized along western
lines was developed in Prague. It contained some 400,000 volumes by 1938, by which time the combined National-University Library in the same city had about a million volumes.
After 1945, under Communist domination, Czech libraries
went through a drastic upheaval. There was censorship of
bookstacks, old libraries were closed and many new ones
were opened. Historic reference libraries were thrown open
for public use, including those at the universities of Olmütz,
Brunn, and Bratislava. By 1970, the National Library in
Prague (the State Library of the CSSR) contained some
4,000,000 items and headed up a national bibliographic and
library service system that covered the nation. Supplementary "national" libraries are in Martin and Bratislava, and
the national library system as a whole includes some 60,000
library outlets of all types. Among major special libraries
in Prague are a National Museum Library (over a million
volumes), a National Medical Library (165,000) and a
Central Agricultural and Forestry Library (450,000).

    In Hungary, the National Library in Budapest and
other major libraries were also rebuilt along Communist
lines in 1945. By 1970, the National Széchényi Library had
over 1,500,000 volumes, while the public (Ervin Szábo) Library in the same city had over 2,000 volumes serviced
through 110 branches. Public library service throughout the
nation stems from large municipal and district libraries and
is channeled through thousands of smaller outlets. Important
university libraries are at Budapest, Szeged, Debrecen, and
Pécs and there is a Central Technical Library and Documentation center in Budapest also. Among many modern special
libraries are a National Agricultural Library of 150,000 volumes and a National Academy of Sciences Library with
800,000.

The Near East

The new nation of Israel has made great library progress since its founding in 1948. The Hebrew University in Jerusalem, which also serves as the National Library, has over a million volumes, including over 200,000 volumes in Hebrew, the largest collection of Hebraica in the world. Other large research libraries are at the University of Tel Aviv (300,000 volumes) and at the Haifa Technion (the Israeli Institute of Technology). There are several specialized government libraries in Jerusalem and Tel Aviv. Public library service is provided from some 700 public and endowed libraries and reading rooms, while the Ministry of Education provides school libraries and libraries for some rural settlements.

Egypt has its National Library at Cairo with over 800,000 volumes and important university libraries at Alexandria, Cairo, and Assiut. The University Library at Alexandria has over a million volumes, while the ancient university of El Azhar has only 80,000, but including some extremely valuable Arabic manuscripts. There are public libraries in the larger towns, and a newly formed National Information and Documentation Center in Cairo.

Syria and Lebanon have some modern libraries, such as that of the American University of Beirut, but also several smaller collections of great value for their contents. The Bibliothèque Orientale at St. Joseph University in Beirut, for example, contains thousands of volumes of rare literature in the Arabic languages. The University of Damascus in Syria also has a growing library, combining both the old and new in contents, and there are small government libraries in both countries. Public and school library services lag in both countries.

Turkey has at Ankara its National Library with some 500,000 volumes, and there are important university libraries in Ankara and Istanbul. Robert College at Istanbul has a modern library of about 100,000 volumes. There are small but important government libraries in both Ankara and Istanbul and in recent years public libraries have been established in most towns. They are small, however, and school libraries are almost non-existent.

In both Iran and Iraq library service is backward according to western standards. The decade after World

War II saw advisors from the United States and from Unesco
attempting to promote the development of public and school
libraries in both countries. Some progress has been made.
Iran has a National Library in Teheran with about 100,000
volumes; the Parliament (Majlis) Library there has about
300,000. Iraq has a valuable university library at Baghdad,
with over 150,000 volumes and notable public libraries in
Baghdad and Mosul. There are other small academic and
public libraries in both countries, but school libraries still
leave much to be desired.

Australia and New Zealand

Australia and New Zealand have quite progressive library systems, including public, school and university libraries. In Australia the public libraries are under state rather
than national control and each of the Australian states has a
large central library. It serves as a reference collection and
as a circulating library for the capital city in some cases.
It also provides extension services in the form of interlibrary
loans and package libraries to outlying villages and farms.
The Public Library of South Australia at Adelaide, for example, has 675,000 volumes. The one in Victoria at Melbourne has over 850,000. The National Library in Canberra,
founded in 1927, is a fast growing collection designed to
serve both as a national library and a parliamentary reference
collection. With about 700,000 volumes it is smaller than
some of the state libraries, but it is supplemented by other,
more specialized governmental collections. There are also
municipal circulating libraries in the larger cities and public
libraries in most of the smaller towns. The University of
Sydney, with over 1,000,000 volumes, has one of the largest
academic libraries, but there are also excellent ones at the
other state universities, and at the National University in
Canberra. School library service in Australia has been
strongly promoted in the past two decades, and the latest ideas
and methods from the United States and England are being
adopted. The University of New South Wales offers a degree
in librarianship and there are also training schools for sub-
professionals and library assistants in some of the larger libraries. The Library Association of Australia, formed in
1937, has been most active in promoting library service of
all types.

In both Australia and New Zealand commercial or
subscription libraries are popular in many cities. New

Zealand in particular has a wide variety of these semi-public collections, some of which receive small public appropriates but still make a small charge for the use of their books. On the other hand, the strictly public libraries also have rental collections of fiction and popular nonfiction. Between the two, however, urban New Zealand has very adequate library service and since 1945 the National Library Service has supplied bookmobile and package library service to virtually all citizens of the two major islands. The National Library Service is divided into four parts: the National Library, the Country Library Service, the School Library Service, and the National Library School. The National Library and its four branches have nearly 3,000,000 volumes at their disposal. Independent of this service, but relying on it for interlibrary loans and bibliographic services, are the municipal libraries of the larger towns and cities. Wellington Public Library, one of the largest, has 11 branches and over 300,000 volumes. The General Assembly Library, also in Wellington, has about the same number and there are four major universities and two colleges in the University of New Zealand system. Their combined libraries total well over a million volumes. A union catalog of non-fiction in the major libraries, as well as a union list of serials, is maintained in the National Library. It also publishes an Index To New England Serials and a current national bibliography as well as many subject bibliographies and reading lists. The New Zealand Library Association is quite active and has been prominent in recent years in a national movement to improve rural school and public libraries.

Republic of South Africa

There are excellent public libraries in Johannesburg and Cape Town and several large university libraries elsewhere in South Africa. The Johannesburg Public Library has over a million volumes and 33 branches, providing service to hospitals and other institutions, and by bookmobile to outlying suburbs. This library, as did many others in South Africa, operated on a fee system until 1938 but since that date it has been a free circulating library. Other public libraries in South Africa are following this lead, but subscription libraries are still popular in most towns and cities. The National Library in Pretoria has over 600,000 volumes, but the South African Library at Cape Town is also considered a national library and with its 400,000 volumes it is the most important historical library in the Republic. There are strong university libraries at Cape Town, Pretoria,

Stellenbosch, Johannesburg and Durban. The University of
Stellenbosch, for example, has some 300,000 volumes,
while the University of the Witwatersrand at Johannesburg
has over 400,000. Regional libraries serve the more rural
areas, particularly in Natal and the Transvaal. Service to
native black Africans is limited, although Johannesburg does
have branch libraries for non-whites and other public libraries are open to them on certain days. There is a South
African Library Association, a library journal, and a library
school at Cape Town. In neighboring Southwest Africa, there
is a public library at Windhoek, the capital, but very little
library service elsewhere.

Central Africa

        On the frontiers of the modern library world are the
newly independent countries of Central Africa and their older
free neighbors, Liberia and Ethiopia. Here are found high
hopes and a few modern libraries, but low incomes, high
illiteracy, and few educators and librarians. Some of the
larger towns have European-style public libraries and there
is usually at least a small "national library" and one or more
college or university collections. Nigeria has a modern
public library at Lagos, a university library of some 220,000
volumes at Ibadan, and a Moslem university in the north at
Zaria, with over 100,000 volumes. Regional libraries serve
most of the nation from district library centers. Ghana has
a national Library Board with a central collection of some
400,000 vloumes at Accra and a regional branch at Kumasi
with over 45,000 volumes. The Balme Library at the University of Ghana, in Accra, has about 150,000 volumes. In
the same city there are several governmental departmental
libraries of a few thousand volumes each. Zaire has a National Library and Archives in Kinshasa with over 600,000
volumes, and a university library of 180,000. Liberia has
a new university library and also a public library in Monrovia, but both are relatively small. The former French
colonies in West Africa, now the independent states of
Senegal, Mali, Upper Volta, Niger and Chad, are provided
with some public library service by the IFAN (Institute Fran-
çais d'Afrique Noir), but these are mostly small except for
the headquarters library in Dakar.

East Africa

There are small public and college libraries in Kenya
and Tanzania. National Library Services were created in
both nations in the 1960s, with aid from Unesco, and plans
are under way for improvement in public, school and college
libraries. The Tanzania Library Service has about 140,000
volumes serviced from its headquarters in Dar-Es-Salaam,
while Kenya's headquarters library in Nairobi alone has
40,000. Nairobi also has an endowed public library, the
McMillan Memorial Library of 65,000 volumes, and a university library of 90,000. Makere University, in Kampala,
Uganda, is one of the largest libraries in East Africa, with
over 130,000 volumes. The East African School of Librarianship in connected with this university. Ethiopia has a small
national library, a university library, and a public library in
Addis Ababa. One of the newest countries in Southern Africa
is Botswana, the former British protectorate of Bechuana-
land. Here a new national library was opened in 1968 with
about 12,000 volumes, and it was noted that at that time
there were hardly 50,000 books in the whole nation of
600,000 people.

North Africa

In the rest of Moslem north Africa, as in Egypt, the
library scene includes a few ancient libraries of rare books,
a few modern ones, and little public or school library service. Algeria has a national library of 600,000 volumes and
a university library of 400,000, both in Algiers. There are
also public libraries of some size in Bone, Constantine and
Oran. Morocco has an ancient and valuable library at the
Kairouine University in Fez, founded in the 13th century.
There is also a national library in the capital city of Rabat.
Both Tunisia and Libya have national libraries, and public
libraries in the larger cities. The national library in Tunis
has over 500,000 volumes, largely in French, but with a
rapidly expanding Arabic collection. Both countries have
governmental agencies for the promotion of library service.

In all of the African nations there are usually foreign
governmental libraries to be found in the capital cities. The
United States Information Service provides collections of books
in many of the countries, as does also the British Council.
The Soviet Union is also entering this field of activity, and
some other countries as well. In 1953 Unesco sponsored a

seminar on public libraries in Africa at Ibadan in Nigeria.
This was a working conference which attempted to ascertain
just what library services were needed, and how they could
be obtained. The results of this seminar were published in
a manual, The Development of Public Libraries in Africa.
The creation of national library services in several countries,
along with programs for library training, national bibliographies, union catalogs and similar ventures, is a direct result
of Unesco programs. The future for library services in
Africa is bright, but lack of economic support, the numerous
languages, and a shortage of librarians will continue to
hamper its development.

China

Turning to the library scene in Asia, it can be seen
that library history in China is almost as ancient as that
nation itself, for the Chinese have always respected learning.
But modern China, partly because of wars and economic
troubles, has been slow to develop a widespread library system. In the 1920s some progress was made, with the development of several large university libraries, many with
American or other foreign aid, and over 500 public libraries
in the larger towns and cities. The years between 1930 and
1950 saw China torn in wars between nationalists and Communists, and between both and the Japanese, so that library
service went backwards instead of forwards. Many libraries
were destroyed, or suffered from moving and neglect. Since
1949, the new Communist government has placed considerable
importance on books and has set up a Bureau of Libraries in
its Department of Cultural Affairs. Between 1952 and 1959,
public libraries increased tenfold, while college and university libraries were more than doubled in number, and tripled
in size. The National Library in Peking has nearly
5,000,000 volumes, and this is supplemented by special collections, including the Central Library of the Academy of
Science with over 2,000,000. Each province has a major
central library, ranging in size from a few hundred thousand
to over a million volumes. Municipal and university libraries are also large in many cases, with the public library in
Tientsin having over 800,000 volumes, and the Peking University Library over 2,000,000. In addition to these there
are hundreds of smaller public and academic libraries, labor
union libraries, commune libraries, collective farm libraries, and reading rooms throughout the nation.

Taiwan

On Taiwan, where the Republic of China has existed
since 1949, there has been considerable library progress.
There is a National Library in Taipei with some 300,000 volumes, provincial libraries at Taipei and Taichung, and 17
other municipal libraries. The provincial library at Taipei
has about 340,000 volumes, and five branches. The National
University in Taipei has a library of about 750,000 volumes
and there are several other universities and colleges with respectable libraries. One of the outstanding special libraries
is that of the Academia Sinica, which has about 300,000 volumes, largely on Chinese history and literature. There are
other special and government libraries of note and also a
Central Educational Materials Center which supplies books
and other teaching materials to educators throughout the island.

Japan

Japanese libraries, before 1945, consisted mainly of
government and academic collections, and the Imperial Library in Tokyo was the largest and most important. Tokyo
had a municipal reference library established in 1908 but it
was burned with its 400,000 books during World War II. It
was not reopened until 1957, but it has now exceeded its
pre-war size. Although public library service in the western
style is still somewhat foreign to Japan, much progress has
been made since the passage of a national Library Law in
1950. Under this act public libraries are under general
government control but with considerable local autonomy, and
libraries are being established at the prefectural and municipal levels. Many of these in the central prefectural level
and in the major cities number their collections in the hundreds
of thousands of volumes. Bookmobiles help to extend library
service to rural areas, but circulating libraries are still the
exception rather than the rule in many parts of Japan. In
some towns and cities central reference collections serve
school students rather than individual school libraries. On
the other hand, college and university library service is quite
advanced in Japan, with some 50 major universities having
libraries up to 2,500,000 volumes, and over 100 other colleges and technical institutes. The National Diet Library includes a Central Library of over a million volumes, the Ueno
Library (former Imperial Library), and two other major
government collections. It publishes a national bibliography
and a periodicals index. A major library school has been

established at the University of Tokyo and there are also
courses for librarians available at several other colleges and
universities.

The Philippines

        In the Philippines, libraries suffered considerably dur-
ing World War II when an estimated 95 per cent of all library
books in Manila were destroyed. Since 1945, aid from the
United States and Unesco has helped in the rebuilding of
Philippine libraries, and considerable progress has been made.
The former National Library has been reorganized as the
Bureau of Public Libraries, and under its direction an attempt
has been made to establish public libraries throughout the islands. The Central Bureau library has about 300,000 volumes,
but most of the libraries are small, and it has been estimated
that not over 25 per cent of all citizens have access to library
service. As an example, even in Manila the largest public library has only about 60,000 volumes. School library service
is under the national Bureau of Educational Services, but
books are so few that there are only about one library book
for every two students in the public schools. Among the major
universities are the University of the Philippines, with about
400,000 volumes in its libraries, and the University of Santo
Tomas, with about 175,000.   The Philippines are virtually
unique in that there are a number of commercially operated
private universities, most of whom offer little or no library
service. There is an Institute of Library Science at the University of the Philippines, a Philippine Library Association,
and as Association of Special Libraries.

South Korea

        Library service in the Republic of Korea has grown
rapidly in the last few years.   Korea has an ancient history,
but has suffered in the 20th century from a long period of
control by the Japanese, followed by a decade of war and in-
ternal conflict.   On the national level in South Korea there is
a Central National Library and a National Assembly Library.
The former heads up a nationwide public library system and
contains some 450,000 volumes.   About a third of this collection consists of the old Royal Korean Library, and is filled
with rare books and manuscripts relating to all phases of
East Asian history and culture.   The National Assembly library
has about 100,000 volumes, and serves as the library for the

government, and also provides some national bibliographic
services.   Korea's national Library Law of 1963 calls for the
rapid development of both public and school libraries, but
funds are scarce and full development of this ideal will take
many years.   However, as of 1967 there were nearly 3000
school libraries with five million books, and 60 major public
libraries averaging about 10,000 volumes each.   There are
117 major academic libraries, ranging from a few thousand
volumes in size up to the 625,000 volumes of the National
University at Seoul.   Several colleges and universities offer
some training in library science, and there is an active
South Korean Library Association.

India

        In India, where the British were in power for
more than two centuries, there are many evidences of English
influence on both public and academic libraries.   The larger
cities have municipal libraries, and there are more than 50
large universities, many with several constituent colleges,
and literally hundreds of institutes, smaller colleges, and
academies.   Central libraries in the universities are not
large by western standards, with such bookstocks as those
of Delhi University with 230,000 volumes, Madras University
with 210,000, and Kerala University with 125,000.   Most
Indian public libraries still resemble European municipal
reference libraries, but since 1950 a model public library
has been in operation in Delhi, with lending services, a children's department, books for the blind, and other western
library customs.   It has over 200,000 volumes, serves some
300,000 users each month, and is slowly being adopted as a
prototype by Indian public libraries.   The National Library of
India is in Calcutta and has over 1,100,000 volumes, but there
is also a Parliamentary library of some 300,000 volumes in
New Delhi.

        India's special libraries range from the ancient and
exotic to the extremely modern.   Among the former is the
Madras Oriental Manuscripts Library with some 80,000 bound
volumes and thousands of manuscripts in Sanskrit and south
Indian languages.   Representing the modern is the Indian
Council of World Affairs library in New Delhi, founded in
1950, and already containing nearly 100,000 volumes.   On the
other hand, development of school and rural library services
in India faces almost insurmountable difficulties.   There are
many different languages spoken in various parts of the heavily

populated country, economic standards are extremely low, and
illiteracy is very high--almost 85 percent of the adults in 1950.
Despite this, Indian library leaders have planned for the
eventual establishment of a nationwide system of school and
public libraries under the direction of a national library service. Dr. S. R. Ranganathan, a leading Indian librarian and
one of the world's outstanding library theorists, has written
widely on library subjects, including a volume on a Library
Development Plan: Thirty-five Year Programme for India.
There is also an active Indian Library Association which is
encouraging library development, the formal training of librarians, and the translation of library literature into the
major Indian languages.

Pakistan

     Elsewhere in southeast Asia, the library picture is
even less advanced than that in India. In Pakistan there is
the new Liaquat National Library in Karachi, with about
50,000 volumes, but one of the largest libraries is the Panjab Public Library in Lahore, founded in 1884 and containing
about 150,000 volumes in 1970. Among the larger university
libraries are those at Hyderabad, Karachi, and Lahore (Panjab University), each with about 100,000 volumes. There are
also a number of public colleges with small working libraries
and there are municipal libraries in the larger towns and
cities. Pakistan has several small but efficient special libraries in Lahore and Karachi, including a National Scientific
and Technical Documentation Center, but adequate public and
school library services are slow in developing.

Indonesia

     The Republic of Indonesia has been very active in attempt-
ing to establish public and school libraries. Before World
War II the Dutch had established a rudimentary public library
system in what was then the Dutch East Indies, but most of
these were abandoned or destroyed in the almost ten years of
war aftee 1941. Since independence was achieved in 1949, the
new government has attempted to set up a system of provincial
or state libraries, county libraries and township libraries.
As of 1968 some 20 provincial libraries were in operation,
and about 1600 of the other two classes, but all were small,
most poorly staffed, and financial support was sometimes entirely missing. There are about 25 publicly supported pro-

vincial universities, and several technical institutes and
teachers colleges, plus about 200 private institutions of higher learning. Most of these are small, while the larger ones
have libraries on the European plan, with small central collections and many institute and departmental collections.
School libraries are also poorly supported, and many have no
books at all besides texts. As in other developing countries,
Indonesia's library scene is one of high hopes, but faced
with economic inflation, political insecurity, and high levels
of illiteracy, the immediate future is not bright.

Bangladesh, Burma, and Thailand

Bangladesh, the former East Pakistan, has university
libraries at Dacca and Rajshani, the former with over
200, 000 volumes. Otherwise library service in this new
country, created with India's help after a revolution in late
1971, remains backward.

Thailand and Burma each have national libraries that
are both archives and libraries, and neither is very large.
The libraries at the University in Rangoon, Burma, total
about 85, 000 volumes, and those at the University of Manda-
lay are even smaller. Public library service in Burma is
poor, but there is some service from privately supported
reading rooms. Much of Burma's pre-war library bookstock
was destroyed during World War II, and although there was
some progress in the immediate post-war years with foreign
and United Nations aid, a change of government in 1962
resulted in a set-back for both education and library services, so that there has been relatively little progress since
that date. The picture in Thailand is more hopeful. Here
foreign aid has been welcomed, and library service, whether
public or academic, is progressive. Some 70 district libraries have been established, and about 250 public collections in
towns and villages, but these average only about 1000 volumes
each. The major university, Chulalongkorn in Bangkok, has
about 200, 000 volumes in its campus libraries. There are
several other universities and colleges, and a number of
special libraries in the capital city. Librarians are trained
at Chulalongkorn University, and the Thai Library Association helps promote the profession throughout the country.

Singapore

      Singapore has a public and national library, formerly
the Raffles Library founded in 1844, with about 200,000 volumes. Branch libraries for suburbs and outlying areas are
being created, and there is the University of Singapore
Library with over 300,000 volumes. School libraries in
Singapore are being strongly promoted. There are some 130
high schools and 480 elementary schools with libraries ranging from a few hundred to a few thousand. In Malaysia
there are sizable public libraries at Penang and Kuala Lum-
pur, with a university and government libraries also at the
latter city. School libraries are also being developed in
Malaysia, but with four major languages and several dialects
to contend with, progress is very slow. Both Malaysia and
Singapore are more prosperous than some of their neighbors,
so library progress with relative rapidity may be expected.

      The United States and Great Britain have placed informa-
tion centers in major cities all over the world since World War
II. These libraries serve as cultural ambassadors and as
models for library service in the countries where they are
located. Other nations are following this lead, and now many
of the developing countries have several of these information
centers in their capitals. Even more important has been the
work of Unesco. This cultural agency of the United Nations
was established with the thesis that since wars begin in the
minds of men, it is in the minds of men that war must be
prevented. Educated citizens and free libraries are twin weapons
in fighting the prejudices, falsehoods and fears that lead to
wars, and for this reason, Unesco is doing everything it can
to promote education and library development all over the
world. In order to promote library service it conducts
seminars and conferences on library development and library
problems and aids in the establishment of model public libraries such as those at Delhi, India, and Medellín, Colombia. It
publishes the Unesco Bulletin for Libraries which serves as
an international exchange of information on library developments and trends. It also publishes two series of library
aids: the Unesco Public Library Manuals and the Unesco Bibliographic Handbooks. To aid intercultural understanding, it
encourages the translation of major literary works into other
languages, and publishes the Index Translationum, a current
bibliography of translated works. In its "Public Library
Manifesto," Unesco has stated the aims of library service for
all countries and in years to come it should be a major factor

in the development of library service throughout the world.

Bibliography

(This list of books and articles is selective rather than exhaustive, since the amount of information currently appearing on world libraries is voluminous. Such periodicals as
Library History, Journal of Library History, Library World,
and the Unesco Bulletin for Libraries, to name only a few,
should also be consulted, as well as indexes and bibliographies such as Library Literature.)

BOOKS

Asheim, Lester. Librarianship in the Developing Countries.
     Urbana, Ill., 1966. 95 p.
Beard, John Robert. Canadian Provincial Libraries.
     Ottawa, 1947. 303 p.
Bixler, Paul. The Mexican Libraries. Metuchen, N. J.,
     1969. 197 p.
Bone, Larry E., ed. Library Education: An International
     Survey. Urbana, Ill., 1968. 388 p.
Burkett, J., ed. Special Library and Information Services
     in the United Kingdom. London, 1961. 200 p.
Burton, Margaret Famous Libraries of the World: Their
     History, Collections and Administrations. London,
     1937. 458 p.
Campbell, H. C. Canadian Libraries. Toronto, 1971.
     90 p.
Chandler, George. Libraries in the Modern World. New
     York, 1965. 172 p.
Collings, D. G. Planning Nation-Wide Public Library Ser-
     vice in Africa. Paris, 1962. 92 p.
Coughlin, Violet L. Larger Units of Public Library Service
     in Canada. Metuchen, N. J., 1968. 330 p.
Dale, Doris C. The United Nations Library: Its Origin and
     Development. Chicago, 1970. 236 p.
Danton, J. P. Book Selection and Collections: A Comparison
     of German and American University Libraries. New
     York, 1963. 204 p.
Ellis, Alec. Library Services for Young People in England
     and Wales, 1830-1970. Oxford, 1971. 210 p.
Esdaile, Arundell, ed. National Libraries of the World.
     London, 1957. 430 p.
Evans, Evelyn J. A. A Tropical Library Service; The Story
     of Ghana's Libraries. London, 1964. 174 p.

Francis, Simon, ed. Libraries in the U. S. S. R. Hamden,
   Conn. , 1971. 182 p.
Friis, T. The Public Library in South Africa, an Evalua-
   tive Study. Capetown, 1962. 357 p.
Garde, P. K. The United Nations Family of Libraries.
   New York, 1963. 252 p.
Harrison, K. C. Libraries in Scandinavia. London, 1961.
   248 p.
Horecky, Paul L. Libraries and Bibliographic Centers in
   the Soviet Union. Bloomington, Ind. , 1959. 307 p.
Jackson, Miles M. , ed. Comparative and International
   Librarianship: Essays on Themes and Problems.
   Greenwood, 1970.
Jackson, William V. Aspects of Librarianship in Latin
   America. Urbana, Ill, 1962. 119 p.
Kaser, David, et al. Library Development in Eight Asian
   Countries. Metuchen, N. J. , 1969. 243 p.
Kesavan, B. S. India's National Library. Calcutta, 1961.
   300 p.
McColvin, L. R. The Chance to Read: Public Libraries
   in the World Today. London, 1956. 284 p.
_____. Public Libraries in Australia. Melbourne,
   1947. 120 p.
Mookerjee, Subodh K. Development of Libraries and Li-
   brary Science in India. Calcutta, 1970. 534 p.
Osborn, Andrew. New Zealand Library Resources . . .
   Wellington, 1960. 70 p.
Ottervik Gösta. Libraries and Archives in Sweden. Stock-
   holm, 1954. 217 p.
Pama, Cornelius, ed. The South African Library. Cape
   Town, 1968. 216 p.
Pan American Union. Books and Libraries in the Americas.
   Washington, 1963. 287 p.
Ranganathan, S. R. Library Development Plan for India.
   Delhi, 1950. 462 p.
Ruggles, Melville J. , and Swank, Reynard C. Soviet Li-
   braries and Librarianship. Chicago, 1962. 147 p.
Saha, Jibananda: Special Libraries and Information Services
   in India and the U. S. A. Metuchen, N. J. , 1969.
   216 p.
Saunders, W. L. , ed. Librarianship in Britain Today.
   London, 1967. 173 p.
Simsova, S. , and MacKee, M. A Handbook of Comparative
   Librarianship. London, 1970. 413 p.
Taylor, Loree. Elizabeth. South African Libraries.
   Hampden, Conn. , 1967. 101 p.
Unesco. Developments of Public Libraries in Africa: The

Ibadan Seminar.   Paris, 1954.   154 p.
_____. Development of Public Libraries in Latin America:
The São Paulo Conference.   Paris, 1952.   192 p.
_____. Public Libraries for Asia: the Delhi Seminar.
Paris, 1956.   166 p.
_____. Directory of Archives, Libraries and Schools of
Librarianship in Africa.   Paris, 1964.   112 p.
_____. National Libraries, Their Problems and Prospects.
Paris, 1960.   125 p.

PERIODICAL ARTICLES

Alksnis, Gertrude.   "Soviet Russian Children's Libraries: A
Survey of Recent Russian Sources," Library Quarterly,
32 (1962), 287-301.
Aman, Mohammed M.   "Libraries in the United Arabic Re-
public,"   Journal of Library History, 4 (1969), 158-
168.
Campbell, H. C., ed.   "Metropolitan Public Library Prob-
lems around the World," Library Trends, 14 (July,
1965), 1-116.
Daniels, Marietta.   "The Promotion of Libraries in the
Americas," Library Quarterly, 30 (1960), 201-208.
Efimova, A. M., et al.   "Librarians and Librarianship in
the Soviet Union," Library World, 69 (1968), 271-300.
Fonotov, G. P. "Libraries of the U.S.S.R. during the Last 50
Years," UNESCO Bulletin for Libraries. 21 (1967), 240-248.
Galloway, R. D.   "Library Experiment in Iran," Library
Quarterly, 30 (1960), 188-200.
Hatch, Lucile.   "Public Libraries in Finland," Journal of
Library History, 6 (1971), 337-359.
Hoppes, Muriel.   "The Library of the League of Nations at
Geneva," Library Quarterly, 31 (1961), 257-268.
Jordan, Alma T.   "Public Libraries in the British Carib-
bean," Library Quarterly, 34 (1964), 143-162, 258-263.
Kase, Francis J.   "Public Libraries in Czechoslovakia
under the Unified Library System," Library Quarterly,
31 (1961), 154-165.
Khan, M. Siddiq.   "Libraries in Pakistan," Journal of
Library History, 2 (1967), 58-65.
Kim, Chin.   "A New National Library: The National Diet
Library of Japan," Journal of Library History, 4 (1969),
225-238.
Lohrer, A.   "School Libraries in Iran and the Near East,"
A. L. A. Bulletin, 63 (1969), 1284-1289.
Ma, J. T.   "Libraries in the People's Republic of China
since 1949," Wilson Library Bulletin, 45 (June, 1971),
970-975.

Nunn, G. R. "Libraries and Publishing in Mainland China,"
  Library Journal, 91 (1966), 3327-3332.
Mearns, David C., ed. "Current Trends in National
  Libraries," Library Trends, 4 (1955), 3-116.
Plumbe, Wilfred J., ed. "Current Trends in Newly De-
  veloping Countries," Library Trends, 8 (October,
  1959), 125-341.
Pourhadi, Ibrahim V. "Iran's Public and Private Libraries,"
  Library of Congress Quarterly Journal, 25 (1968),
  219-229.
Rao, K. Ramakrishna. "Library Developments in India,"
  Library Quarterly, 31 (1961), 135-153.
Sawamoto, T. "Recent Japanese Library Developments,"
  College and Research Libraries, 24 (1963), 213-218.
Shepard, M. D. "Report on Latin American Libraries,"
  Wilson Library Bulletin, 40 (1966), 538-542.
Tauber, Maurice F. "Survey of Resources of Australian
  Libraries," Stechert-Hafner Book News, 16 (1962),
  53-55.
Verner, Mathilda. "Librarianship in Western Germany,"
  Journal of Library History, 2 (1967), 144-151.
Vladimirev, Lev I. "The Libraries of the United Nations,"
  Journal of Library History, 1 (1966), 209-219.
Vosper, Robert. "European University Libraries: Current
  Status and Developments," Library Trends, 12 (1964),
  475-623.

XIV

MODERN AMERICAN LIBRARIES

Library services have made tremendous progress in the United States in this century. Free public libraries have almost covered the nation; school libraries are an accepted part of the educational process; government and research libraries abound; and new special libraries are being created as aids in strengthening the not only national but global process of storing and retrieving knowledge. To graphic communication in all its forms, today's libraries are more and more adding electronic controls at every stage.

The public library in particular has grown from a 19th-century experiment into an increasingly important segment of the social and cultural scene. In this respect, the largest public library in the country is typical: the New York Public Library is almost entirely a 20th century achievement. It had been created in 1895 with the combining of the already-owned Astor and Lenox reference libraries and with the aid of the Tilden Fund. At first there was no central library, although Andrew Carnegie in 1901 gave funds for the construction of some 65 branch libraries. Plans for a central library were finally realized when the building now known as the New York Public Library was completed and opened to the public in 1911. This building is mainly a reference library, housing the Lenox, Astor, Tilden and other major research collections, but it is one of the busiest libraries in the world. By 1913, the entire public library system contained over 2,000,000 books and pamphlets, and circulated more than 8,000,000 items to 343,000 registered borrowers. Its annual budget had already passed $1 million and it was rapidly becoming one of the most important libraries in the nation. By 1970 the New York Public Library was serving Manhattan, the Bronx and Richmond (Staten Island) with over seven million volumes and 80 branches. Also in the metropolitan area were the Brooklyn Public Library with 2,750,000 volumes and 55 branches, and the Queens Borough Public Library system, almost as large.

Elsewhere in the nation the first decade of the century saw public libraries firmly established in the larger cities and well under way in many others. The subscription libraries continued to decline as the public libraries increased in size and services and many of them merged into the newer institutions. This was not always easily accomplished, as for example in Philadelphia. There was a move in that city to merge the strong Mercantile Library into the Philadelphia Free Library as early as 1900, but it was not until 1944 that it was finally accomplished. Old established libraries were offering new services--open stacks, children's collections, public catalogs--while new public libraries were being created. For example, Louisville, Kentucky, opened its Free Public Library in 1902, and Galveston, Texas, did likewise in 1904. A few brave librarians were experimenting with branches and even with rural library service. The U. S. Office of Education, taking stock of the nations libraries in 1913, proudly reported 3062 free public circulating libraries of over 1000 volumes each. It is interesting to note though that the great majority of these were in the Northeast and Middle West while in the South and West public libraries were few and far between.

The coming of the First World War slowed down the development of public library service somewhat, but it did bring about another event in library history that was to have a lasting effect. This was the creation of libraries for the use of service men in army camps, on ships, and overseas. Over $1,600,000 was raised by public subscription to finance this venture and its direction was placed in the capable hands of the American Library Association and the American Red Cross. With the A. L. A. -A. R. C. books thus purchased or donated by libraries and individuals, 47 major camp libraries, staffed for the most part by trained librarians, were set up at training bases and overseas headquarters. Additionally, 261 smaller libraries and over 2500 supply points, consisting of 50 to 100 books each, were placed on board ships and at Red Cross canteens. These books were well used, and there can be little doubt that many soldiers and sailors, who were thus introduced to library service during their military careers, came home with an increased interest in reading and libraries. At any rate, the return of peace and relative prosperity in the 1920s saw many smaller towns opening their first public libraries, while others extended their services to rural

areas, acquired new buildings, or explored new fields of
service to the public.   Library extension, in particular,
came into its own during the post-war decade and county libraries in many parts of the nation moved out of the experimental stage.   State library commissions were active but
public funds for library service remained small and trained
librarians were still scarce.

In 1926, the American Library Association published a
serious study of the   libraries of the nation in its survey of
Libraries in the United States.   It was mainly a factual summary but it emphasized the fact that library service was
still far from what it should be.   Over 3000 libraries of
5000 volumes or larger were queried as to administration,
staff, services and facilities and a wide variety of replies
were received.   This report made few recommendations as
to how services could be improved but it did serve as a
solid basis on which to plan for the future.   Had it not been
for the depression years that followed, it would have quite
probably been followed by a period of noticeable library
progress.

The depression years that began in 1929 at first
brought severe difficulties for public libraries.   Budgets were
reduced and services were curtailed.   Branches were closed
in many cases, and bookmobiles discontinued.   But the depression also brought with it new demands for library services from unemployed who desired to improve their chances
for jobs or who simply wanted reading matter for their enforced leisure.   After 1933 the federal government entered
the library scene tentatively with the Federal Emergency
Relief Administration employing unskilled workers for public
agencies, including libraries.   In 1935 the Works Progress
Administration appeared and specific library programs were
inaugurated at federal expense.   In some cases new library
buildings   were constructed; in others, library demonstration
projects were carried on, bookmobiles were put into service,
new books were purchased, and old ones mended.   Many
professional librarians found their first employment in the
1930s on federal library projects and many future librarians
found their first interest in library work while employed as
W. P. A. or National Youth Administration library assistants.
Not the least important to libraries were the efforts of the
W. P. A. Federal Writers Project which produced local histories, state tour guides, and other useful aids for the student and librarian.   Another federal agency, the Tennessee
Valley Authority, began a regional library experiment in the

seven states touched by the Tennessee River, and brought
public library service to many counties that had hitherto
had none. The establishment in 1936 of the Library Services Division in the U. S. Office of Education gave the
nation a central clearing house for library information and
statistics and a source of guidance and planning for all
types of libraries. A number of states added considerably
to library progress by providing direct aid for public library
service in the 1930s. All in all, 1939 found 3,000,000
more Americans with library services than in 1934, thanks
largely to the library efforts of federal agencies. Nevertheless, there was still nearly one-third of the nation without
public library service. Only one county in eight offering
county-wide service in 1940.

These effects of the depression years, both favorable
and unfavorable, can be seen in the U. S. Office of Education's public library statistics for 1938-1939. Bookstocks
and circulation were up but staffs were still small and budgets stretched considerably to meet the demands. Statistical-
ly, there were 6880 public libraries reporting in that year
and their bookstocks totalled more than 104 million volumes.
Some 24 million registered borrowers had taken home over
400 million volumes and 7,000,000 new books had been added to public library shelves in the last year reported. The
Northeastern and Middle Western states still had the largest
number of libraries, but the remainder of the nation was
increasing its library service at a rapid rate. The South
lagged most noticeably in this respect, but its larger cities
were developing stronger libraries and rural library services were expanding.

Between the depression years and mid-century came
the long years of the Second World War. Unlike the First
World War, it did not hamper the development of public library service in the United States. Indeed, it tended to
encourage service. There were shortages of personnel in
most libraries and in some war industry areas the rapid
growth in population resulted in restricted library service.
But generally speaking, public library service expanded and
went far beyond the usual passive offering of educational and
recreational reading. In maintaining public morale, in
serving business and industry, and in the broad fields of
adult education and public information, America's public libraries more than proved their worth to the nation during
the trying days of World War II.

After the war public libraries saw a rapid return to
normal conditions and then a progressive surge ahead with
new buildings, new branches, and new services. New challenges arose as well, with television and the millions of
paper-backed reprints that flooded the book market. Post-
war shifts in population added thousands of patrons to some
libraries and subtracted them from others. Two groups in
particular--those under 21 and those over 65--increased
out of proportion to the rest of the population and they provided a ready and willing public for the library's services.
But in the main, these challenges have been met, and the
public library is the stronger for them. Television has
been welcomed as a communication ally and even as a tool
for library service through book reviews and book talks over
educational stations. The paper-backed thriller relieves the
public library in part of its task in supplying purely enter-
tainment reading and, in reinforced library bindings, it
often supplements the library bookstock at economical prices.
The population changes have been met with improved services to children, and special departments for teen-agers
and for the elderly.

For library service in rural areas and in towns of
10, 000 or less population the Library Services Act of 1956
produced a remarkable advance. It originally provided for
federal government aid to library extension in those areas
over a trial period of five years, but its aid has been extended by subsequent acts. As an example of one immediate effect of aid from the Library Services Act, the book
circulation in a rural Georgia county jumped from 35, 000 in
1955 to over 300, 000 in 1959. New books, new branches,
new personnel and even new library systems have resulted
all over the United States from the assistance provided by
this one act alone. In 1964 it was renewed as the Library
Services and Construction Act, and as late as 1970 there
was $16, 500, 000 available from it. By that year almost
90 per cent of the American people were receiving public
library services, although half of them were still not receiving adequate services according to the standards of the
American Library Association. Still there were nearly
6000 public libraries with incomes of over $2000 annually,
and they contained over 200 million volumes for the use of
some 52 million registered borrowers.

One progressive step in the recent development of
public library service has been the improved services available to minority groups throughout the nation. For example,

in 1913 only 14 public libraries in the South offered library
service to the Negroes of their areas. Larger cities gradually opened branches to serve them, but as late as 1947
only 188 out of a total of 597 Southern libraries offered
blacks any type of library service at all. After the decision of the Supreme Court in the school desegregation case
in 1954, Southern libraries began opening their doors to
Negroes, and this movement was finally completed after the
passage of the Federal Civil Rights Act of 1965. Today
not only are all Southern libraries open to all citizens, but
particular efforts are being taken in most of them to meet
the specific needs of all minority groups. Elsewhere in the
nation other minority groups, such as the Spanish-speaking
population of the Southwest, or the American Indians, are
receiving not only library services, but encouragement
toward their use.

        College and university libraries have also progressed
rapidly since 1900. The average college library of that
date was small and consisted almost entirely of the classics
and contemporary textbooks. It was staffed with only one
or two librarians, was little used by the students and was
usually housed in a room or wing of the college administration or classroom building. With the exception of a few
major universities, the concept of the college library as a
research center was almost entirely absent. The idea of
the college library was that of a storehouse of knowledge,
where books were preserved rather than used. The librarian was only a curator of a repository of ancient items. But
changes were rapidly taking place in college library practices: separate buildings were erected, the hours of opening and lending policies grew more liberal, and additional
services were rendered to students. Students and faculty
alike were demanding and receiving more books and more
service. The 20th-century college library was gradually
taking shape.

        Harvard University Library had, by 1900, been sur-
passed in size by the Library of Congress, but it was still
by far the largest university library in the nation. Its
bookstock then numbered 560,000, including the main library
and all departments or special libraries on the campus, and
it was far ahead of Yale (285,000 volumes) and the University of Chicago (329,000). Other major university libraries
at the turn of the century included those at Princeton,
Cornell, Johns Hopkins, Dartmouth, and the Universities of
Michigan, California (Berkeley) and Pennsylvania. In 1915,

Harvard moved into the new Widener Library building, designed to fill its library needs for an indefinite period. But
within 15 years it was filled to overflowing, and it has been
supplemented by the Houghton Library for rare books and
manuscripts, the Lamont Library for undergraduates and
some 70 other departmental and associated libraries elsewhere on the campus.

On other university campuses, libraries in the first
half of the 20th century were growing similarly, although
usually on a much smaller scale. There was a constant
striving, with varying success, to keep bookstocks, buildings, and staffs in line with the growing numbers of faculty
and students. Gradually the college library ceased being a
museum and became an active part of the academic program.
Newer teaching methods called for more student use of the
library and more faculty participation in book selection. For
the undergraduates, the college library had to provide re-
served books for required course readings and a wide variety
of source materials for term papers. For the graduate
students there was no end to the demand for research materials, rare and expensive books and periodicals, and the
publications of learned societies. Above all, the books had
to be readily available and to this end libraries had to be
better organized, and in many cases completely recataloged
and reclassified. Open stacks, seminar rooms, faculty
studies and student carrels became more common as new
buildings were constructed. Fortunately, the changes came
at a time when library philanthropy was still alive, and
most of the major university libraries and many of the minor
ones received substantial gifts in books, buildings and money.
The Carnegie Corporation, in particular, gave money for
buildings, for books, library surveys, recataloging projects
and publications.

The 1920s saw a number of the university libraries
in the South and West beginning to compete in size and importance with the older ones in the Northeast. Similarly,
the libraries of teachers' colleges and agricultural and
technical institutions took on more importance, and although
not equal in size to those of the universities, they increased their significance in their own fields. Library and
laboratory were growing together and their interdependence
was being widely recognized. On many campuses there was
a conflict between those who wanted departmental libraries
and those who wanted everything in a central collection.
Each type of organization had its good points and its weak

points, but down to 1940 the departmental libraries were the
more common in the larger institutions. As the donations
of books and funds from the library philanthropists became
smaller and fewer, many libraries turned to the formation
of Friends of the Library groups, where many could make
small gifts to take the place of the few large ones formerly
received. The coming of the depression decade of the 1930s
hurt the college and university libraries as much as it did
the public libraries. Staffs and budgets were curtailed and
plans for expansion and improvements were often put off indefinitely. Here too the W. P. A. and the N. Y. A. programs
brought temporary relief, enabling some colleges to go on
with binding, cataloging, indexing and other long delayed
projects. The W. P. A. public records projects provided outstanding library research materials in their indexes and ab-
stracts of public records on the local, state and Federal
levels. Sometimes federal funds were available for the
construction of library buildings, usually public.

        In order to extend the services which their strained
budgets could not provide, university libraries experimented
with cooperative buying programs, in which neighboring collections shared expensive materials or coordinated their
buying of rarer works. Union catalogs and inter-library
loans furthered this cooperation, and photographic means of
reproducing printed materials were introduced in the larger
libraries. By the time the effects of the depression were
wearing off, World War II came with all its problems.
As colleges and universities were called upon to supply the
special training needed for soldiers and specialists in a nation at war, their libraries felt the strain. Funds were
usually plentiful but staff problems increased and the demands for books and services for the new programs, the
newly organized academic departments, and the war information centers severely taxed the abilities of all but the
largest libraries. Under the pressure of need, however,
new methods were employed, new tools were developed,
thousands of new workers were introduced to the library
field, and the end of the war found the nation's colleges
and university libraries stronger than ever. Everywhere
academic libraries were taking stock of their assets, accomplishments and aims, and were planning for sound and
useful service in the postwar years.

        After 1945 thousands of war veterans flooded the
college campuses and both undergraduate and graduate enrollments rose to new highs. Moreover, these older stu-

dents, usually more serious than their non-veteran class-
mates, made fuller use of all library facilities. Hard put
at first to meet this demand, the libraries soon adjusted,
and once again went into a program of new buildings, an-
nexes and departmental collections. Scores of new library
structures graced campuses from Maine to California, with
most of them designed in the newer forms of modular construction, open shelf arrangement, and subject divisional
organization. Bookstocks, library staffs, and library budgets far surpassed the expectations of even a decade earlier.

The nation's largest university library at Harvard had
by 1969 passed the 8,000,000 mark in its volume count,
while Yale's collection approached 5,500,000. Some 50 other
university libraries passed the million mark, and the collection of a half million volumes was becoming almost a norm.
Harvard's annual budget for library purposes approached
$8 million while at least two other universities, Yale and
Berkeley, had library budgets of over $5 million. Several
scores of other university libraries had budgets in the millions and staffs of hundreds, indicating that on the university level, libraries were distinctly big business. On the
other end of the scale, however, dozens of junior and community colleges were getting along with only one professional
staff member and hundreds of others had only two or three.
Each year in the 1950s and 1960s new colleges were being
established and each of these required staff, books and
quarters. Money was the problem.

In the 1960s aid from the federal government was
available to hard-pressed college and university libraries as
student enrollment continued to grow rapidly. The Higher
Education Facilities Act, passed in 1963, made funds available to aid in the construction of many libraries as well as
other college buildings. Even more institutions received
federal aid through the Higher Education Act of 1965. Here
funds were available for purchasing books and other library
materials under Title II-A and for aid in the training of
more librarians under Title II-B. With this aid, and with
higher library budgets in general, facilities and bookstocks
at most academic libraries grew rapidly as student enrollment doubled and almost redoubled in the post-war years.
By 1972, there were in the United States over 2500 college
and university libraries, serving 8,800,000 students with a
total bookstock of 383 million volumes. Total library budgets for these institutions had passed the half billion dollar
mark, and 30 million volumes were added in the 1971-72

school year alone. It was a far cry from the library scene
of 1900.

As bookstocks reached unmanageable proportions, many
university libraries turned to space-saving devices such as
various types of storage plans for little used material.
Compact shelving, storage in nearby buildings, and wide use
of micro-forms helped out in many cases, while more drastic measures were necessary elsewhere. In New England
and the Middle West cooperative interlibrary storage centers
were developed, with ownership and control jointly invested
in several university libraries. The New England Deposit
Library in Boston is maintained by Harvard, Massachusetts
Institute of Technology, Boston Public, and the Massachusetts State Library. In it are deposited newspapers, state
and foreign documents, runs of periodicals, sets of little
used works, and similar marginal materials. Much of this
material is not duplicated in any of the member libraries,
but is available to any of them. The Hampshire Inter-
Library Center, in Western Massachusetts, does much the
same service for Amherst, Mt. Holyoke, Smith and the
University of Massachusetts. In Chicago, the Center for
Research Libraries (formerly the Midwest Inter-library
Center) is the result of cooperation among some 20 Midwest
university libraries. With a capacity of over two million
volumes, this Center goes a step beyond simple storage; it
has the task of collecting certain types of little used materials itself, thus relieving its constituent libraries of
that operation. The volume of printed material made available by the "information explosion" of the mid-20th century
is at least partially offset by the use of micro-forms. On
microfilm, microfiche, microcard, miniprint, or other reduced form, resource materials are being produced that
even the medium-sized college library can afford, from the
standpoint of either budget or space. This makes more information available to more people, but it also adds new
problems in handling and servicing non-book materials.

Reversing an earlier trend toward concentrating all
college library services into one central library, not only
are university libraries today decentralized by subject content into professional, college, or department libraries, but
their materials are being decentralized by use or clientele.
For example, undergraduate libraries are being built on
many campuses, while much of the recreational reading is
being relegated to dormitory or student center libraries.
The undergraduate library of around 100,000 volumes

provides most of the needs of the average student without
the bewildering enormity and complexity of million-volume
research collections.

Many of the larger universities are also fortunate in
having on their campuses special research libraries, often
privately endowed. These are usually housed and staffed
completely separate from the main libraries, but are available for research use to faculty and students. Examples of
these are the William Andrews Clark Memorial Library at
the University of California at Los Angeles, the Hoover Library of War, Revolution and Peace at Stanford University,
and the Furness Memorial Library at the University of
Pennsylvania. The Clark Memorial Library consists mainly
of rare and important works in English literature, and today
contains over 60, 000 volumes. The Hoover Library, endowed by former President Herbert Hoover, centers its holdings around primary source materials, especially those dating from 1900 on, relating to the themes of war, revolution
and peace. It holds thousands of volumes of periodicals and
government documents from other countries, including files
of over 6000 newspapers, in addition to over 900, 000 books,
pamphlets, and other printed items. Pennsylvania's Furness
Library on the other hand is built around a Shakespearean
collection and English literature of the 16th century. At
Baylor University in Waco, Texas, there is a Robert Browning Library that is justly renowned. The University of
Cincinnati has the Burnam Classical Library of some 80, 000
volumes, and on many other university campuses there are
special libraries, privately endowed and separately managed,
but adding to the total research materials available. In almost every case these collections owe their existence to the
efforts of one man, a book collector and scholar who made
his own hobby and interest a cultural asset for the benefit
of thousands of future students.

The school library as we know it today in the United
States is almost entirely a 20th-century development. The
1800s had seen academy libraries, school district libraries
and Sunday school collections, but at the turn of the century
there were few public schools with anything like workable
libraries. There was still a debate as to whether the public library should serve the children with year round library
service, or whether there should be libraries in the school
as well. By 1910, however, changes in the philosophy and
methodology of public education had decided the question in
favor of libraries in the schools, or at least in favor of

250 Communication

books in the school. The introduction of such new educational programs as the platoon school, the Winnetka plan and the Dalton plan, all involving the development of initiative on the part of the pupil, called for books at hand all the time. The concept of developing and educating the child through freedom rather than compulsion made the use of books, both for instruction and for pleasure, a necessity in the new methods of classroom teaching. By 1910, the standard goal of schools was a centralized library of at least 1000 volumes, supervised by a librarian or teacher-librarian and under the general direction of the school principal or superintendent. Unfortunately, this goal was not reached to any great extent until well after World War I.

In 1913, the nation's schools reported only 3265 libraries of over 1000 volumes, only 607 of which were staffed by full-time librarians. The total bookstock of some 6,000,000 volumes sounds impressive, but a description of the average secondary school library, which was included in the report by the U. S. Office of Education, gives another picture:

> Secondary school libraries are weighed down with books long since out of date, or with antiquated books. . . . Most of them are small collections of reference and text books, poorly quartered, unclassified, and neither catalogued or readily accessible for constant use.

The better libraries were in the larger cities, where they were often organized into city-wide systems with trained library supervisors. On the other hand, the small town and rural areas, particularly in the South and West, had schools whose library service was either weak or entirely lacking.

School libraries progressed gradually in the 1920s and most of the new school buildings of that decade provided quarters for library service. But still services were not up to the demand and in 1935 when the U. S. Office of Education compiled what was probably the most complete set of statistics ever gathered on the nation's schools, there was a noticeable deficit in libraries. A total of 27,724 schools reported libraries containing more than 28 million volumes in all, for an average of slightly more than 1000 each. But of these only 3808 reported full-time librarians; 8770 were in the charge of part-time librarians. This left some 15,000 "libraries" that were nothing more than unsupervised book

collections. There was still a long way to go in school library service and in most cases the individual schools were
financially unable to find answers to their library problems.

Fortunately, aid and advice on school library service
has been available from a number of outside sources. On the
national level both the American Library Association and the
National Education Association have been most active in encouraging the development of school libraries, the training of
librarians and the establishment of school library standards.
Particularly in the publishing of helpful handbooks and texts
these organizations have supplied a long felt need. The National Council of Teachers of English in 1914 appointed a
standing committee on school libraries and the A.L.A. in the
same year established its School Library Section. N.E.A.
in 1920 published a pamphlet on Standard Library Organization
and Equipment for Secondary Schools, giving librarians and
school administrators a goal toward which they could aim their
library development. This report, which received the en-
dorsement of the A.L.A., provided standards of size and
contents for libraries of junior and senior high schools of
various enrollments. This was followed by another N.E.A.
pamphlet in 1925 which was on Elementary School Library
Standards, also approved and republished by the A.L.A. In
addition to these, state departments of education, state education and library associations, and library schools made
surveys, studies and reports that added to the information
available on school library services and standards.

Aside from standards and statistics, however, there
were other significant developments in school libraries, often
on a more practical level. Charitable foundations, such as
the General Education Board and the Rosenwald Fund, give
financial aid to school library demonstration projects in various parts of the nation, particularly in those areas where
school library service had lagged behind. For example, in
1929 the Rosenwald Fund provided aid for 11 county libraries
in the South to demonstrate public library service to rural
schools. The Carnegie Corporation's aid to library schools
also furthered the training of school librarians and the improvement of school libraries. Most of the states gave aid
and encouragement to the development and improvement of
school libraries. In some cases this took the form of a
state school library supervisor; in others, the supplying of
books for school libraries, either in permanent desposits or
in rotating collections. Almost all states published school
library standards, handbooks, and booklists and gave some

form of certification or recognition to those schools whose
libraries met certain requirements. The federal government
aided the schools and their libraries through the Office of
Education, which published literature, collected statistics,
and after the 1930s provided a school library specialist in
the national office.

Particularly in rural areas, past cooperation between
school and public libraries has provided answers to many of
the problems of both. Sometimes there is a single library
system, including a public library in the county seat, which
supplies all county schools with books. There are many advantages to this--lower administrative costs, lower processing and operating costs, and the advantage of having to supply only one set of children's books for both school and public library use. In other areas, public libraries or branches
are located close to schools and the children are allowed free
use of the public library facilities. Also sometimes the re-
verse is true--the libraries are in the schools and are open
to the public after school hours. Either way, the benefits are
obvious, particularly when the cooperative system includes
centralized purchasing and processing. Professional libraries for teachers are often incorporated into the larger library systems. By the 1950s, many public libraries, particularly in the larger cities, were being deluged with high school
students whose school libraries were inadequate in book
stock or open hours or both. In these cases compromises
have had to be made between school and library officials and
better library services for both have usually resulted.

Recent years have found the public school library expanding beyond the medium of books and into the field of
audio-visual and other teaching aids. In fact, the instructional materials center, or learning resources center, or
some other term for a multi-media collection and multi-ser-
vices approach to school libraries, is rapidly replacing the
book-centered library. Such a center will supply all the instructional needs of either student or teacher, including books,
pamphlets, periodicals, pictures, slides, films, filmstrips,
film loops, disk recordings, tape recordings,television tapes,
programmed teaching materials, and even three-dimensional
models and materials. A large high school library today
may well consist of a suite of rooms (or even a separate
building on the new campus-style high school grounds) including reading rooms, reference room, browsing room,
conference rooms and work rooms. Audio-visual aids are
available for either individual or group use. Student carrels

may provide teaching machines, television receivers, ear-
phones from tape and record players and other learning devices. Among its 20 to 30 thousand books and other items
there will also be microfilm, microprint and miniprint. Its
field of service will include all the graphic and auditory arts;
its staff will include librarians, teaching media specialists,
and even subject specialists as well as clerical and mechanical
sides. Another approach in large high schools is toward de-
centralization, with several separate libraries in specific subject areas. Many school libraries have far to go to reach
such levels of service, but the multi-media approach is much
more common in the 1970s than ever before.

As late as 1963, only about 60 per cent of the nations
schools had central libraries and only about 40 per cent had
school librarians. Of the elementary schools, only 45 per
cent had school libraries, and only about 21 per cent had
school librarians. Over ten million elementary children had
no school libraries and of all the school children in the United
States fully 25 per cent attended schools with no central libraries. This meant that whereas some schools had excellent
libraries, many had none at all, and in the 1960s the efforts
of the nation's educational leaders were directed toward equal-
izing and improving school opportunities all over the nation.
Aid from the federal government has been available, including
the National Defense Education Act (particularly the amond-
ments of 1964), the Elementary and Secondary Education Act
of 1965, and various other federal laws. Title II of the ESEA
particularly has provided funds for the purchase of books and
other instructional materials for public schools. Aid has
also been available for training school librarians through fellowships, loans and summer institutes. One significant attempt to show what excellent school libraries can do has been
demonstrated by the Knapp School Libraries Project. In
1964 the Knapp Foundation of New York City made a grant of
over $1 million to the American Library Association for a
five-year project in demonstration school libraries. Eight
pilot libraries were selected to show how schools that meet
the national standards for school library service could improve their educational programs. Other librarians and educators were invited to visit these demonstration libraries to
observe their methods and services. The project was completed in 1968 and declared an unqualified success.

With these concerted efforts toward improving school
libraries, the end of the 1960s saw definite changes for the
better. In 1968 alone over 3200 new school libraries were

opened, and 61,000 others were improved or expanded.
Under ESEA in that year $82 million was spent to purchase
22 million books for the nation's schools. This did not include audio-visual materials and other instructional aids.
By 1970, it was estimated that 95 per cent of the public
schools in the nation had some form of library service, and
some 70 per cent of them had formal libraries or media
centers. Still, scarcely over half of them were under the
management of trained librarians. To aid in the movement
toward full service instructional centers, the A.L.A. in
1969 published Standards for School Media Programs.

  Paralleling the growth of public, college and school
libraries in the 20th century has been the rapid progress in
special libraries, including those of the federal government.
The realization that necessary books and source materials
should be at hand for all government agencies has led to the
establishment of a multitude of special libraries not only in
Washington, but at regional headquarters throughout the nation.

  The Library of Congress is tha nation's greatest library and one of the two or three largest in the world. Its
growth this century has been phenomenal. The huge building
completed in 1897 was rapidly filled and in 1938 a new annex more than doubled the available space. In 1937 the
opening of the new National Archives building had removed
from the Library of Congress most of the public records
and manuscript materials, but this dual expansion of space
was to suffice for only a few decades. As of the late 1960s,
a third major addition was under construction to help house
the immense amount of graphic and electronically recorded
information in its files. As of 1970, the Library contained
some 60 million items, of which nearly 15 million were
books and pamphlets, while the remainder included maps,
prints, music scores, recordings, pictures, motion picture
and other items. Its acquisitions increase at a rate of
some 2,000,000 items per year and its services directly
or indirectly reach almost every citizen of the United States
through such means as inter-library loans, publications, services to the blind, and printed catalog cards. Two other
major libraries in Washington, the National Agricultural Library and the National Library of Medicine, are among the
largest libraries in the world in their respective field.
The former serves the U. S. Department of Agriculture and
the nation with its 1,300,000 volumes and over 20,000 files
of periodicals and newspapers. The latter, which moved

into a new building in nearby Bethesda, Maryland, in 1962, makes its 1,400,000 volumes available to all medical and health agencies in the country through loans, photo-copies, and bibliographic services. Since 1963 it has operated MEDLARS (Medical Literature Analysis and Retrieval System), a computer based program of storage and retrieval of bibliographic citations in the field of medicine and related sciences.

There are approximately 100 other federal libraries in the Washington area, ranging from a few thousand to a million volumes in size, and serving clienteles ranging from a few score to the general public. All together they form a bibliographic center than can hardly be surpassed anywhere in the world. Many of the federal government's libraries are not located in Washington, but are scattered throughout the nation and in fact around the world. The armed services, for example, have libraries at army, navy and air force installations in many countries, and the U. S. Information Service operates libraries wherever they are still welcomed. Inside the United States there are large libraries at the service academies, and all permanent military and naval bases have both popular and technical libraries, as do the service hospitals. The larger naval vessels have libraries on board and the smaller ones have rotating collections made available through the Navy Department's Library Services Branch. Other federal agencies, such as the Tennessee Valley Author ity, the Atomic Energy Commission, and the National Aeronautics and Space Administration have developed notable research libraries in various parts of the nation. The TVA has since its founding in 1933 developed a technical library of some 56,000 volumes in Knoxville and has also maintained libraries at each of its construction points and encouraged the development of public library service throughout its area. The Atomic Energy Commission has several libraries scattered throughout the United States, with the largest at Germantown, Maryland (near Washington), and at Oak Ridge, Tennessee. NASA has research libraries at each of its major centers, including one of 65,000 volumes at Houston, Texas, and another of 28,000 volumes and 200,000 documents at Cape Kennedy in Florida. Examples of other federal government libraries outside Washington include those in veterans' hospitals, federal prisons, Department of Commerce regional offices, and many others.

Not to be ignored in a discussion of government libraries are those of the states. State libraries are usually devoted primarily to history or law or both, but they have in

many instances grown into important reference and research
collections. Ordinarily they serve as reference libraries
only but their books may be available to citizens of the state
through mail or inter-library loans. In many cases the
state libraries serve as library commissions to encourage
the development of library service in all parts of the state.
Other libraries operated by states include such special collections as supreme court libraries, legislative reference libraries, and libraries of various state departments, such as
agriculture and education. In some states the best collection
of public documents is found in the library of the department
of state. State archival agencies, which are in fact specialized manuscript libraries, are sometimes found connected
with the state library and sometimes are maintained as
separate institutions. New York has probably the largest
state library, in Albany, with more than 4,000,000 items
including books, pamphlets and manuscripts. Hawaii has a
statewide library system with all public, school and governmental libraries developed into a coordinated and cooperative
system headed up by the state library.

In a general sense, all government libraries are special libraries in that their collections are specialized, or
their functions, or their reading public, or all three. However, the libraries most generally considered as special libraries are those of professional associations, professional
schools or departments of universities, public institutions
such as hospitals and prisons, and those of industrial or financial corporations. These libraries, many of which are
quite large, serve only a limited clientele but are considered
so important to that small number that they often have large
staffs. Outstanding among the special libraries are the endowed libraries, often semipublic in nature, such as the
Newberry and John Crerar libraries in Chicago, the Folger
Shakespeare Library in Washington, and the Huntington Library in California. The Crerar Library is a technical and
scientific reference collection of 1,100,000 volumes now
serving also as the library of the Illinois Institute of Technology. The Newberry Library is a reference collection
devoted to literature, history, philosophy and music. It is
particularly strong in American history and contains over
900,000 volumes. In San Marino, California, the Henry E.
Huntington Library and Art Gallery is largely a rare book
collection but as such it is one of the finest in the nation,
and many of its 430,000 volumes are not duplicated elsewhere.
The Folger Shakespeare Library, opened in Washington,
D. C., in 1932, is devoted to material by and about William

Shakespeare, the theater, and the era in which Shakespeare
lived. It has among its 260,000 volumes the largest single
collection in the western hemisphere of books printed in
England or in English before 1641. The Pierpont Morgan Library in New York City is another endowed reference library,
strong in incunabula, history and early Americana, while the
Lloyd Library and Museum in Cincinnati has some 165,000
books and over 100,000 pamphlets devoted to botany, chemistry, pharmacy and related sciences. One of the most recently established of these endowed li braries is the Linda Hall
Library of Kansas City, Missouri, largely devoted to science
and technology. These libraries and a few other similar ones
throughout the nation are usually open to serious students,
although almost all are strictly reference libraries and some
have other restrictions as to use.

Almost as valuable as the endowed libraries are those
of the historical and other professional societies throughout
the nation. Many of these had their beginnings in the 19th
century or earlier, and their holdings are extensive and important. The Wisconsin State Historical Society is one of
the largest, with over 390,000 volumes, an equal number of
pamphlets, and more than 2,000,000 manuscripts. The New
York Historical Society Library in Albany has over 4,000,000
items, including books, pamphlets, periodicals and manuscripts. The Boston Athenaeum, essentially an historical library, contains over 450,000 volumes and several other historical collections in the nation number over 100,000 volumes
each. In addition to the historical societies, many scientific
organizations have libraries noteworthy for their size and
contents. The New York Academy of Medicine Library has
some 380,000 volumes, plus an additional 172,000 pamphlets.
The Engineering Societies Library in the same city has
nearly 225,000 volumes. In Philadelphia, the Academy of
Natural Sciences Library with 150,000 volumes, and the
American Philosophical Society Library with 130,000 are
noted for their research collections, while the Franklin Institute Library is even larger with 250,000 volumes. Throughout the nation there are literally hundreds of other technical,
scientific, legal and religious libraries ranging in size from
a few hundred to several hundred thousand volumes. For
example, there were over 1700 hospital libraries in the
United States in 1970, with an average of 4000 volumes
each.

A recent addition to the field of special research libraries is the Presidential library, containing the books and

258 Communication

papers of ex-Presidents of the United States. The Franklin
D. Roosevelt Library at Hyde Park, New York, is the oldest
of these and contains some 38,000 bound volumes and nearly
20 million manuscripts and other items. Other Presidential
libraries are those of Harry S Truman at Independence, Missouri; Dwight D. Eisenhower at Abilene, Kansas; Herbert
Hoover at West Branch, Iowa; and Lyndon B. Johnson at
Austin, Texas. Plans are underway for a memorial library
for John F. Kennedy near his home in Massachusetts. The
Presidential libraries are all under the general supervision
of the National Archives and Records Service. A very special library is that of the United Nations in New York. This
library, named in honor of the late Dag Hammarskjold, U. N.
Secretary General, contained some 300,000 volumes in 1970.

Another type of special library has appeared on the
American scene. This is the business or technical library
maintained by the large corporation. Consisting of highly
specialized books and materials, this type of library is
ordinarily used by the personnel of a particular company but
it may be available to other serious students on request.
Banks, insurance companies and newspapers were among the
first businesses to realize the importance of having their own
reference libraries but industrial firms were soon to follow.
The New York Times has a large library of books and pamphlets, backed up by information files containing more than a
million items. The DuPont Company has libraries at each
of its major plants in addition to a large one at its headquarters in Wilmington, Delaware. The General Electric
Company Library in Schenectedy, New York, is outstanding
in the field of electronics, while the American Telephone and
Telegraph Company Library in New York City is equally
strong in the field of communications. Most of the large oil
companies have technical libraries to serve their staffs of
researchers, as do also the steel, rubber, chemical, auto-
motive and mining corporations. These technical libraries
range from a few hundred volumes to many thousands and from
part-time librarians to large staffs of specialists. Besides
books, periodicals and pamphlets, they must deal with micro-
materials, thousands of processed reports, and various forms
of mechanically and electronically recorded information. To
control a multitude of materials and a mountain of information, the technical librarians have led the way in experimenting
with new methods of storing and retrieving information. They
were among the first to try punched cards, and went on through
various mechanical and electronic methods to computerized
devices for informational storage, searching and print-outs.

Library service has made tremendous strides in the United States since 1900. Whether in public, school, college, government or special libraries, progress has been made in both numbers and services that could hardly have been imagined a half century ago. Yet in spite of this growth--in fact, because of it--the library profession is faced with more problems today than ever before. More and more, librarians are realizing their social obligations--seeing themselves as something more than mere "keepers of books." As the number of libraries and librarians increase rapidly, the library associations and their members are constantly reassessing their roles. The library scene is changing in more ways than one, but the future of librarianship in the world of communication is brighter than ever, as knowledge itself becomes ever more the world's true commerce.

Bibliography
BOOKS

(The periodical literature on modern American libraries is immense. See particularly such journals as Library Journal, Wilson Library Bulletin, American Libraries (formerly A.L.A. Bulletin), Library Quarterly, Library Trends, and College and Research Libraries, as well as other publications of national, regional and state library associations. The key to much of this literature is found in Library Literature. Again, the following bibliography is introductory, rather than complete.)

Adams, Frederick B., Jr. An Introduction to the Pierpont
      Morgan Library. . . . New York, 1964. 64 p.
American Association of School Librarians. Standards for
      School Media Programs. Washington, 1969. 66 p.
American Library Association. College and University Li-
      braries and Librarianship. Chicago, 1946. 152 p.
      . Minimum Standards for Public Library Systems.
      Chicago, 1967.
      . National Inventory of Library Needs. Chicago,
      1965. 72 p.
      . A Survey of Libraries in the United States.
      Chicago, 1926. 4 v.
Asheim, Lester, ed. Forum on the Public Library Inquiry.
      New York, 1951. 281 p.
Bobinski, George S. Carnegie Libraries; their History and
      Impact on American Public Library Development.
      Chicago, 1969. 257 p.

Bostwick, Arthur E. The American Public Library. New
York, 1929. 471 p.
Brough, Kenneth. Scholars' Workshop; Evolving Concepts of
Library Service. Urbana, Ill., 1953. 197 p.
Brown, Eleanor F. Bookmobiles and Bookmobile Service.
Metuchen, N. J., 1967. 471 p.
Cecil, H. L. School Library Service in the United States,
An Interpretative Survey. New York, 1940. 334 p.
Daniel, Hawthorne. Public Libraries for Everyone: The
Growth and Development of Library Services in the United
States. . . New York, 1961. 192 p.
Davies, Ruth Ann. The School Library; a Force for Educa-
tional Excellence. New York, 1969. 386 p.
Ellsworth, Ralph E. The School Library. New York, 1965.
116 p.
Evans, Luther H., ed. Federal Departmental Libraries, a
Summary Report. . . . Washington, 1963. 150 p.
Gaver, Mary Virginia, Patterns of Development in Ele-
mentary School Libraries Today. Chicago, 1969. 76 p.
Gleason, Eliza A. The Southern Negro and the Public
Library. Chicago, 1941. 218 p.
Jamieson, John. Books for the Army; the Army Library Ser-
vice in the Second World War. New York, 1950. 335
p.
Johns, Ada W. Special Libraries: Development of the Con-
cept, Their Organization and Their Services. Metuchen,
N. J., 1968. 245 p.
Johnson, Elmer D. A History of Libraries in the Western
World. Metuchen, N. J., 1970. 2nd ed. 521 p.
Jordan, Robert T. Tomorrow's Library: Direct Access and
Delivery. New York, 1970. 200 p.
Landheer, Bartholomeus. Social Functions of Libraries.
New York, 1957. 287 p.
Kroll, Morton, ed. College, University and Special Libraries
of the Pacific Northwest, Seattle, 1961. 310 p.
_____, ed. Libraries and Librarians of the Pacific
Northwest. Seattle, 1960. 271 p.
Lacy, Dan. "The Library of Congress: A Sesquicentenary
Review," Library Quarterly, 20 (1950), 157-179;
235-258.
Leigh, Robert D. The Public Library in the United States.
New York, 1950. 273 p.
Lee, Robert Ellis. Continuing Education for Adults Through
the American Public Library, 1833-1964. Chicago,
1967. 158 p.
Leigh, Robert D. Governor's Study of Public and School
Libraries in the State of Hawaii. Honolulu, 1960. 83 p.

Lowrie, Jean E. Elementary School Libraries. Metuchen,
    N. J. , 1970. 238 p.
Lydenberg, Harry M. History of the New York Public Library.
    New York, 1932. 643 p.
Marshall, John David, ed. The American Library History
    Reader: Contributions to Library Literature. Hamden,
    Conn. , 1961. 464 p.
Nelson Associates, Inc. Public Library Systems in the
    United States. A Survey of Multi-Jurisdictional Systems.
    Chicago, 1968. 384 p.
Knight, Douglas M. , ed. Libraries at Large: Tradition,
    Innovation and the National Interest. New York, 1969.
    664 p.
Prostano, E. T. The School Library Media Center. New
    York, 1971. 256 p.
Salamanca, Lucy. Fortress of Freedom. Philadelphia, 1942.
    445 p. (A popular history of the Library of Congress.)
Schenck, Gretchen K. County and Regional Library Develop-
    ment. Chicago, 1954. 272 p.
Sanford, Edward B. Library Extension under the W. P. A.
    Chicago, 1944. 284 p.
Sullivan, Peggy, ed. Realization: The Final Report of the
    Knapp School Libraries Project. Chicago, 1968.
United Nations. The Dag Hammarskjold Library. New York,
    1962. 167 p.
Wright, Louis B. The Folger Library, Two Decades of
    Growth. Charlottesville, Va. , 1968. 300 p.

XV

THE GROWTH OF THE PROFESSION
OF LIBRARIANSHIP

A profession is usually characterized as having a body
of specialized knowledge, advanced facilities for specialized
education, and a professional association to improve services
and to increase the quality and quantity of services and of
professional personnel. In each of these respects, the field
of librarianship qualifies eminently as a profession.

The development of a body of specialized knowledge,
in the form of professional tools and technical aids for librarians, has closely paralleled the growth of libraries themselves, particularly in the modern era. Classification manuals, subject heading guides, bibliographies, indexes, and
textbooks in library methods all aid the librarian in serving
the reading public. Professional studies, library surveys,
library statistics, and works on the history of the profession
add to the professional literature. More recently a wide
variety of more theoretical works on information science and
the role of the library in human communication have been
added to the librarian's working tools.

It has already been noted that 1876, an important
year in American library history, saw the beginning of the
Library Journal and the first appearance of Melvil Dewey's
Decimal Classification System. Those useful library aids
were followed in a few years by the first volume of the
American Catalog, a current record of books in print. The
American Catalog continued to appear at intervals until 1910,
but before that date it had been superseded by the H. W.
Wilson Company's United States Catalog of Books in Print.
In its last one-volume edition, which appeared in 1928, the
United States Catalog listed more than 190,000 titles. Its
supplement, the Cumulative Book Index, keeps this national
bibliography up to date, and provides a current author, sub-
ject and title index to books and pamphlets published in the
United States or elsewhere in the English language. Another
exhaustive bibliographic tool is the R. R. Bowker Company's

262

Publishers' Trade List Annual, which is a compilation of all
available publishers' catalogs for a given year, bound together. In recent years this has been made more useful by
means of an author and title index, Books in Print, and by a
Subject Guide to Books in Print. The increasing numbers of
paperbacked books has led to similar inclusive bibliographies
in this field, although these publications are also included in
the more general tools.

    The Dewey Decimal Classification System went through
several editions before 1900 and by that date it had been
widely adopted by public, school and college libraries throughout the nation. As the new editions grew longer and more
complex, an abridged edition was issued for the use of smaller libraries. The development of the Library of Congress
Classification System provided a more easily expanded arrangement for larger and more specialized collections. Many
of the university and technical libraries turned to this system, particularly after the publication of the L. C. Classification in revised and expanded editions. To supplement the
classification guides came the A. L. A. Catalog Rules of 1908,
and Subject Headings for Use in Dictionary Catalogs. Just
as important to the average library was the service rendered
by the Library of Congress in preparing and selling printed
catalog cards. These cards, available after 1901, provided
full author information, title, collation, L. C. Classification
number, and suggested subject headings. In later years the
Dewey Classification number began to be added to them.
L. C. cards are available for most American publications
and many foreign ones, and have gradually been expanded to
include all cataloged books in the Library of Congress. The
average library can now purchase cards for almost all books
added to its collection. The Library of Congress also publishes its own Guide to Subject Headings, and other indexes
and bibliographic aids for the use of its own staff and other
librarians who care to purchase them. Since the 1940s a
printed catalog of all Library of Congress holdings has been
available, kept up to date by both author and subject supplements. After 1956 this was expanded into the National Union
Catalog, which includes not only books cataloged in the Library of Congress but many more received by other major
libraries. Printed catalog cards have also been available
from some private companies in recent years.

    Other sources of bibliographic aids for librarians ap-
peared early in the century. Possibly the most used book
selection tool was the A. L. A. Catalog. First published in

1893, it was revised in 1904 to include some 8000 titles, all
suitable for use in the public library. It remained the standard guide for small libraries, and was continued by new editions and supplements down to 1949. Another useful aid in
book evaluation and selection is the Book Review Digest,
which first appeared in 1905. It provides a brief summary
of several reviews for each of hundreds of the more popular
and important books published each year. Serving as an index
to book reviews, as well as a selected subject guide to the
new books, the Book Review Digest has proved to be a most
valuable library aid. Even more selective in approach is the
H. W. Wilson Company's Standard Catalog series. This
series began with the Children's Catalog in 1909, the first
time an extensive but selective bibliography of current children's literature was made available. The Children's Catalog
was followed by the Standard Catalog for Public Libraries in
1918 and the High School Catalog in 1926. Each of these
provides a classified selection of the latest books in each
field, with a dictionary catalog of authors, titles, and subjects, and is kept up to date by supplements and new editions.
There are brief annotations and some collections are analyzed
to provide further information for librarians. Classification
numbers and subject headings are included to make them even
more indispensable, with the result that they are basic purchases for libraries in their respective fields. Along with
other Wilson publications, they appear in cumulative form,
with a basic volume about every five years, kept up to date
by semi-annual and annual supplements.

    The H. W. Wilson Company aids already mentioned
are only a small part of the library service program provided
by that organization. In the field of periodical indexing,
Poole's Index to Periodical Literature, begun in the mid-19th
century, was the only thing available before 1900. However,
it proved not satisfactory, since it was very selective, difficult to use, inaccurate in places and rather erratic in its
publication, and after many tribulations, it ceased publication
in the early 1890s. Several attempts at a successor failed,
and finally in 1901, H. W. Wilson took over the task and
began the publication of the Reader's Guide to Periodical
Literature. This succeeded after some difficulties, largely
because the Wilson Company adopted the custom of charging
for its publications according to the value of each to a particular library. This service basis of prices enabled smaller
libraries to obtain the Wilson publications at lower prices;
hence their use was widespread. Another useful feature of
the Wilson publications was the system of cumulative issues

and cumulative indexes that reduce the number of places to
look for a particular item of information.

The next Wilson index after the Reader's Guide was
the International Index to Periodicals, begun in 1907. This
index, started as a supplement to the Reader's Guide, indexed a selected list of periodicals largely of a scholarly or
technical nature in the humanities and pure sciences. These
were periodicals not usually received in the smaller libraries and did not need to be included in the Reader's Guide, but
which were needed in the larger public and college libraries.
The need for special indexing in another field was met in 1908
with the Index to Legal Periodicals and other subject fields
have been covered by the Industrial Arts Index (begun in 1913),
the Agricultural Index (1916), the Art Index (1929), the Education Index (1929), Library Literature (1936), and the Bibliographic Index (1938). In recent years the Industrial Arts
Index has been divided into the Applied Science and Technology Index and the Business Periodicals Index, while the International Index came to concentrate more on two specific
fields and took the name Social Sciences and Humanities Index
in 1965. Meanwhile the Agricultural Index has broadened its
field somewhat and become the Biological and Agricultural
Index.

Current Biography, a collection of sketches of currently important people, was begun in 1940. It was supplemented, beginning in 1946, by the Biography Index, which
lists biographical material appearing in some 1500 periodicals,
plus numerous collected biographies and pamphlets. Other
important Wilson library aids include the Essay and General
Literature Index (started in 1931), which indexes books of
essays and collected articles in all fields, the Fiction Catalog
(1908), the Abridged Reader's Guide (1935), and the Catalog
of Reprints in Series (1940), taken over by Scarecrow Press
in 1961. The Union List of Serials, begun in 1927, contains
about 120,000 serial titles and indicates the holdings of these
titles for some 650 large libraries. This was compiled with
the aid of the American Library Association and revised in
a 1943 edition with later supplements. In addition, Wilson
has published over the years hundreds of books and pamphlets
on various phases of library service, along with many study
guides and bibliographies. By no means the least important
of their publications is the Wilson Library Bulletin, a monthly
periodical devoted to the interest and needs of librarians.

Another important firm in the library publishing field

is the R. R. Bowker Company of New York, which since
1870 has issued the Publishers Weekly, a current index to
books and pamphlets appearing in the United States. This is
a most complete record of current and forthcoming books
and as such is a standard tool both for booksellers and librarians. The Bowker Company also has published the
Library Journal since early in that periodical's history, making of it one of the most generally useful of all library periodicals. Regular features of the Library Journal include
selected and annotated lists of new books, news about libraries and librarians, and articles of practical and professional
interest to librarians. Since 1954 Bowker has also published
the School Library Journal, appearing monthly from September to June. Other Bowker publications include the American
Library Directory, which is a guide to the location, personnel and resources of libraries, large and small, all over the
United States and Canada; and Ulrich's Periodical Directory,
which lists periodicals of all types and all countries. As the
interests of librarians have widened to include non-book materials, Bowker has also entered this field, with publications
such as Resources for Learning: A Core Media Collection
for Elementary Schools.

The American Library Association is also a major
publisher of library tools. These include the Booklist and
Subscription Books Bulletin, long separate publications but
now joined together; and American Libraries, (formerly the
A.L.A. Bulletin), the professional journal of the association.
The Booklist is a selected and annotated list of current books
suitable for purchase by the average library, while the Subscription Books Bulletin is a critical guide to new reference
works, particularly those sold on a subscription basis. American Libraries provides news of the Association's activities,
publishes articles of general library interest, and serves as
a sounding board for discussion of current library problems.
Since 1904, A.L.A. has published a Guide to Reference
Works, first edited by Alice B. Kroeger, later by Isadore G.
Mudge, and then by Constance M. Winchell. Through several
editions this has been a standard textbook for students in
reference classes, and a handy guide for all librarians. A
list of Subject Headings for Use in Dictionary Catalogs was
issued in 1893, with later editions to 1911. When the Library
of Congress began publishing its own greatly expanded list of
subject headings, the A.L.A. allowed its list to go out of
print. Fortunately, the Wilson Company filled the gap in
1923 with the publication of Minnie E. Sears' List of Subject
Headings for Small Libraries. In addition to the publications

of A. L. A., which include many books on all phases of librarianship, the various divisions of the national library organization also have publications of their own. For example, the Association of College and Reference Librarians publishes a quarterly, College and Research Libraries. In addition, most of the state and regional library associations have their own publications, as do also the national special library groups.

Several other important periodical and bibliographical aids for the librarian have been and are published by other companies. The Library Bureau from 1896 to 1921 published a general library periodical entitled Public Libraries (later simply Libraries), which was ably edited by Mary Eileen Ahern. The University of Chicago Press has published a number of important books in the library field, especially the symposiums of its various annual library institutes, and has issued the Library Quarterly since 1930. The F. W. Faxon Company of Boston publishes the Bulletin of Bibliography, and has also published such indexes as the Dramatic Index and the Annual Magazine Subject Index. In 1952 another most useful library periodical was started by the University of Illinois Press, with the title Library Trends. Later Florida State University joined the field with the Journal of Library History. The Scarecrow Press of Metuchen, New Jersey, the Shoestring Press of Hamden, Connecticut, and Gale Research Company of Detroit, all publish indexes, bibliographies and general works of particular interest to libraries and librarians. The National Information Center for Educational Media, at the University of Southern California, publishes indexes to various non-book media, such as 16mm films, filmstrips, and educational recordings. In recent years, the McGraw-Hill Company of New York has joined in the publication of several useful works for the librarian, including the Educational Media Index, published in 1964 in 14 volumes. In addition to American library publications, there are a number of excellent works published in England, particularly by the Library Association there, and also in Canada, Australia and New Zealand, keeping the English-speaking library world well supplied with professional literature. Most of the West European countries also have professional journals and the Soviet Union has a well-organized system of library publications. To meet the need for library tools in Asia, Africa and Latin America, Unesco is aiding in the writing and translating of suitable library tools in all the major languages.

As far as specialized education and training are concerned, the field of librarianship also qualifies as a profes-

sion. Before the present century the librarian was for the
most part a scholar, more concerned with learning than with
the techniques of librarianship. His interest was in the contents of books, their subject matter, and he worked with
books because he loved and needed them. His interest in the
use of books by others was secondary to his own use of
books or to his desire to preserve them for future use.
Hence, even in the 19th century the librarian was often considered to be a book keeper, a protector of the storehouse
of knowledge, rather than an educator, eager to have books
used and read. Good librarians of that century became
such because they trained themselves or were fortunate enough
to have worked under other great librarians. Library processes and methods varied from institution to institution;
usually, each one developed its own method of arranging books
and circulating them. Librarianship was an occupation but
it was hardly a profession in the last century.

Library education in England in the 19th century took
the form of apprenticeships and the prospective librarian
simply learned his trade by working in a library. This
method of library training was also preferred by many American libraries during the same period and it was widely held
that apprenticeship was preferable to classroom training as
late as 1900. In Europe, on the other hand, the education of
the librarian was the same as that of the scholar, and considerable emphasis was placed upon a wide range of training
in the liberal arts, with knowledge of languages, bibliography
of all subjects, rare books and even paleography. In the
United States, library education, when it did develop, generally took the form of a combination of these two plans, with
training both in the liberal arts and in the practical techniques
of library operation.

Some American colleges had offered courses in bibliography, particularly historical bibliography, in the years
immediately after the Civil War. The U. S. Bureau of Education's monumental report on Public Libraries in the United
States in 1876 had some interesting notes on the subject of
library training:

> It is clear that the librarian must soon be called
> upon to assume a distinct position as something
> more than a mere custodian of books, and the sci-
> entific scope and value of his office be recognized
> and estimated in a becoming manner. . . . To
> meet the demands that will be made on him should

he be granted opportunities for instruction in all
the departments of library science.

This instruction in library science was slow in coming, however. A few universities did begin to offer courses in "reference and bibliography" or "books and reading, " but it was not
until 1887 that the first school of librarianship was opened.
Melvil Dewey had proposed a formal library school at the
Buffalo meeting of the American Library Association in 1883,
and in the fall of 1887 he opened such a school at Columbia
University in New York City.   This location was not satisfactory, so in 1889, Dewey moved his school to Albany when
he became librarian of the New York State Library there.
He gradually built up a competent faculty and soon had a student body of 30 to 50 each year.   His curriculum was a
practical one, in line with the general educational tendency
toward technical training that was then in vogue. He taught
the actual processes of selecting, acquiring, processing,
arranging and circulating library books. His courses included
phases of library work now considered clerical rather than
professional, such as typewriting, library handwriting, book
lettering and book repairing.

In the 1890s, three "institutes" began offering courses
in library science. These were Pratt in Brooklyn, Drexel in
Philadelphia, and Armour in Chicago. They were joined in
the next decade by schools at Syracuse University, Western
Reserve in Cleveland, the University of Wisconsin, and the
University of Illinois (transferred from Armour). About the
same time the public libraries of several cities began formal
training classes for librarians--among them were New York,
Atlanta, St. Louis and Los Angeles. Still another type of
library training could be obtained at summer schools held at
several colleges and universities before 1920. Wherever it
was taught, library training in the early years of the century
emphasized the practical aspects of librarianship, and the
highest prerequisite for library courses was usually the junior
year of college.

In 1913, the U. S. Bureau of Education reported rather
fully on the status of library training in the nation and noted
the small number of colleges offering library science courses.
Of some 900 colleges and universities queried, only about a
dozen offered full courses in the field, with a few more offering summer library institutes or courses designed especially
for teacher-librarians.   About one college in ten offered
some type of training in the use of books and libraries,

although there was considerable variance in the length and
content of the courses given and in the credit or degrees
granted for library training. Courses ranged anywhere from
a few months to two years in length and most classwork
continued to emphasize the practical side of library work.

Prior to 1920, library training presented a most confused picture. There was no general agreement on what
should be taught in library science courses or at what stage
in one's formal education they should be given. Library
training was being offered variously in public libraries, technical institutes, liberal arts colleges, teachers colleges,
and universities, and no one was sure who was doing the best
job. Some thought that any educated person could learn the
necessary routines to run a library in short order, while
others considered sound training in the techniques of operating
a library more important than knowledge of the contents of
books. This confusion tended to work against the professional standing of the graduates of the various schools, so
there soon arose a demand for standardization of library
schools and their curricula. In 1915, ten library schools
joined together to form the Association of American Library
Schools, with the purpose of standardizing entrance requirements and reforming curricula. This still did not solve the
problems, however, and in 1919, Carnegie Corporation aid
was obtained for a thorough study of the library training
field. Charles C. Williamson, then on the New York Public
Library staff, had been an outspoken critic of current library
training methods, and was selected to do the necessary research for the Carnegie study.

Williamson's report was completed and most of it published in 1923 (the complete version--The Williamson Reports
of 1921 and 1923--was issued in 1971 by Scarecrow Press).
In many respects it marked a turning point in the modern
era of library training. Williamson surveyed the library
school curricula, entrance requirements, teaching staffs,
methods of instruction, and textbooks. He found confusion
between professional and clerical training and recommended
that library schools teach professional courses only, while
training classes conducted by libraries could be used for
teaching library techniques to clerical workers. He recommended more standardization in the library school curricula,
particularly in the first year. Finding only two schools that
required a college degree for admission, he recommended that
all should have this requirement. Concerning the teaching
staffs in the library schools, Williamson noted that only 52

per cent were college graduates themselves, only 7 per cent
of them had ever had any training in teaching and nearly a
third had had little or no practical experience in library work.
He particularly noted the lack of adequate textbooks and the
reliance on the lecture method of teaching. He recommended
better qualified teachers, more class discussion, more and
better supervised field work, and improved textbooks. The
need for more library schools and more students was pointed
out, as well as the need for certification of professionally
trained librarians. Finally, the need for postgraduate library
courses in specialized and advanced fields was recognized
and considerable emphasis on cultural rather than technical
courses was encouraged. On the whole, Williamson's findings concerning library training were not flattering to the
profession but his recommendations were sound and they were
adopted in considerable degree, if gradually, over the next
decade.

Along with the funds for Williamson's study, the Carnegie Corporation provided support, over a ten-year period,
for the promotion and extension of library training. A Board
of Education for Librarianship was established by the American Library Association in 1924 and this group proceeded to
plan for the accreditation of library schools. It also aided
and encouraged the development of new library schools. In
1926, the New York State Library School at Albany was returned to Columbia University where it became the School of
Library Service. Dr. Williamson became its head and was
able to carry out some of his own recommendations. The
Carnegie Corporation made available funds for the establishment of two Southern library schools, one at Hampton Institute, Virginia, for Negroes and one at the University of North
Carolina. It also aided in the establishment of the graduate
school of library science at the University of Chicago. By
1930, graduate library courses--that is, courses beyond the
first year--were offered at Michigan, Illinois, California,
Columbia and Chicago, and Carnegie fellowships are available
for the best qualified students applying for admissions at any
of these schools. With the beginning of advanced library study
leading to M.A. and Ph.D. degrees, the training of librarians entered a new phase.

In 1926, there were only 14 library schools accredited
by the Board of Education for Librarianship, but this figure
had reached 30 by 1942. These accredited schools were
divided into three classes. Type I schools required college
graduation for admission and/or gave advanced library

courses beyond the first year. Type II schools had the same
entrance requirements, but gave only one year of library
training. Type III schools admitted college undergraduates,
usually at the senior year and gave only one year of library
courses. In addition to these, however, there were a number of other colleges, particularly teacher training institutions,
that offered undergraduate courses in library science, usually
for the training of school librarians.

        Along with the idea of accreditation for library schools
came the plea for certification of librarians, although this
was somewhat slower in gaining general approval. By 1938,
21 states and the District of Columbia were legally requiring
certification for school librarians, while a few states were beginning to certify public and county librarians or librarians
in state-owned college and universities. By 1952, school
librarians in 31 states were required to have certificates,
while 14 states called for legal certification of public librarians. Standards for libraries, that related holdings, staff,
buildings, and hours to the population or clientele served
were also slow in being adopted, but some progress was
made. In 1933, the American Library Association adopted
standards for public libraries and in 1937 the Carnegie Corporation Advisory Group drew up recommended standards
for junior college libraries. State departments of education
and regional associations of colleges and secondary schools
have set up standards for high school and college libraries.
Various national accrediting groups also have requirements
for library holdings and service in their respective fields.
The American Library Association and its various divisions
have continued to provide standards for all types of libraries, as for example the Standards for School Library Programs, published in 1960. Much of the progress made by
American libraries in the last few decades can be attributed
to this development in certification and accreditation.

        World War II brought on an increased demand for
trained librarians; to meet this demand, more non-accredited
library schools were begun and various innovations were introduced into the curricula of the established schools. This
led to a period of confusion in the years after 1945. As
early as 1926, most of the library schools had agreed to
offer only an A.B. or B.S. degree in library science for
the first year of graduate work and to require two years for
the M.A. or M.S. in L.S. After the war, some schools
began to offer the master's degree for the first year of
graduate library courses in order to make the library degree

equal to the fifth year M.A. available in most other fields.
This trend gradually met general acceptance and by 1952 the
majority of the accredited schools were also giving the fifth
year M.A.

In 1946, Joseph L. Wheeler, retired librarian of the
Enoch Pratt Free Library in Baltimore, surveyed the field
of library education again at the expense of the Carnegie
Corporation, and reported on his findings. In his volume,
Progress and Problems in Education for Librarianship,
Wheeler noted that there was still much criticism of library
schools for teaching too much detail, for being too elementary,
too theoretical, and too slow in meeting the changing demands
of the profession. He found also that not all these criticisms
were justified and that the library schools were making head-
way in meeting those that were. However, he still felt that
the library education picture was confused and librarians
themselves were undecided as to what type of training they
wanted for their new assistants. Wheeler's recommendations
included more strength and life for the Board of Education for
Librarianship and more standardization in methods, requirements and curricula for the schools. If necessary, fewer
and better library schools would be preferable to more with
lower standards. Yet he called for a strong program for
recruiting potential librarians and better salaries and working conditions to make the library field more attractive to
young people. And strong throughout all his recommendations
was the basic thought that, above all, librarians should know
and love books.

Since the old standards of accreditation for library
schools were outmoded by 1950, the Board of Education for
Librarianship set up new standards in 1951 and began a program of school visitation designed to set up a new accredited
list. Forty-four library schools had been accredited under
the new standards by 1968, along with five schools in Canada.
The new standards took into consideration the organization
and administration of the schools, their faculty and staffs,
their physical facilities and particularly their curricula. By
1956, the Board of Education for Librarianship was replaced
by the A.L.A. Committee on Accreditation, and a policy of
continuous reappraisal of the library education field was
adopted. In 1962 an A.L.A. Commission on a National Plan
for Library Education was formed for long-range planning
in the field and with a grant from the H. W. Wilson Company
this was made permanent in 1966 as the Office of Library
Education.

Communication

Other developments in library training in recent
years have been numerous. In addition to the M.A. and Ph.D.
programs, several library schools have begun to offer a
sixth-year degree, designed either to meet the increased
needs for specialization in library positions, or to train
teachers for schools of library science. As a sort of "doc-
torate without the dissertation," this degree is becoming
increasingly popular. Other means of providing subject and
activity specialists for widening library fields have included
recruiting subject specialists to take library science courses,
and encouraging librarians to take further degrees in subject
fields. The need for special talents in library services, such
as public relations, adult education, or even library architecture, is being reflected in library school offerings. To
reach librarians already in service, summer workshops,
special institutes and conferences are being held at many institutions. Aid in the form of scholarships and expenses for
such institutes has been available in many cases from the
Federal government, as for example under the terms of the
1965 Higher Education Act. At the other end of the library
training spectrum, junior colleges are now offering "library
technician" programs for the potential library assistant.
Probably the most dramatic change in library education in
recent years, however, has been in the trend toward the
relatively new field of information science. Discussed for
years--and implemented to some degree--under the designa-
tion "documentation," information science came into its own
in the 1960s. Several library schools in the United States
and Canada have redesignated themselves as "Schools of
Library and Information Science" or similar terms.

The third attribute of the profession, that of an active
and representative professional association, is very much in
evidence in the field of librarianship. In fact, the development of librarians' professional associations has been closely
associated with the growth of librarianship since the mid-
19th century. In the United States, the major library organization has been, since 1876, the American Library Association. From its hundred or so members at the beginning, it has grown steadily, reaching about 2000 members by
1920 and over 30,000 by 1970. Very early in its history the
organization saw the need of specialized sub-divisions, with
a College and Reference Library Section, and a Trustees'
Section before 1890. Later on, sections for Catalogers and
Classifiers, Public Librarians, Junior College Librarians,
Children's Librarians and other special groups were added.
Outside of A.L.A., but cooperating with it in many ways,

The Profession of Librarianship 275

are such groups as the Music Library Association, the Theatre
Library Association, the Special Libraries Association, the
Catholic Library Association, and other special groups. In
addition, the A.L.A. and its members often cooperate with
such related groups as the National Education Association,
the Adult Education Association, and the Bibliographical Society of America. In recent years there have been a number
of more specialized organizations supplementing those more
definitely in the library field. The American Society for Information Science (formerly the American Documentation Institute) is one of the more active of these. In the international field, American Librarians have joined in such organizations as the International Federation for Documentation,
the International Association of Music Libraries, and the International Federation of Library Associations.

Besides its component divisions, the American Library
Association also ties together a nationwide system of state,
regional and local associations. Each of the states has a library association, which usually meets annually or biennially,
and many of them have their own publications. Moreover,
several parts of the United States have active regional library
organizations, such as the Southwestern Library Association
and the Pacific Northwest Library Association. In many of
the larger cities and metropolitan areas there are local library organizations, sometimes largely social, but often
professionally active.

The organization of the American Library Association
has been changed several times in its history, but its basic
objectives have remained the same. The first goal of promoting library service for all Americans has still not been
completely achieved, but great progress has been made so
that today over 90 per cent of the people of the United States
are in reach of library service, which is not all, however,
completely adequate. Other objectives of raising library
standards, improving library methods, increasing the number of trained librarians, assuring the professional status of
librarianship, and providing helpful professional literature
and library tools for working librarians, have all been
generally achieved, although all need continued attention. In
recent years, the A.L.A. through its Washington office, has
taken a prominent role in promoting federal legislation of
benefit to libraries and education in general. The Library
Services Act of 1956 and more recent legislation of value to
librarians are at least partially the result of this activity.
The promotion of international cooperation in library services

and of international good will and understanding through books
and libraries is another outstanding objective of the Association.

Professionally, the American librarian has come far
since 1876. He has achieved professional recognition and a
respected place in the cultural and educational structure of
the nation. There are still many problems concerning the
recruitment, training and placement of librarians, and concerning their duties, salaries and welfare after they are
placed, but these problems are gradually being solved. Today many librarians feel that the professional librarian has
social obligations over and beyond his library duties and that
he should speak out and join with others taking action toward
the solution of public problems. Whatever their social and
political viewpoints, all librarians agree that quality as well
as quantity is needed in the profession and that the role of
the librarian in the general task of preserving and transmitting knowledge has never been more important.

Bibliography

BOOKS

American Association of School Librarians. Standards for
      School Media Programs. Washington, D. C., 1969.
      66 p.
American Library Association. College and University Li-
      brary Accreditation Standards. Chicago, 1957. 48 p.
      _____. The Preparation of Teacher-Librarians. Chicago,
      1937. 48 p.
Anders, Mary Edna. The Southeastern Library Association,
      1920-1950. Atlanta, 1956. 58 p.
Anderson, F. The Carnegie Corporation Library Program,
      1911-1961. New York, 1963. 115 p.
Asheim, Lester. The Core of Education for Librarianship.
      Chicago, 1954. 68 p.
Benge, Ronald C. Libraries and Cultural Change. London,
      1970. 278 p.
Berelson, Bernard, ed. Education for Librarianship.
      Chicago, 1949. 307 p.
Beust, Nora E. Professional Library Education. Washing-
      ton, 1937. 95 p.
Bone, Lerey E., ed. Library Education: An International
      Survey. Champaign, Ill., 1968. 388 p.
Bremley, Gerald. A History of Library Education. London,
      1969. 131 p.

Butler, Pierce. An Introduction to Library Science. Chi-
    cago, 1933. 118 p.
Carroll, E. Edward. The Professionalization of Education
    for Librarianship . . . 1940-1960. Metuchen, N. J.,
    1970. 368 p.
Danton, J. Periam. Between M. L. S. and Ph. D. A Study
    of Sixth-Year Specialist Programs in Accredited Library
    Schools. Chicago, 1970. 103 p.
_____. Education for Librarianship. New York, 1949.
    97 p.
David, Lily M. Economic Status of Library Personnel.
    Chicago, 1950. 117 p.
Dewey, Melvil. Simplified Library School Rules. New York,
    1904. 96 p.
Evans, Henry R. Library Instruction in Universities, Col-
    leges and Normal Schools. Washington, 1914. 38 p.
Friedel, J. H. Training for Librarianship. Philadelphia,
    1921. 224 p.
LaMontagne, Leo F. American Library Classification.
    Hamden, Conn., 1961. 433 p.
Lawler, John. The H. W. Wilson Company: Half a Cen-
    tury of Bibliographical Publishing. Minneapolis, 1950.
    207 p.
Leigh, Robert D. Major Problems in the Education of Li-
    brarians. New York, 1954. 116 p.
Metcalf, Keyes D. The Program of Instruction in Library
    Schools. Urbana, Ill., 1943. 49 p.
Munn, Ralph. Conditions and Trends in Education for Li-
    brarianship. New York, 1936. 49 p.
Munthe, Wilhelm. American Librarianship from a European
    Angle. Chicago, 1939. 191 p.
Pettee, Julia. Subject Headings; the History and Theory of
    the Alphabetical Subject Approach to Books. New
    York, 1947. 191 p.
Rantz, James. The Printed Book Catalogue in American
    Libraries, 1723-1907. Chicago, 1963. 144 p.
Reece, Ernest J. Programs for Library Schools. New
    York, 1943. 64 p.
_____. The Task and Training of Librarians. New
    York, 1949. 91 p.
Swanson, Don R., ed. The Intellectual Foundations of Li-
    brary Education. Chicago, 1955. 98 p.
Trautman, Ray. A History of the School of Library Service,
    Columbia University. New York, 1954. 85 p.
Utley, George B. 50 Years of the American Library Associ-
    ation. Chicago, 1926. 29 p.

Vann, Sarah K. Training for Librarianship before 1923.
    Chicago, 1961. 242 p.
Wasserman, Paul. The new librarianship: a challenge for
    change. Ann Arbor, 1972. 300 p.
Wheeler, Joseph L. Progress and Problems in Education for
    Librarianship. New York, 1946. 97 p.
White, Carl M. The Origins of the American Library School.
    New York, 1961. 211 p.
Williamson, Charles C. The Williamson Reports of 1921 and
    1923. Metuchen, N. J., 1971. 276, 165 p. (Originally
    published, New York, 1923.)

PERIODICAL ARTICLES

(The amount of periodical literature on the subjects of library
education and librarianshp as a profession is immense, particularly in such magazines as The Journal of Education for
Librarianship, Library Trends, American Libraries and the
Library Journal. The following articles are merely representative.)

Boaz, M. T. "Current Developments in General and Library
    Education," Special Libraries, 62 (1971), 179-184.
Gitler, Robert L. "Accrediting and Education for Librarian-
    ship, developments of 1951-57," A.L.A. Bulletin, 52
    (1958), 273-274.
Graham, C. R. "1876-1951, Seventy-Five Years Later,"
    Library Journal, 76 (1951), 459.
Howe, Harriet E. "Two Decades in Education for Librarian-
    ship," Library Quarterly, 12 (1942), 557-570.
Huckaby, Sally. "Education for Librarianship in Italy: An
    Historical View," Journal of Library History, 6 (1971),
    5-21.
Keppel, F. P. "The Carnegie Corporation and the Graduate
    Library School," Library Quarterly, 1 (1931), 22-25.
Lancour, Harold. "The Librarian's Search for Status,"
    Library Quarterly, 31 (1961),   369-381.
_____, and Harrison, J. C. "Education for Librarianship
    Abroad in Selected Countries," Library Trends, 12
    (1963), 121-355.
Mitchell, Sydney B. "The Pioneer Library School in Middle
    Age," Library Quarterly, 20 (1950), 272-288.
Putnam, Herbert. "Education for Library Work," Independent,
    52 (1900), 2773-2776.
Ryan, D. E. "Library Education in the Soaring Seventies,"
    Southeastern Librarian, 20 (1970), 232-240.
Scott, Edith. "IFLA and FID--History and Programs,"
    Library Quarterly, 32 (1962), 1-18.

Walbridge, E. F. "Milestones of Library History," Library
    Journal, 76 (1951), 460-463.
Wasserman, Paul. "Professional Adaptation," Library
    Journal, 95 (1970), 1281-1288.
Wilson, L. R. "The American Library School Today,"
    Library Quarterly, 7 (1937), 460-463.
Winger, Howard W. "Aspects of Librarianship: A Trace
    Work of History," Library Quarterly, 31 (1961), 321-
    335.

XVI

CURRENT TRENDS IN BOOKS AND LIBRARIES

The world of books and libraries finds itself rapidly changing in the 1970s. While millions of people are still not receiving the minimum of library service, some recent library school graduates are finding it difficult to locate responsible positions. While many libraries are automating their technical processes, using the latest of electronic devices, others are begging for just a few more books, just a little larger budget, to meet current demands. Some of the newly emerging countries are starting documentation centers before they have adequate textbooks, much less libraries, for their schools. The library world is caught between two seemingly irresistible forces, the population explosion and the information explosion. On the one hand there are more people than we can serve with standard types of library service and on the other hand there is more information in recorded form than we can make available to the ones who would benefit from it. There are more books, pamphlets, periodicals; more audio, video and micro-materials than ever before; and more people to use them. Can the librarian meet the challenge? Do we have to become information scientists instead of librarians? Do we have to put the books on tape and the tape into push-button machines? Or is there a place for both the book and the electronic brain, the librarian and the information scientist?

Long before we solve these problems, we are rapidly becoming aware of others facing the library profession. The people whom we serve want more than facts--they want ideas. They want more than a machine can give them. Librarians of the future must be more than collectors, preservers, and dispensers of information. They must be educators, leaders, and at the same time, servants, of an enlightened people. They must be alert to the problems not only of their profession, but of society as a whole, and active participants in their solution. To begin with, not only are the numbers of people increasing, but the percentage of people using libraries

280

is rapidly increasing. No longer can the public library consider an educated 10 per cent as its major clientele; it must
serve all ages and all types of readers. From the kindergarten
to the post-Ph.D., and from the casual Sunday reader to the
astronaut, the library of today must serve the total population.
No longer will the latest novels, a few children's books, and a
"handyman's shelf" suffice to meet the public's needs. Instead, the public library today must consider the ages, the
educational level, the social and economic background, and
the occupations or professions of its readers. The needs of
the teenager and the golden-ager, the drop-out and the genius
must all be met. The unemployed, the unskilled and the poorly
educated require perhaps more attention than the successful
and highly trained. The library must not be content to sit and
wait for the public to use it; it must go out and reach those
needing its services, particularly the ethnic and social minorities who would ordinarily not visit the library or expect it to
meet their needs. Such a wide range of needs strains public
library staffs, budgets and buildings with the volume and variety of the materials required and the services to be rendered.

     How are the libraries of the 70s meeting these new
demands and problems? The old answers of more money and
larger staffs does not suffice; they help, but new methods, new
viewpoints, even new philosophies of librarianship are needed.
Branches meet the needs of the sprawling suburbs, and bookmobiles, the rural communities; specialized collections or
rooms meet the needs of particular groups. Different types
of books--in native languages for the foreign born, in easy
reading for the newly literate, in large type or Braille for
the nearly blind--all help the library serve its public. Audio
or video, tape or film, map or chart--whatever is needed
must be supplied. Of course, few libraries are large enough
or adequately financed to provide all of these services, so
cooperation must be the answer. Regional library systems,
information networks, inter-library loans and union catalogs
are only a few of the methods used to combine efforts toward
a common goal. Region-wide borrowers cards, ready information by telephone or teletype, and liberal use of photocopying
are other methods widely used. Perhaps in the near future it
will be possible to sit in one library and read a book in
another by means of closed circuit television. In the field of
services to minorities, the answer lies not so much in tools
as in the approach. Library units in the areas where the
minorities live, geared to their interests and cultural back-
grounds and preferably staffed at least partially by their own
people seem to be a logical solution. The Model Cities

Library Materials and Cultural Centers being tried in Albuquerque, New Mexico, points in this direction, as do many
branch libraries in black portions of metropolitan areas.

The public library is of course faced with many other
problems. How far should it go in meeting the needs of
school and college students? Where does the responsibility
of the academic library end and the public library begin?
If the public library serves all ages, why not the student with
his term paper requirements? Perhaps the answer to this
lies in unified school and public library services, such as
that in use in Charlotte, North Carolina, or in the new statewide library services in Hawaii. In the latter case, a single
system serves public and students from the kindergarten
through the graduate level, and in all educational media as
well as books. Another question for the public library is,
how far should it go in meeting the demands of the public for
purely recreational reading? Should it stock multiple copies
ofthe latest "best-seller?" Can it rely on the paperback and
the commercial rental collection to fill this need or does it
still owe a duty to the public in the field of reading for enter-
tainment? Different libraries and different librarians have
opposing viewpoints on this question and practice varies considerably among libraries. Certainly it would seem that the
library's obligation for purely recreational reading diminishes
as other sources become available, but it is still a moot
question. Then there is the question of censorship. Public
libraries are particularly vulnerable to such attacks since
their services are open to all and since they have a duty to
serve the very people who attempt to censor their holdings.
What one reader wants another decries as pornographic or
subversive. Even the librarian himself comes under the
charge of censorship at times, since he must, willingly or
unwillingly, select some books and reject others in the
process of acquiring his library's bookstock. The question
of censorship, entering as it does into the fields of morals
and social mores, is at best a difficult one to answer. Not
only are court decisions and permissive legislation necessary,
but more and broader education is needed before a social
climate in which censorship will not be a problem can be
achieved.

For libraries in institutions of higher education, the
1970s bring problems equally as difficult as those in the public sector. One problem is related to the simple matter of
growth and progress: more students, more colleges, more
libraries, more information to be collected, organized and

dispensed. From the world's authors and scientists the amount of literature and recorded research that appears each year is amazing, even for the largest libraries. It is virtually impossible for any library to keep up with all the information appearing in even a few chosen fields. Not only is it difficult to procure the recorded literature in the first place, because of its volume, varied source and forms, but the organization of this material, the classifying and cataloging, the coding and indexing, is a task that staggers the imagination. Research libraries are looking in many directions for solutions. One answer lies in cooperation in the field of acquisition, along the lines of the Farmington plan. According to this arrangement, major research libraries divide their acquisitions in certain fields so that all material appearing anywhere in the world is acquired by one or more of the institutions cooperating. Along with this cooperative acquisition program will go services in photocopying, inter-library loans, telephone and teletype, to make these materials readily available to researchers at any of the cooperating units. Another approach is through cooperative information networks such as those of the New England Library Information Network or the Ohio College Library Center. Libraries in relatively close proximity are opening their doors to each other's students and faculties, multiplying the facilities available with no great expense. An example of this is CLIC--Cooperating Libraries in Consortium--in Minnesota, where ten large academic and public libraries are making their collective resources available to a collective clientele.

Since the 30s many librarians have felt that the ultimate answer to the information explosion lies in the development of electronic information storage and retrieval devices. The ultimate goal would be a single machine that would store all the knowledge ever recorded by man and make it instantly available on request. Certainly the current computer age has advanced considerably in this respect. Library and information science journals are filled with news of acronymic organizations (MARC, LARC, MEDLARS, ERIC, etc., just to name a few) that always seem on the verge of a breakthrough to the ultimate control of all information. Yet, the more we learn about the machine control of information, the more we realize that it is not the final answer. It helps, but it doesn't really solve the problem. One writer has said, "Scholars can produce machines, but machines cannot produce scholars." Only scholars can provide the spark that turns inquiring students into great minds; only man himself can provide the true connecting link between preserved

information and the ultimate user. Even if there were electronic solutions to the information problem for the scientist
and researcher, what about the students and the public who
are not yet ready for, or will never need, such sophisticated
equipment? Shall we install vending machines for required
reading materials? Or program our computers to answer
the standard reference questions? These or similar services
could be provided if it were felt that they were worth the cost.
But for the multiplicity of students, the trained librarian is
still the required element, the necessary link between the
book and its reader, or the fact and its user.

Of all libraries, the public school one is perhaps
facing the greatest era of change in the 70s. Education itself
is in a period of change, and the role of the library in the
school is closely allied with this change. Even while thousands
of schools are still not adequately served by "book libraries,"
other thousands are moving to establish programs from kindergarten to college built around the learning materials provided
from "media centers." The multi-media methods of teaching
are replacing the textbook approach, and the task of the librarian or media specialist is to have those materials ready as
needed, whether they be books, films, or three-dimensional
models. Some schools are trying "learning in the round,"
with central libraries serving classrooms that radiate outward
like spokes in a wheel. In this way, each classroom has a
door opening on the library. Others have a divisional approach, with science libraries or materials centers, humanities libraries, or social science libraries, each surrounded
by the related classrooms. Individual learning centers, with
audio and video facilities connected to a central source, can
provide the slow student with extra help, or enable the superi-
or student to forge ahead on his own. In such a system,
bright fifth graders can do "research" in a manner that once
would have pleased senior high school teachers, and some high
school students can write papers that would not long ago have
been accepted in college.

The experimental work of the Knapp School Libraries
of the 1960s have pointed the way toward schools that are
really "library centers" and now Phase II of the Knapp program is aimed toward demonstrating how personnel for such
media centers can be recruited and trained. Federal aid
under the several educational acts of recent years has provided
funds for building better school library programs, and the
advice and guidance of the Bureau of Libraries and Educational Technology in the U. S. Office of Education will aid in

carrying them forward. Whatever its name, school library
or media center, the school of the 1970s will be built around
a central supply of teaching materials and librarian-educators
of many skills will be needed to staff them.

The special library in its myriad forms is also feeling
the forces of change, but fortunately it is usually in a better
position to profit by them. As a relatively new member of
the library family, the special library has fewer traditions to
uphold, or fewer established systems to break away from.
Although it ordinarily has a restricted clientele and provides
a limited type or subject field of information, it often has
funds available to make the changes as needed. For this
reason it has been the special libraries who have usually led
the way in experimenting with new library methods and devices. From punched cards to punched tape, these libraries
have usually been the first to make use of innovations, often
while they were still in the experimental stage. Thus it is
not surprising that special libraries, particularly those of
the federal government, are leading the way in the development of information storage and retrieval systems. Under
the National Science Foundation, the Commission on Scientific
and Technical Information (COSATI) serves as an overall guid-
ing and advisory agency to direct the development of bibliographic and information controls in its area in all cooperating
governmental agencies. ERIC (the Educational Resources Information Centers) is an agency under the Office of Education
to control and disseminate information on all phases of education. The National Aeronautics and Space Administration
(NASA) maintains several space research centers throughout
the nation to dispense information relating to aerospace ex-
ploration. These are only a few of the major information
systems and programs underway among federal libraries.
The importance of libraries and information control to the
nation is emphasized by the creation in 1970 of the National
Commission on Libraries and Information Control. This
Commission has the task of recommending any and all programs necessary to provide fully adequate library and information services for all the people of the nation.

The non-governmental special library also offers a
picture of rapid change in the 1970s. For every governmental development in the use of automation to control information supply and demand, there are doubtless similar
advancements in at least two private organizations. Commercial and non-profit information networks in virtually
every technical field are either already in use or in the planning stage. Although some of these are valuable assets to

their subscribers, others are hastily formed, inadequately
organized, and soon fade from the picture or also drastically
change their services. On the other hand, such commercial
services indicate that there is a need for information control
that has profit-making possibilities, and unless the public
libraries and information centers meet this demand, private
enterprise will take it over. The special library in the business field is a commercial proposition, and more money will
be invested in it if it produces results. Time is money to
the business man and information control devices that save
time are very desirable. Hence the rapid use of automation,
computers, and similar devices in special libraries of private
industry, and the fortunate spin-off of their services to special libraries in service to government, education and professional organizations. One example of this is in the computer networks through which any computer-stored information
at any point on a nation-wide hook-up can be instantly available to any other computer in the network.

Somewhat different is the scene in the many special
libraries associated with professional societies and institutions of higher learning. Here, in many cases, budgets are
not keeping up with demands for service and with the cost of
materials needed and available. Many society and departmental libraries once considered adequate are lagging behind
as the flood of research materials in their fields outgrows
their capacity to acquire and digest. Many of them are finding solutions in cooperation with other collections, in donations of money and services from private businesses that
benefit from their activities, and often in restricting their
services or even charging for them.

Some of the most drastic changes affecting the library
profession in the 70s will probably come in the profession and
philosophy of librarianship itself. Certainly the problems
now facing the profession can hardly be postponed and solutions
must be found sooner or later. For example, what is the relationship of the librarian to the information specialist on the
one side or to the media specialist on the other? Can librarianship encompass both fields, or must there be three (or
more) separate professions in the collection, organization
and dissemination of recorded knowledge? If one field, how
broad can library education become? If separate fields, who
will train the media or information specialists. Where does
librarianship end and other professions begin? Even in the
more generally accepted field of librarianship, who is to be
the special librarian? Is he to be a subject specialist with

incidental library training or a librarian with incidental subject knowledge? Who trains the library technicians? Junior
colleges may train library assistants, but what about the
staff to operate sophisticated automated equipment? Must
the librarian or library administrator need also to be a computer specialist? (Perhaps not, but he must know enough
about it to select and supervise the necessary personnel.)
The more complicated the equipment used in a library, the
more exacting--and demanding--the profession of librarianship will become.

Aside from the complications brought on by technical
progress, there are other professional problems to concern
the librarian of today. The academic librarian, for example,
still faces the question of academic standing ("faculty status").
Does he rank with the professors or does he not? Librarians, both academic and public, have also been asking themselves, will organization into library employees' unions bring
better working conditions, better hours, higher salaries,
greater recognition of the profession? Or is descent into the
sordid world of unions beneath the dignity of professional librarians? As for the overall philosophy of librarianship,
what is the true role of the librarian--is it comparable to
that of the pharmacist or that of the physician? Does he
merely fill the prescription for educational tools as required
by the teacher, meanwhile giving over-the-counter service
to the informational and recreational reading needs of the
public? Or does he take a truly professional role, diagnos-
ing the informational needs of society, anticipating them and
directing their ultimate fulfillment? (Or does his role go even
further, beyond the informational needs of the public to their
social problems?) In a world of war, poverty, disease, ignorance, intolerance, and ravished environment, what is the
role of the librarian?

In the 1960s, the American public was introduced to
the "Library of the future" in two world's fairs, at Seattle
and New York. "Library 21" at Seattle provided the visitors
with a pictorial history of communication from cave painting
to computer, and then provided the latter with a staff of
operators to show how it could be used in dispensing information. There was also a conventional "ready reference center,"
an adult browsing area, and the Children's World, with the
latter being by far the most popular area with the general
public. At New York, "Library/USA" was a combination of
books, librarians, and machines, demonstrating particularly
the potential role of the computer and other data processing

equipment in the modern library. Here, as in Seattle, one of the most successful parts of the library display was an exhibit of children's literature in a library atmosphere. Possibly the great success of the two exhibitions was not so much the demonstration of the "library of the future" as the impression made on the millions of visitors concerning the significance of libraries in the 1960s.

While technological advances seem to bring the "push-button library" nearer to reality each year, most thoughtful librarians and information specialists feel that its accomplishment in reality is a generation away--perhaps even more. But even so, other far-seeing scientists are already anticipating more startling developments--for example, the eventual transferral of sensory perception directly to the human brain, bypassing both eyes and ears. The therapeutic value of this for the physically handicapped or mentally disturbed, might be remarkable, but for the normal human being its possibilities are frightening to say the least. Extending this line of reasoning, one could foresee direct thought transferral from one person to another, thought control by one person of another, direct implanting of knowledge in the human brain by electronic or chemical means, and memory erasure by similar means--all equally frightening possibilities. Mass indoctrination and complete control of society in a manner never yet achieved by politics or military force could easily be expected if such a process were devised. Man's potential in the field of communication is almost unlimited. How he chooses to develop that potential is the only question.

Whatever forms the recorded knowledge of the future may take, there will always be the problem of preserving it, storing it, organizing it, and making it available for future use. Whether it will be the librarian, the information scientist, or the members of some yet un-named profession, the "keepers of the books" will always be needed. Most authorities feel that the book itself, in its present format, will be around for a long time, although aided and extended by a multitude of other forms of communication. The future shape of the profession may not be crystal clear, but its value to mankind will never diminish.

Bibliography
BOOKS

American Library Association. National Inventory of Library
    Needs. Chicago, 1965. 72 p.
_____. Library Automation: A State of the Art Review.
    Chicago, 1969. 175 p.
Asheim, Lester, ed. Persistent Issues in American Librari-
    anship. Chicago, 1961. 114 p.
Becker, Joseph, and Hayes, R. M. Information Storage and
    Retrieval: Tools, Elements, Theories. New York,
    1963. 448 p.
Becker, Joseph, ed. Interlibrary Communications and In-
    formation Networks. Chicago, 1971. 347 p.
Clapp, Verner. The Future of the Research Library.
    Urbana, Ill., 1964. 124 p.
Coplan, Kate, and Castagna, Edwin, eds. The Library
    Reaches Out. Dobbs Ferry, N. Y., 1964. 430 p.
Dupuy, Trevor N. Modern Libraries for Modern Colleges.
    Washington, D. C., 1968. 122 p.
Dyer, Christopher. The Role of School Libraries in Educa-
    tion. Hamden, Conn., 1970. 181 p.
Gipe, George A. Nearer to the Dust: Copyright and the
    Machine. Baltimore, 1967. 290 p.
Hicks, Warren B. Developing Multi-Media Libraries. New
    York, 1970. 199 p.
International Federation of Library Associations. Libraries
    in the World: A Long-Term Programme for the I. F. L. A.
    The Hague, 1963. 62 p.
Jordon, Robert T. Tomorrow's Library: Direct Access and
    Delivery. New York, 1970. 200 p.
Kent, Allen: Textbook on Mechanized Information Retrieval.
    2nd ed. New York, 1966. 371 p.
Knight, Douglas M., ed. Libraries at Large: Tradition,
    Innovation, and the National Interest. New York, 1969.
    664 p. (The Resource Book based on the materials of
    the National Advisory Commission on Libraries.)
Lacy, Dan. Freedom and Communications. Urbana, Ill.,
    1961. 93 p.
Licklider, J. C. R. Libraries of the Future. Cambridge,
    Mass., 1965. 219 p.
McLuhan, Marshall. Understanding Media: the Extensions
    of Man. New York, 1964. 359 p.
Meise, Norman R. Conceptual Design of an Automated Na-
    tional Library System. Metuchen, 1969. 234 p.
Monypenny, Philip. The Library Functions of the States.
    Chicago, 1966. 178 p.

Moon, Eric, ed. Library Issues: the Sixties. New York,
    1970. 400 p.
National Association of Secondary School Principals.
    Libraries in Secondary Schools: A New Look. Wash-
    ington, 1966. 122 p.
Saracevic, Tefko, ed. Introduction to Information Science.
    New York, 1970. 751 p.
Schick, Frank L., ed. The Future of Library Service:
    Demographic Aspects and Implications. Urbana, Ill.,
    1961. 286 p.
Sharp, J. R. Some Fundamentals of Information Retrieval.
    New York, 1965. 224 p.
Shera, Jesse H. Libraries and the Organization of Knowledge.
    Hamden, Conn., 1965. 216 p.
Sullivan, Peggy, ed. Realization: the Final Report of the
    Knapp School Libraries Project. Chicago, 1968. 398 p.
U. S. Library of Congress. A Preliminary Report on the
    MARC (Machine Readable Cataloging) Pilot Project.
    Washington, 1966. 101 p.
Voight, Melvin J., ed. Advances in Librarianship. New
    York, 1970. 294 p.
Wellisch, Hans, ed. Subject Retrieval in the Seventies:
    New Directions, an International Symposium. Westport,
    Conn., 1972. 180 p.

PERIODICAL ARTICLES

(The periodical literature on the subject of this chapter is quite
large. In addition to the articles mentioned below, and to
the periodicals mentioned in earlier chapter bibliographies,
such library journals as Special Libraries, Library Trends,
Library Resources and Technical Services, and the Journal
of Information Science should be consulted along with the
Encyclopedia of Library and Information Science and such
yearbooks in the field as the Annual Review of Information
Science and Technology.)

Campbell, H. C., ed. "Developments in National Documen-
    tation and Information Services," Library Trends, 17
    (1969), 227-338.
Ebersole, J. L. "An Operating Model of a National Informa-
    tion System," American Documentation, 17 (1966), 33-
    40.
Graham, Mae, ed. "The Changing Nature of the School
    Library," Library Trends, 17 (1969), 343-338.
Lewis, Philip, ed. "New Dimensions in Educational Tech-
    nology for Multi-Media Centers," Library Trends, 19

(1971), 399-523.
"Operations Research: Implications for Libraries," <u>Library
Quarterly</u>, 42 (1972), 1-160.

INDEX

Aarhus (Denmark), University of, 215
Abelard, Peter, 53
Aberdeen (Scotland), University of, 103, 207
Academia Sinica Library (Taipei, Taiwan), 229
Academy of Natural Science Library (Philadelphia), 177, 257
Acton, Lord, 103
Adams, James, 128
Adams, John, 142, 162
Adams, John Quincy, 162
Advocates' Library (Edinburgh), 106, 111, 207
Ahern, Mary Eileen, 267
Alabama, University of, 150
Albany, N. Y., Institute of Science Library, 152
Albrecht V, Duke of Bavaria, 87
Albuquerque (New Mexico) public libraries, 282
Alcuin, 50-51
Alexander, Bishop of Jerusalem, 38
Alexandrian Library, 32-34
Alfred, King of England, 45
Algeria, National Library (Algiers), 96, 227
Almanacs, 120-124, 143, 192
Alphabet, 15, 17, 19-20, 65-66
Alsted, Johann Heinrich, 97
Amadeo, Vittorio, II, 83
American Academy of Arts and Sciences (Boston), 152
American Antiquarian Society (Worcester, Mass.), 152
American Library Association, 168, 175, 178-180, 240-241,
    243, 251, 253-254, 265-267, 269, 272-276
American Memorial Library (West Berlin), 211
American Philosophical Society Library (Philadelphia), 140,
    152, 257
American Red Cross, 240
American Revolution, 130, 135, 137-138, 140, 142, 147-148
American Society for Information Science, 275
American Telephone and Telegraph Co. libraries, 258
Amherst College (Massachusetts), 149, 248
Amsterdam, University of, 93
Anne, Princess of England, 136
Antiochus the Great, 32

293

Antwerp (Belgium) Public Library, 92
Appleton-Century-Crofts Co., 192
Appolonius of Rhodes, 33
Archer, John, 112
Archives, 9, 28, 39, 108, 254, 256.
    See also: Manuscripts
Argentina, National Library (Buenos Aires), 203
Aristophanes of Byzantium, 33
Aristotle, 31-32, 73, 76
Armaria, 48, 55
Armour Institute Library School (Chicago), 178, 269
Artois, Count d', 86
Ascham, Roger, 104
Association of American Library Schools, 270
Assurbanipal's Library, 30-31
Astor, John Jacob 171
Astor Library, New York, 171, 178, 182, 239
Atlanta, Carnegie Library, 269
Audio-visual aids, 199, 252-254, 267, 280, 284
August, Duke of Wolfenbüttel, 88
Augustus Caesar, 35
Australia, National Library (Canberra), 224
Austria, National Library (Vienna), 88, 92, 219
Azilian pebbles, 13

Balboa Heights (Panama Canal Zone) Public Library, 206
Balcarres, Earl of, 107
Baltimore, Library Company of, 172
Bamberg (Germany) State Library, 88
Barcelona, University of, 94, 217
Barnard, John, Jr., 136
Baronius, Cardinal, 84
Basel (Switzerland), University of, 216-217
Baskerville, John, 112, 114
Bates, Joshua, 170-171
Bavaria, State Library (Munich), 87-88, 210
Bay, Jacob, 127
Bayle, Pierre, 96
Beckley, John James, 160
Behistun, Rock of, 17
Belgium, Royal Library (Brussels), 92, 217
Benedict, Saint, 45
Benjamin Franklin Library (Mexico City), 201
Bergen (Norway) Public Library, 216
Bergrave, Thomas, 133
Berkeley, George, 134
Bessarion, Cardinal, 83

Borromeo, Federigo, 83
Boston, John, 55
Boston Athenaeum Library, 152, 169, 179, 257
Boston Mercantile Library, 169
Boston Public Library, 135-136, 140, 168, 170-171, 175, 178, 248
Boston Social Law Library, 153
Boston Society for Medical Improvement, 153
Boston Society of Natural History, 152
Botswana, National Library, 227
Bowditch, Nathaniel, 171
Bowdoin, James, 149
Bowdoin College, Brunswick, Maine, 149
Bowker, R. R., Co., 193, 262-263, 266
Boyd, James, 103
Boyd, Zachary, 103
Bracciolini, Poggio, 56
Bradford, Andrew, 127
Bradford, John, 128
Bradford, William (governor), 139
Bradford, William (printer), 121-122, 127-129
Braud, Denis, 122, 128
Bray, Thomas, 108-109, 136-137
Brazil, National Library (Rio de Janeiro), 202
Bristol (England) Public Library, 108
Bristowe, the Rev., 135
British Council Libraries, 201, 227, 234
British Museum (London), 16, 28, 47, 104-107, 111, 207-208
Broadsides, 77, 96, 106, 120, 122, 124-125, 130, 192
Brooklyn Public Library, 239
Brothers in Unity Society Library (Yale University), 179
Brown, John, 148
Brown, John Carter, 162-163
Brown, Nicholas, 148
Brown, Samuel, 110
Brown University (Providence, R. I.), 135, 148, 169, 174, 181
Browning Library (Waco, Texas), 249
Brunswick, Duke of, 90
Brussels Public Library, 92
Bucharest public libraries, 95
Budapest public libraries, 222
Budé, Guillaume, 85
Buell, Abel, 127
Buenos Aires, University of, 203
Buffalo (N. Y.) Public Library, 174
Bulgaria, National Library (Sofia), 95

Bullock, William A., 187
Bulmer, William, 114
Burgundy, Duke of, 92
Burma, Royal Library (Rangoon), 95
Burnam Classical Library (Cincinnati), 249
Bury, Richard de. See: De Bury, Richard
Bushell, John, 122
Byrd, William, II, 141

Caesar, Julius, 35
Caldwell, David, 163
California, University of (Berkeley), 174, 244, 247, 271
Calligraphy, 59, 69
Callimachus, 33
Cambridge University, 56, 101-103, 111, 207
Camden, William, 107
Campbell, John, 125
Canada, National Library (Ottawa), 199
Caracas, Central University of, 205
Carey, Matthew, 194
Caritat's Circulating Library (New York), 157
Carnegie, Andrew, 181-182, 239
Carnegie Corporation, 213, 245, 251, 270-273
Carnegie Institute Library School (Pittsburgh), 269
Carter, Robert, 141
Cartoons, 192
Casanato, Girolamo, 83
Caslon, William, 112, 114
Cassiodorus, Magnus Aurelius, 45-46
Catalog cards, 176, 180-181, 220, 254, 263
Catalogs and cataloging, 6, 10, 31, 33-34, 48-49, 55, 59,
    82, 88, 90-91, 104-106, 134-135, 139, 143, 148, 150,
    154, 160, 169, 171, 176, 178-180, 214, 220, 262-264,
    283
Catherine the Great, Queen of Russia, 94
Cave drawings, 11-13
Caxton, William, 72, 75, 77
Cennini, Bernardo di, 72
Censorship, 96, 100, 111-112, 123, 194, 211-212, 220,
    282. See also: Freedom of the press
Center for Research Libraries (Chicago), 248
Certification of librarians, 252, 271-272
Chained books, 47, 49, 52
Chalkley, Thomas, 140
Chambers, Ephraim, 97, 113
Champollion, Jean François, 16, 18
Chap-books, 81

Fair Trade Laws, 194
Farmington Plan, 283
Faxon, F. W. , and Co. , 267
Federal aid to libraries, 243, 247, 252, 275, 284-285
Federigo, Duke of Urbino, 57, 84
Federov, Ivan, 72
Fichet, Wilhelm, 71
Finland, National Library (Helsinki), 216
Fitzhugh, William, 141
Flags, 8
Florence, National Library, 83, 214
Folger Shakespeare Library (Washington, D. C.), 256-257
Folsom, Charles, 169
Force, Peter, 162, 175
Fort Monroe (Va.) Library, 161
Footer, John, 120, 128
Fourah Bay College (Sierra Leone), 96
Fourdrinier, Henry, 188
Fourdrinier, Sealy, 188
Fowle, Daniel, 128
Fox, Justus, 129
France, National Library. See: Bibliothèque Nationale
Francis I, King of France, 85
Franklin, Ann, 129
Franklin, Benjamin, 121-123, 126-129, 135, 137, 139-140,
    161-162
Franklin, James, 128
Franklin Institute Library (Philadelphia), 152
Franklin D. Roosevelt Library (Hyde Park, N. Y.), 257-258
Fraser Valley Library (British Columbia), 199
Frederick the Great, King of Prussia, 87
Frederick William, Great Elector of Brandenburg, 87
Free University of West Berlin, 211
Freedom of the press, 124, 130, 194, 213, 220. See
    also: Censorship
French Revolution, 84-87, 89
Friends' Library (Philadelphia), 140
Friends of the library groups, 246
Froben, Johann, 72, 74-75
Fugger, Ulrich, 88
Furness Memorial Library (Philadelphia), 249
Fust, Johann, 69-72, 77

Galveston (Texas) Public Library, 172, 240
Garamond, Claude, 75
Gazi Husrev Beg Library (Sarajevo, Yugoslavia), 218

Johnson, Samuel, 140
Johnston, Gabriel, 141
Johnston, James, 121, 128
Johnston, Samuel, 140-141
Johnston, William, 141
Joseph II, Emperor of Austria, 92
Julius, Duke of Brunswick, 88

Kairovine University (Fez, Morocco), 227
Keayne, Robert, 135-136
Kennett, White, 107
Kenya, National Library (Nairobi), 227
Kerala, India, University, 231
Kharkov (Russia) public libraries, 95
King's Chapel Library, Boston, 136
King's College. See: Columbia University
Klosterneuberg (Austria) Monastery Library, 219
Knapp School Libraries Project, 253, 284
Koberger family, 74
Koblinger, Stephen, 72
Kolurov State Library, Sofia, Bulgaria, 221
König, Friedrich, 186
König, Wilhelm, 72
Königsberg (Germany), University of, 90
Koran, 40
Korea, National Library (Seoul), 230
Korf, M. A., 94
Kooter, Laurens, 70

Langley Marish (England) Public Library, 108
Language. See: Speech; Writing
Laud, Archbishop, 102
Laurens, Henry, 142
Laurentian Library (Venice). See: Biblioteca Laurentiana
Lea and Febiger, Inc., 192
Legal deposit, 85, 93, 94, 103-104, 106, 111, 163, 176,
    208, 211
Leibniz, Gottfried Wilhelm, 88, 90-91
Leicester (England) public libraries, 108
Leiden (Netherlands), University of, 93
Leipzig, University of, 90
Lenin Institute of Economic Sciences (Bucharest), 221
Lenin State Library (Moscow), 219
Lenox, James, 163, 171
Lenox Library (New York), 171, 239
Leo XIII, Pope, 84

Lessing, Gotthold Ephraim, 88
Lettou, John, 72, 76
Lexington (Mass.) Youth Library, 157
Leypoldt, Frederick, 180
Liberia, University (Monrovia), 96
Librarians and librarianship, 6, 10, 29-30, 35-37, 48, 51,
    57, 77, 81, 84-85, 90-91, 104-105, 135, 138-139, 150-
    151, 157, 160, 168-169, 174, 176-179, 213, 228, 250,
    253-254, 259, 262-276, 280-281, 286-288
Librarian's Conference of 1852, 168-169, 179

Libraries (Arranged by Location):
    Africa, 40, 59, 76, 226-229.
        See also names of specific countries
    Albania, 218
    Algeria, 96, 227
    Argentina, 202-204
    Asia Minor, 32-35, 38-40, 221
    Assyria, 29-31
    Australia, 96, 224
    Austria, 92, 219
    Babylonia, 28-30
    Bangladesh, 233
    Belgium, 92, 216-217
    Botswana, 227
    Brazil, 202-203
    Bulgaria, 95, 221
    Burma, 95, 233
    Canada, 182, 198-200
    Chile, 202, 204
    China, 40, 59, 95, 228-229
    Colombia, 205
    Constantinople (medieval), 38-39, 45, 50, 58
    Cuba, 205
    Czechoslovakia, 56, 222
    Denmark, 93, 215
    Egypt, 28-30, 32-36, 39, 45, 59, 96, 223
    England, 50, 52, 55-57, 101-115, 182, 207-209
    Ethiopia, 96, 227
    Finland, 93, 216
    France, 49-52, 54-57, 85-87, 209-210
    Germany, 51-52, 56-57, 87-91, 210-213
    Ghana, 226
    Greece, 31-32, 35-36, 218
    Hungary, 57, 222
    India, 59, 231-232
    Indonesia, 232

306

Iran, 223-224
Iraq, 223-224
Ireland, 46, 103, 106, 110-111
Israel, 223. See also under Palestine (ancient)
Italy, 46, 52, 56, 83-85, 213-215. See also under
   Rome
Japan, 59, 95, 229-230
Kenya, 227
Korea, 230
Latin America, 199-206.
   See also names of individual countries
Latvia, 95
Lebanon, 223
Liberia, 96, 226
Libya, 227
Malaysia, 234
Mexico, 200-201
Morocco, 227
Moslem countries (medieval), 39-40, 52-53, 58-59, 93
Netherlands, 92, 216-217
New Zealand, 224-225
Nigeria, 226
Norway, 93, 216
Pakistan, 232
Palestine (ancient), 38-39
Panama, 205-206
Pergamum, 32, 34
Peru, 204-205
Philippines, 230
Poland, 56, 94-95, 220-221
Portugal, 93-94, 217-218
Rome (ancient), 35-38, 44, 58
Rumania, 95, 221
Russia, 94-95, 219-220
Scotland, 102-103, 106, 110, 111, 182
Sicily, 33
Singapore, 95, 234
South Africa, 96, 225
Spain, 40, 52-53, 93-94, 217-218
Sweden, 89, 93, 215-216
Switzerland, 52, 216-217
Syria, 33, 223
Taiwan, 229
Tanzania, 227
Thailand, 233
Tunisia, 227
Turkey, 223
Uganda, 227

309

311

New York Apprentices' Library, 155, 171
New York City Hospital Library, 177
New York Historical Society Library (Albany), 171, 177, 257
New York Mercantile Library, 169-171
New York Public Library, 163, 171, 181, 239-240
New York Society Library, 138, 140, 147-148, 171
New York State Library (Albany), 161, 177, 256, 269
New York State Library Association, 179
New York Times Library, 258
New Zealand National Library Service, 223
Newberry, Walter L., 181
Newberry Reference Library (Chicago), 181, 256
Newbery, John, 113
Newcastle (England), Library and Philosophical Society, 109
Newspapers, 77, 96-97, 112-113, 122-127, 129-130, 138,
    151, 160, 187-188, 191, 248-249
Newton, Isaac, 134
Niccoli, Nicolo, 57
Nicholas V, Pope, 58
Nigeria, Regional Central Library (Enugu), 226
Nodier, Charles, 86
North Carolina, University of (Chapel Hill), 149, 174, 271
Norway, National Library (Oslo), 216
Norwich (England) public libraries, 110
Notary, Julian, 76
Nürnberg Chronicle, 75, 77
Nuthead, Dina, 129
Nuthead, William, 121, 128-129

Odessa (Russia) public libraries, 95
Offset printing, 190, 193
Ohio College Library Center, 283
Ola, 23-24
Old South Church Library (Boston), 140
Omar, Caliph, 34
Oporto (Portugal) public libraries, 94, 218
Organization of American States, 206
Orsini, Fulvio, 84
Oslo public libraries (Deichmann Library), 93
Oslo, University of, 93
Oxford, University, 57, 101-103, 111, 135, 207

Pablos, Juan, 119
Paine, Thomas, 77, 130
Pakistan, National Library (Liaquat), (Karachi), 232
Palatine Library (Heidelberg), 84, 88, 89

Palatine Library (Rome), 37
Palimpsests, 48
Palmart, Lambert, 72
Pamphlets, 77, 96, 109, 112, 120, 124, 130, 191-192
Panizzi, Anthony, 105-106
Panjab Public Library (Lahore, Pakistan), 232
Pannartz, Arnold, 71-72
Paper and paper making, 40, 53, 64, 66-67, 112, 119, 121,
  127-128, 188-189
Paper-backed books, 191-192, 195, 243, 263, 282
Papyrus, 15-16, 20-23, 28-29, 33, 38, 44, 59, 66, 92,
  106, 207
Parchment, 22-23, 38, 44, 47, 54, 59, 66
Paris, University of, 54-55, 60, 209. See also: Sorbonne
  Library (Paris)
Parker, James, 128
Parker, Matthew, Archbishop, 102
Parks, William, 121, 128
Paulmy, Marquis de, 86
Paulus, Aemilius, 35
Pauper's Bible, 68
Peabody Institute Library (Baltimore), 172
Peking University, 228
Pennsylvania Hospital Library (Philadelphia, 152
Pennsylvania State Library (Harrisburg), 161
Pennsylvania, University of (Philadelphia), 244
Pens, 21, 22, 24
Pergamum Library, 34
Periodical indexes, 179, 220, 225, 229, 264-265
Periodicals, 77, 96-97, 113, 127, 138, 151, 154, 173, 187,
  191, 193, 248-249
Perry, Michael, 143-144
Peru, National Library (Lima), 204
Peter the Great, Czar of Russia, 94
Peterborough (N.H.) Public Library, 157
Petrarch, Francesco, 56, 76
Pfister, Albrecht, 72
Philadelphia Apprentices' Library, 155
Philadelphia College of Physicians' Library, 177
Philadelphia Free Library, 172, 240
Philadelphia Historical Society Library, 178
Philadelphia Law Association Library, 153
Philadelphia Library Company, 137-138, 140, 169, 172
Philadelphia Mercantile Library, 155, 172, 240
Philip the Good, Duke of Burgundy, 57
Philip II, King of Spain, 53, 93
Philip V, King of Spain, 93

314

Philippines, National Library (Manila), 230
Philodemus, 36
Phonograms, 14-15, 18-19
Photo-copying, 246, 255, 281, 283
Photo-engraving, 114, 190
Piccolomini, Enea Silvio, 92
Pictographs, 8-9, 14-19, 64
Pierpont Morgan Library (New York), 257
Pisistratus, 31
Pius II, Pope, 92
Pius XI, Pope, 213
Plantin family, printers, 74, 82
Playing cards, 66
Poland, National Library (Warsaw), 221
Pollio, Caius Asinius, 35
Poole, William Frederick, 169, 172, 179, 264
Pornography, 194
Portland (Oregon) Library Association, 173
Portugal, National Library (Lisbon), 94, 217-218
Prague public libraries, 222
Pratt, Enoch, 181
Pratt Institute Library School (Brooklyn), 178, 269
Prince, Thomas, 140, 171
Prince Edward Island, Canada, public libraries, 199-200
Princeton University, 135, 147-148, 173, 244
Printer, James, 120
Printing and printers, 9, 64-77, 96-97, 111-112, 114-115,
    119-130, 186-196
Prints, 190
Ptah, Temple of, 29
Ptolemy, Pharoah of Egypt, 33, 34
Public documents. See: Government publications
Publishing, 59, 191-196, 262-267
Putnam, Herbert, 180
Pynson, Richard, 72, 76

Québec Public Library Service, 199-200
Quills, 22, 24
Quipu, 13
Qumran Library, 38

Radio, 7, 195
Raffles Library (Singapore), 95
Raleigh, Sir Walter, 107
Ranganathan, S. R., 232
Rangoon (Burma), University of, 233

317

319